A Diverse Assembly

A Diverse Assembly

The Debate on a Scottish Parliament

Lindsay Paterson

Edinburgh University Press

© Lindsay Paterson, 1998

Edinburgh University Press
22 George Square, Edinburgh

Typeset in Goudy Old Style
by Hewer Text Ltd, Edinburgh, and
printed and bound in Great Britain by MPG Books, Bodmin

A CIP record for this book is available from the British Library

ISBN 0 7486 1007 3 (paperback)

The right of Lindsay Paterson
to be identified as author of this work
has been asserted in accordance with
the Copyright, Designs and Patents Act 1988.

Contents

Preface

The debate about a Scottish parliament has been intense for three decades, and yet much of it remains inaccessible because it has taken place in periodicals, newspapers, speeches and interviews. In the relatively small marketplace of Scottish intellectual life, periodicals go out of print, newspapers languish without indexes, and speeches go uncollected. So bringing together some representative texts can help to ensure that in the next phase in this discussion – an unprecedented stage, since a parliament is imminent – the new generation of discussants will not forget where the ideas for that parliament came from.

The selection here was shaped by themes, summarised in the Introduction: these are, in the editor's view, the dominant concerns of the debate. So the book is not a source book, and neither does it offer a literature review (for which, see the excellent account by Mitchell, 1996). It is a selection influenced by a particular way of interpreting events and influences. It is selective also in the sense of being primarily about politics and policy: debates about culture, history or society, for example, appear only insofar as they are refracted through the reductive spectacles of political polemic.

Within that broad framework the intention is to provide a balanced account. There is strong representation here from each of the main points of view on Scottish government between the late 1960s and the autumn of 1997, and also from all four of Scotland's main political parties. In keeping with the principle of concentrating on themes, the balance is with respect to ideas and arguments, not necessarily to people or factions. Indeed, in an attempt to ensure breadth of coverage, a general principle was adopted of not including anyone more than once. Nevertheless, many of the key figures in Scottish political debate over the three decades are here. Two are in fact represented twice: John P. Mackintosh because of his pioneering work on bringing together social democracy and the campaign for home rule, and Tom Nairn because he has probably been the most influential nationalist intellectual in Scotland and because his own position has changed in ways that are revealing for the whole debate. A further two are here twice, too, although once in disguise: Alec Douglas Home in his own right and through the Scottish Constitutional Committee which he chaired, because he was the Conservative politician who did most to try to find a position on Scottish government that would satisfy both his own party and the country; and Donald Dewar both in his own right and through his leading the Labour government's home rule proposals in 1997. There are also some other hidden overlaps – for example, Neil MacCormick was on the committee which produced the *Claim of Right*, and Yvonne Strachan was on the STUC Women's Committee which produced the paper on women and a Scottish parliament.

Such intersecting activities shape the character of public debate in Scotland. None of the voices represented here is wholly independent of any other, even across the apparently unbridgeable divide between supporters of a Scottish parliament and its opponents. That familiarity with each other helps to make the debate intense and searching, but it also can make it introspective (as Tom Nairn observes in his 1970 essay here). So far as possible, introspection has been avoided in this selection, but it cannot be wholly absent. One way in which the introspection of intellectuals has been overcome is through having a preference for contributions which were made for a reasonably large audience. Thus newspapers and periodicals are preferred to academic journals; indeed, academics are present here only insofar as they were taking part in public debate. The academic debate itself can be followed in collections of essays such as Carty and McCall-Smith (1978), Hodge (1994), MacCormick (1970), and MacKay (1979), in the *Scottish Government Yearbook* from 1977 until 1992, and in the quarterly journal *Scottish Affairs* thereafter (both series published by the Unit for the Study of Government in Scotland, Edinburgh University).

Most of the contributions here have been edited, again in order to be able to include as much breadth as possible. For similar reasons of economy of space, two big sources of contribution have been omitted. There are no views from abroad (although there are several from England), and so the debate represented here is an overwhelmingly Scottish one. And the technical aspects of debate about financing Scottish government have been omitted, because they need a book to themselves (but debate about the principles of finance is included). Other restrictions on coverage are less obvious but still important. Any selection which is based on surviving texts is bound to be biased against people and ideas which tend not to be recorded. Thus there are far fewer women here than there are men, and no-one from minority ethnic communities. The absence of extant records does not imply that social groups such as these were not debating the issues; it simply reflects the very traditional character of Scottish public life – both political and intellectual – until very recently indeed.

The book is arranged chronologically, grouped into four parts. Each of the parts is opened with a short editorial introduction which relates the items that have been selected to the political events of the times. These introductory essays are no substitute for a full political history, for which see Bennie et al. (1997), Brown et al. (1998), Finlay (1997), Fry (1987), Hanham (1969), Harvie (1998), Hodge (1994), Keating (1996), Kellas (1986), Linklater and Denniston (1992), Marr (1992), McCrone (1992), Midwinter et al. (1991), Mitchell (1996) and Paterson (1994); books such as these, and their extensive bibliographies, are required to understand fully the context and therefore the implications of the extracts here. The starting point of the mid-1960s is not entirely arbitrary, because it does mark an unusually clear threshold in this debate. However, none of the themes here are wholly absent in earlier periods, as these same histories explain, and as can be traced in the much more historically extensive selection of documents by Scott (1997).

On the first page of each item is a note of where the piece came from; explanation of the significance of each piece, however, is in the introduction to the Part and in the overall introduction. Where words have been omitted from an original, this is indicated by three dots. Words inserted by the editor are surrounded by square brackets. If the original author referred to other texts, these are included in the general bibliography at the back of the book.

Although the final selection is the editor's, valuable advice was received from numerous people. Both broad comments and detailed suggestions came from Alice Brown, John Fairley, Neil MacCormick, David McCrone and three anonymous readers to whom Edinburgh University Press sent the book proposal. David McCrone also made helpful comments on the full manuscript. Specific suggestions of items to include were received from Neal Ascherson, Malcolm Bruce, Menzies Campbell, Roseanna Cunningham, Tam Dalyell, Donald Dewar, Winifred Ewing, William Kerr Fraser, Michael Fry, Maria Fyfe, Christopher Harvie, The Earl of Home, Peter Jones, Michael Keating, Charles Kennedy, Janet Law, Isobel Lindsay, Stephen Maxwell, John McAllion, David Millar, Tom Nairn, Malcolm Rifkind, Jim Ross, William Storrar, Jim Wallace and John Young. Finding elusive items was greatly aided by the helpful staff of the National Library of Scotland,

and transcription from the originals was undertaken by Lesley Scullion. Nicola Carr of EUP was a patient source of advice on administrative matters (including securing copyright clearance, as detailed below). Ian D. L. Clark's copy-editing was perceptive, ensuring consistency and accuracy in the ways in which the extracts have been presented.

Lindsay Paterson

Acknowledgements

The editor and publishers wish to thank the following for permission to reproduce material as below; full details of the original source are given at the beginning of each item.

Robert Crawford and Chatto and Windus for 'A Scottish assembly'; *The Herald* for 'The claim of Scotland' and 'Why enmity and conflict?'; Sir Edward Heath for 'The declaration of Perth'; Tom Nairn for 'The three dreams of Scottish nationalism'; Scottish Labour Party for 'The government of Scotland'; Scottish Liberal Democrats for 'Forms and consequences of federalism'; Scottish Conservative and Unionist Party for 'An assembly'; Her Majesty's Stationery Office for 'A scheme of legislative devolution', 'Our changing democracy', 'Speech to parliament' and 'Scotland's parliament' (Crown copyright is reproduced with the permission of the Controller of Her Majesty's Stationery Office); *New Statesman* (copyright holder) and Una Maclean-Mackintosh for 'The new appeal of nationalism'; STUC for 'Scottish government' and 'Women's issues and the Scottish assembly'; Una Maclean-Mackintosh for 'A parliament for Scotland'; *New Statesman* (copyright holder) and Christopher Harvie for 'The devolution of the intellectuals'; Isobel Lindsay for 'Nationalism, community and democracy'; Tam Dalyell for 'The slide to independence'; Stephen Maxwell for 'The trouble with John P. Mackintosh'; *The Herald* and Sir Teddy Taylor for 'Why it must be "No" when assembly is put to the vote'; Scottish Conservative and Unionist Party, Lord Pym and Sir Leon Brittan for 'The Conservative Party and devolution'; The Earl of Home, the BBC and James Cox for 'Speech and interview' with Alec Douglas Home; *The Spectator* and Vernon Bogdanor for 'The defeat of devolution'; Baroness Smith for 'Interview: portrait of a devolutionist'; Robin Cook for 'Interview: devolution'; *The Spectator* for 'Scotland: omega one'; Alan Lawson for 'Towards a Constitutional Convention'; Allan Stewart for 'The devolution maze'; Donald Dewar for 'Lecture'; Neil MacCormick for 'Unrepentant gradualism'; Jock Stein and the Handsel Press for 'The government of Scotland' and 'Church and nation: a Catholic view'; Jim Sillars for 'Independence in Europe'; David McCrone for 'Thatcherism in a cold climate'; Alice Brown and Yvonne Strachan for 'The implications of a Scottish parliament for women's organisations in Scotland'; James Kellas for 'The Scottish Constitutional Convention'; Christine Richard for 'The Scottish question'; Lord Lang for 'Taking stock of *Taking Stock*'; Centre for Scottish Public Policy, Bernard Crick and David Millar for 'To make the parliament of Scotland a model for democracy'; Sir Michael Forsyth for 'The governance of Scotland'; Rosemary McKenna for 'A Scottish parliament: friend or foe of local government?'; Charles Gray for 'Scottish local government in Europe'; Graham Leicester for 'Fundamentals for a new Scotland Act'; Peter Jones and *Prospect* (4 Bedford Square, London, WC1B 3RA) for 'Scotland's next step'; Tom Nairn and *New Left Review* for 'Sovereignty after the election'; *New Statesman* (copyright holder) for 'What's the story?'; *The Herald* and David Martin for 'Three-level path to flourish in Europe'; *The Herald* and Joyce McMillan for 'Losing sight of Tinkerbell'; *The Scotsman* and Baroness Thatcher for 'Don't wreck the heritage we all share'; *The Herald* and Michael Fry for 'Free, on our own terms'; *Independent on Sunday* and Neal Ascherson for 'Some poetry, pipers and politics for the people'.

A Scottish Assembly

Robert Crawford

Circuitry's electronic tartan, the sea,
Libraries, fields – I want the lot

To fly off and scatter, but most of all
Always to come home to roost

In this unkempt country where a handicapped printer,
Engraver of dog collars, began with his friends

The ultimate encyclopedia.
Don't expect any rhyme or reason

For Scotland remaining an explosion reversed
Or ordinariness a fruited vine

Or why I came back here to choose my union
On the side of the ayes, remaining a part

Of this diverse assembly – Benbecula, Glasgow, Bow of
    Fife –
Voting with my feet, and this hand.

(from *A Scottish Assembly*, London: Chatto and Windus, 1990)

Introduction

Four broad themes have characterised the debate about a Scottish parliament over the last three decades. At its most rational, the debate has been about good and effective government, how best to manage the affairs of Scotland and, more widely, the UK or Europe. The argument has, however, never been merely about sensible planning or enlightened democracy: it has always, right across the political spectrum, drawn on emotion, usually through competing national identities, Scottish and British. It has also, especially since the 1980s, been about the nature of community, about whether Scotland has a particularly strong attachment to community, and, if so, whether that sentiment requires a Scottish parliament or would be threatened by one. But, despite the acrimony of the political rhetoric, there has also been agreement that autonomy is always partial, provisional and evolving: the debate has been about which institutional structures can best ensure that the resulting negotiations are conducted in ways that protect Scottish interests in an inter-dependent world.

This introduction explains these themes, and points to the places where they appear in the texts. Of course, the texts also deal with many other matters, and they could be summarised according to different themes from those used here. Some of these other matters are about high affairs of state, such as the best way of preserving the unity of the UK or of securing the integrity of the Scottish nation. Others are nakedly partisan, such as the bitter dismissal of the Scottish National Party by its unionist opponents, or – during most of the period – the SNP's equally inveterate hostility towards cooperation with other parties. The four themes used here, however, do seem to provide a reasonably broad way of understanding the debate, a way of interpreting it which does not prejudge its outcome. The introduction ends with some comments about the way in which the discussions summarised here might continue to shape the debate after the Scottish parliament is elected in 1999.

– Good Government –

In one very obvious sense, the theme of good government is important because it eventually won the day for the supporters of a Scottish parliament: belief that a parliament would improve social policy and would make government more effective and responsive was the main explanation of why the result of the referendum in September 1997 was emphatically in favour of home rule (Surridge et al., 1998). The debate around the referendum was concerned above all with this matter, as the items in Part IV show.

It is important also, however, because it was present from the start. On the one hand, the supporters of a parliament have recurrently claimed that it was needed because of the growth of governmental bureaucracy. The problems of bureaucracy in the democracies of the twentieth century are most eloquently stated in the 1975 pamphlet by John Mackintosh, but it can also be found in, for example, Edward Heath's 1968 speech to the Scottish Conservatives, in Donald Dewar's long-standing advocacy which is exemplified here in a speech from 1988, and in the planning for the parliament that was endorsed in the 1997 referendum. In this tradition, a Scottish parliament is seen as a way of making the bureaucracy more accountable. Indeed, responsive government is at the core of the whole case for home rule. This argument is found from Heath and several of his Conservative associates – notably in the report of the Scottish Constitutional Committee (chaired by the former prime minister Alec Douglas Home), in the remarkably open and unprejudiced discussion of all the constitutional options in the 1978 pamphlet by Francis Pym and Leon Brittan, and, much more recently, in the arguments of Christine Richard in 1993, one of the small group of Conservatives who maintained the tradition on this matter started by Heath, Home, Pym and Brittan. It is also found in the Labour government's white paper of 1975, *Our Changing Democracy*, in Donald Dewar's speech of 1988, and in the 1995 discussion by Bernard Crick and David Millar of the internal workings of any new parliament. Very recently, a new version of the good government theme has been found in the argument that a Scottish parliament could be more responsive to women, and, because of that, could be more democratic and more effective for both men and women: this case is put by the report of the STUC Women's Committee in 1989 and in the report by Alice Brown and Yvonne Strachan of a discussion on these matters held in 1991. And the argument that a Scottish parliament would make good government is found from nationalists, in Jim Sillars's pamphlet of 1989 or in H. J. Paton's quite traditional advocacy of home rule in his book of 1968: despite claims by some of its opponents, the SNP and other nationalists have been interested in the structure of government as well as in the stark matter of achieving independence.

All these proponents of a parliament have also unanimously agreed that it would make better policy and would, in particular, help the regeneration of the Scottish economy. This can be found from the STUC's response to Kilbrandon in 1974, from all of John Mackintosh's writing, from John Smith's 1981 reflections on the way forward, and from the *Claim of Right* of 1988.

Those advocates of a Scottish parliament who have not favoured a separate Scottish state have also tended to argue that home rule would be good for UK government as well. There have been two versions of this. On the one hand has been the belief that Scotland could provide an example for the rest of the UK, as in the Liberal Party's 1970 submission to the Kilbrandon Commission, and in the report of the Constitution Unit in 1996, summarised by Graham Leicester. On the other has been the view that changing the structure of government in Scotland would force the rest to change too: we find this from John Mackintosh in 1975, from Alick Buchanan-Smith in his 1976 speech, from Vernon Bogdanor in his analysis of the 1979 referendum, and in Donald Dewar's speech of 1988. Stephen Maxwell, nationalist critic of Mackintosh, claimed in his 1977 article here that a concern with reforming British government can in fact be an impediment to finding the best form of Scottish government.

Nevertheless, partly because the goals of good and responsive government have come to be the main element in the case for home rule, its opponents have advocated different means to the same ends as ways of arguing against an elected body. In the early years dealt with here, the suggestion that bureaucracy needed to be made accountable was not automatically associated with a tendency to support a parliament, as can be seen in the Labour Party's submission to the Kilbrandon Commission (1970) and even in the 1974 article by the home ruler John Mackintosh. Later, Conservative politicians tried to find ways of making the bureaucracy of Scottish government accountable that would not require an elected body: that is the whole tenor of the reforms introduced by Ian Lang (reviewed by him here in a speech from 1994) and taken forward by Michael Forsyth (1995 speech). Thus they were building on ideas that had been proposed not only by their Conservative predecessors such as Pym and Brittan and Alec Douglas Home in his 1980 interview, but also by Labour before it was irrevocably converted to home rule in the 1980s. This same strand of thinking also viewed a Scottish parliament as bad government, and thus was directly counter to the claims of its supporters: this argument is most cogently put by Tam Dalyell (1977) and Ian Lang (1994), but can be found also in the articles by Teddy Taylor (1978) and by Allan Massie (1984), and the pamphlet by Allan Stewart (1987). The political right have also claimed, notably, that it would be bad government because it would be bad for business: see Teddy Taylor in 1978, Allan Stewart in 1987, Michael Forsyth in 1995, and Margaret Thatcher during the referendum campaign in 1997.

Just as the need for good and responsive government has been used by all sides, so has the case for greater popular responsibility. Again, the obvious uses are by the supporters of a parliament, especially those on the political right – Edward Heath in 1968, Michael Fry in 1997. But it is also found among opponents: Tam Dalyell claims that financing a parliament with a block grant induces dependency, and, in fact, that is the basis of Fry's argument that the parliament should be responsible for raising all its own revenue. The journalist Peter Jones, writing in 1997, foresees that one effect of an elected parliament will be to force people in Scotland to take responsibility for their own decisions: England or Westminster or whatever will no longer be available to blame. Michael Forsyth (1995) might disagree so far as a merely home rule parliament is concerned: he claims that it will deepen dependency because it will encourage the blaming of London, and so help the SNP's case for independence.

– Nationalism –

If this discussion had only ever been conducted as an academic seminar on good government, it would have got nowhere. The emotional fuel on all sides has come from some version of politicised national identity, verging on nationalism even among people who would disavow that word. Perhaps the most remarkable feature of the whole debate is how frequently history is invoked, not only by Scottish nationalists in support of a separate state, but also by home rulers (such as in the *Claim of Right* of 1988) and by opponents of any elected assembly (such as the Labour Party in 1970 and Conservatives Esmond Wright in 1968 and Ian Lang in 1994).

A romantic nationalist tradition that traces its origins to the nineteenth century was still alive at the beginning of the period, and is found in the article by H. J. Paton (1968) and in some of the allusions in Edward Heath's speech (1968). But that was dying, aided on its way by Tom Nairn's polemic of 1970, an essay which many people know without having read it, so deeply have its arguments entered the Scottish intellectual world.

Replacing that romantic strand has been something more modern, more 'genuine' (the term used by Stephen Maxwell to reject John Mackintosh's claim that Scottish nationalism cannot be taken seriously). The core philosophy of this new nationalism is summed up in the title of the 1988 report that led to the Constitutional Convention and hence to the ultimately successful commitment of the Labour government to establish a parliament: a 'claim of right'. Seeking to avoid the vague romance of old Scottish nationalism – and, in the case of many advocates, seeking to avoid nationalism altogether – these new home rulers have sought a Scottish tradition of contractual rights (see also Hearn, 1998). The Scottish people, according to this argument, have contracted with each other, through the idea of a covenant (Church of Scotland, 1989), and they have then contracted with the sovereign power. If the sovereign breaks that agreement, then the people have the right to start again. A sense of a broken bargain underlay a great deal of the frustration with the Thatcher government in the 1980s, as analysed by David McCrone in 1989. Whether home rule will stabilise as the new contract depends on whether Donald Dewar's 1988 optimism or Tom Nairn's 1997 caution is the more valid.

Alongside this project to reinvent Scottish nationalism has been an attempt to rescue British identity in Scotland. Most contributors here would agree with John Mackintosh's well-known assessment that Scots have dual identities, both British and Scottish. Home rulers such as Mackintosh and Donald Dewar would claim that a domestic parliament would consolidate Britishness, and, indeed, that it was a way of modernising Britain. Opponents of any elected assembly fear that it would destroy Britishness permanently (Tam Dalyell, Ian Lang, Margaret Thatcher). One of the reasons why the referendum of 1997 was decisive, in contrast to that of 1979, was that people were persuaded that a Scottish parliament was consistent with being British (Surridge et al., 1998).

Multiple identities are becoming more complex, however, and the European dimension of allegiance has, like the British, been used by all sides. Edward Heath uses prospective UK membership of the then European Economic Community as an argument against separation in 1968, whereas Jim Sillars uses the same fact in exactly the opposite direction in 1989 (and was arguing the same point from 1976). Sillars, and also the Conservative Allan Stewart, use the EEC or European Union as an argument against limited self-government, while these new contexts are an argument in favour of home rule for Donald Dewar in 1988, Charles Gray in 1996, and David Martin in 1997.

The point, in other words, is that identity and allegiance do not ineluctably point in any particular direction: they are available to be appropriated by whichever side in the argument is most skilful at invoking emotion. The main reason why the strongest emotions have been on the side of home rule since the early 1980s has probably been, simply, that Scottish culture has shifted its allegiance wholesale from straightforward unionism to a much greater ambivalence. At the start of the period, it was common to assume that culture was quite a separate matter from politics: this is argued by the Labour Party in its submission to Kilbrandon. Nationalism is even seen as a threat to the vitality of Scottish culture by Esmond Wright. According to many people, a self-governing Scotland could be provincial: we find this from Wright, from the 1970 analysis by Tom Nairn, from John Mackintosh in 1974, and from the Labour Party's view in 1970 that what mattered to socialists was internationalism. Such views have not vanished, as can be seen in the speech by Michael Forsyth from 1995. But it has mostly been replaced by a cultural revolt against the idea of Britain, as noted by Isobel Lindsay in 1976. It was around that time that the Scottish cultural activists switched wholesale to support for autonomy, as discussed by Christopher Harvie in 1976. Jim Sillars (in 1989) sums up a common view, that self-government is now the way of rescuing Scotland from provincialism, and is by no means a threat of cultural marginalisation. These changed perceptions in the 1980s and 1990s have created a quite different type of nationalism from the one defined by Stephen Maxwell in 1977. It was thereafter no longer true that the broad campaign for a Scottish parliament paid little attention to culture; indeed, as Peter Jones notes in his 1997 essay looking back on it all, culture is one of the few areas of Scottish life which does not lack self-confidence. The title of this book, drawing on a poem created by one of this new generation of writers, is intended to reflect that process too; the full text is reproduced as an epigraph.

– COMMUNITY AND CIVIL SOCIETY –

The new nationalism with its roots in culture and contractual claims has also paid a great deal of attention to ideas of community and to the institutions of Scottish civil society. This was not the case at the start. For the Labour Party in 1970, community was a reason to oppose any elected assembly, and this view persisted on the political right (Allan Massie in 1984, Michael Forsyth in 1995). The occasional voice on the left could also be heard still articulating the old view, such as John Lloyd in 1997. Another reason why the idea of a Scottish community was not automatically associated with support for home rule was expressed by Tom Nairn in 1970: he sees the traditional pillars of the Scottish community – the church, the law, and education – as deeply conservative and provincial, and in need of destruction before Scotland can move towards genuine autonomy.

But in his 1997 essay, Nairn reflects the profound change that took place in the meantime, so that, for the Scottish majority, civil society became the expression of popular sovereignty and a bulwark against the encroachments of an unpopular Conservative government. (The change in Nairn's position can be traced through Nairn (1977, with second expanded edition in 1981) and Nairn (1997).) This view can be found emerging in John Mackintosh's 1975 pamphlet and in John Smith's view from 1981 that the powers of an assembly mattered less than that it should be popularly elected. The opposition between the Scottish community and the British state began to be expressed in language of the type used by Isobel Lindsay in 1976 or (more cautiously) the STUC in 1974. Vernon Bogdanor notes presciently in the aftermath of the debacle of 1979 that the SNP would become adept at using the bare majority achieved then as a way of challenging the very legitimacy of the state. He was wrong only in not predicting that the sense of people against the state would come to extend right across the Scottish left, as in the 1988 *Claim of Right* and as summed up in the analyses by James Kellas (1992) and David McCrone (1989). New versions of the theme emerged with the entry of the women's movement into the debate in the late 1980s: see the paper by Alice Brown and Yvonne Strachan. And local government, from being reluctant to oppose itself to the existing structures of power in the 1970s, came to identify with the campaign for a parliament in the 1980s (Rosemary McKenna in 1996).

Nevertheless, although Nairn reflects this shift, he retains enough of his initial scepticism about Scottish civil society to raise the possibility that the coming of a parliament will provoke a confrontation with the traditional Scottish institutions (see also Nairn, 1997, Part IV). This prognosis can be deduced also from John Smith's noting in 1981 that the Scottish middle class are reluctant to follow through their institutional identity with support for anything politically radical. The scope for a popular rebellion against the very institutions which have helped to achieve a parliament is examined by Joyce McMillan during the 1997 referendum. A flavour of the links that this could build with dissenting Scottish culture is given by Neal Ascherson's graphic reportage on the busful of intellectuals who toured Scotland during the referendum agitating for a new kind of politics.

– NEGOTIATED AUTONOMY –

So there will be battles ahead. But that these are more likely to be constructive than internecine can be inferred from the final point – the appreciation shown by all the contributors of the limited nature of sovereignty and of the need for a small country to engage in negotiation and compromise.

On the one hand, the debate in the early years still reflects an assumption that the UK will be flexible enough to accommodate special Scottish interests and institutions: we find this from H. J. Paton in 1968, from the reply by Esmond Wright which talks about a 'federal society', from Alick Buchanan-Smith in 1976, and from the Labour Party's submission to Kilbrandon. A similar expectation underlies the proposals for a more formal type of federalism or quasi-federalism from the Conservatives' Scottish Constitutional Committee in 1970 or from the Liberal Party in 1970. All these people and organisations offer, as it were, a new contract to the state – that, in return for special treatment, Scots will be 'responsible citizens' (the words of the Scottish Constitutional Committee) and will seek to make the compromise work.

Although faith in the flexibility of the UK state declined with the coming to power of Margaret Thatcher, a sense that there was a need to return to that more accommodating statecraft pervades the thinking of the people who constructed the scheme for a parliament that was endorsed in the 1997 referendum – not only from Labour politicians such as Donald Dewar (1988) and from their advisors such as Graham Leicester (1996), but also from gradualist nationalists such as Neil MacCormick (1989). Even the more intransigent nationalists now accept the reality of limited sovereignty: Jim Sillars's great contribution to this whole debate has been the concept of 'independence in Europe' (1989), an intrinsicaly limited form of self-government.

The precise mechanisms for ensuring that a new balance can be achieved have always been a matter of dispute, notably on the role of the Secretary of State for Scotland after a parliament is established: the Kilbrandon report (1973) proposes to retain the office, as does the Labour government's white paper in 1997; the STUC proposes to abolish it (1974), and opponents of a parliament believe that the post will become redundant (Tam Dalyell in 1977 and Michael Forsyth in 1995). Similar controversy surrounds the role of Scottish MPs at Westminster (Tam Dalyell most famously, but also Allan Stewart in 1987 and Michael Forsyth). Acrimonious though these discussions are, the very fact that they have taken place shows that a concern with mechanisms through which autonomy is negotiated is at the heart of all the arguments around a proposed parliament.

If supporters of a parliament must show how their schemes can respect the nature of partial sovereignty, the problem for opponents has been to demonstrate that they are not simply surrendering all autonomy to London. Again and again, they insist that administrative autonomy is real, that special arrangements for Scottish business at Westminster are not merely tokens, and that retaining full Scottish participation in the UK government is the best way of gaining influence inside the Cabinet. The sincerity of these beliefs is evident throughout, from the Labour Party in 1970, Teddy Taylor in 1978, Francis Pym and Leon Brittan in 1978, Alec Douglas Home in his speech just before the 1979 referendum, Ian Lang in 1994, Michael Forsyth in 1995 and even Margaret Thatcher in 1997. Despite what is often claimed by their opponents, these unionists have genuinely believed that the accommodating Union could be reinvented, and was a better way of achieving a balance between Scottish autonomy and the constraining wider world than any unstable scheme for an elected assembly.

– Conclusions –

Four points emerge in conclusion. The first is the simple observation that the debate is long-standing. It was already intense and well-informed at the beginning of the period, already far ahead of what is still, in 1998, the inchoate discussions of English regionalism (Elcock and Keating, 1998; Payton, 1993; Tindale, 1996).

But – second – the Scottish debate has also moved on. It has become more subtle. It has recognised in more complex ways the partial nature of autonomy, as can be seen from a comparison of (for example) the exchange between H. J. Paton and Esmond Wright of 1968 with the dialogue between Donald Dewar and Michael Forsyth in the 1980s and 1990s. It has had to confront stark choices, forced on it by Margaret Thatcher's period in power. On the one hand, this required home rulers to re-examine the nature of the UK state, and to find principled ways of re-founding it: that process was crystallised by the *Claim of Right*, but it was also present in thinking in the churches (Church of Scotland, 1989, and Tim Duffy, 1989), in local government (Rosemary McKenna, 1996, and Charles Gray, 1996), and among people concerned to locate Scottish reforms in a wider process of UK constitutional change (Graham Leicester, 1996). On the other hand, it also forced nationalists – for whom the experience of Thatcher confirmed the need for separation – to find other ways of avoiding the romantic illusion that a small country could ever be fully independent. This is solved in different ways by pragmatic philosophers such as Neil MacCormick (1989) and by active radicals such as Jim Sillars (1989), but each position more fully acknowledges the realities of power than did the older nationalist tradition represented here by H. J. Paton (1968).

The third point is that this subtlety has developed because none of the four themes traced in this Introduction has been unchanging. That is the main reason, in fact, why a selection from original texts is useful: it protects against anachronism. The theme of good government has taken account of new currents from feminism and from the revolution in information technology (so that the scope for popular participation mentioned by Bernard Crick and David Millar is much greater than it would have been in the 1970s). The theme of accountability which started as a rather dry commentary on Scottish Office bureaucrats acquired political urgency during the 1980s when that Office was controlled by a party for which Scots had unambiguously not voted (David McCrone, 1989). The nationalism that then emerged was quite different, quite distinct from the old romantic styles that were still around in thinkers such as H. J. Paton at the beginning of the period, and which dominated the SNP during its electoral successes in the 1970s. The new nationalism was already being prefigured at that time by writers such as Isobel Lindsay (1976) and Stephen Maxwell (1977); it grew far beyond the SNP in the 1980s, to permeate the Scottish majority: its most eloquent statement is not in any SNP document, but in the *Claim of Right*. Along with this new nationalism has emerged a new conception of community and of culture – not only a positioning of Scottish culture firmly on the political left, but also the finding in the idea of community a political principle which seemed to offer a new foundation for Scottish government. And the old awareness of autonomy as a negotiated process acquired new perspectives, for example acknowledging the importance of the European dimension (Jim Sillars, 1989, and David Martin, 1997), or insisting that a Scottish parliament should not arrogate power to itself but should form a partnership with communities and social sectors (Charles Gray, 1996, and Joyce McMillan, 1997).

As the themes have changed, so have their proponents, most starkly Labour and the Conservatives. The Labour story is apparently simple – a move from old unionism to enthusiastic support for home rule. It will be interesting, nevertheless, to see whether and how their unionist inheritance complicates their role in the new parliament. At least, though, Labour will have the luxury of having won the debate. Surveying the texts collected here, the greatest sense of loss is in relation to the Conservative Party. As late as the end of the 1970s, they had the strongest claim to being the most creative thinkers on Scottish government, and yet that was buried in the rigidity of the Thatcher years. Ian Lang (1994) and Michael Forsyth (1995) did resurrect some of that imagination as they tried to reform the existing system in the mid-1990s, but their party had lost too much ground because it had neglected to till it, and the scheme which eventually triumphed in the 1997 referendum owed nothing to recent Conservative thinking. Despite that, there were signs immediately after the 1997 referendum that the Conservatives might be about to find their constitutional imagination again, led by the small vanguard of people such as Michael Fry (1997) and Christine Richard (1993) which had stuck to its home rule principles all along.

These points about the future of Labour and the Conservatives bring us to the last conclusion. The character of the debate as it will continue to evolve when the Scottish parliament is set up will be shaped by its recent history as reflected in the texts collected here. Good government will continue to be a prime goal, and a strong expectation: failure to deliver it could cause the parliament grave problems. Nationalism will continue to lie in the background of most of Scottish politics, but will also change its character to accommodate to the new structures. The SNP, in particular, will have to reconcile the gradualism which has always been the principled position of some of its members and a majority of its supporters (Brown, McCrone, Paterson and Surridge, 1998, chapter 6) with a fundamentalism that regards home rule as a charade. Civil society will continue to operate independently of the state, and so could be awkward for the parliament just as it was for Margaret Thatcher. And the whole of Scottish political debate will find new ways of discussing the nature of partial autonomy, taking forward the difficult task of reconciling popular sovereignty with interdependence. Although the referendum of 1997 – and the elections to the parliament in 1999 – do mark the beginning of a new era, the discussions that took place during these past three decades will continue to live on in people's memories. Politicians may crumble, and constitutions may be radically reformed, but debate continues to have a life of its own, stubbornly resistant to changes in political fashion.

Part I: Beginnings, 1968–74

Introduction

The first decade of debate here responds immediately to political and economic events of the 1960s. Politically, the most notable feature was the rise of the SNP, from being on the fringes as recently as the 1966 general election to Winifred Ewing's winning the Hamilton by-election in 1967. The kind of nationalism which the party embodied at that time is exemplified by the article from H. J. Paton (based on a book which was well-received when it was published, for example by *The Scotsman*, 29 February 1968, p. 8). All the parties responded to the SNP's strength, while denying that it had much to do with their actions. Most commentators would have agreed with Magnus Magnusson, writing in *The Scotsman* on 30 October 1967 (p. 6), that, without the SNP, there simply would not have been a Scottish political agenda. Few people were, as yet, in favour of independence: even Ewing, in her victory speech in Hamilton, made more of giving Scotland 'an independent voice at Westminster' than of a separate Scottish parliament (quotation from BBC recording). But there was beginning to be a feeling, as expressed by Paton, that unless there was some reform of Scottish government, there might be a slow movement of popular feeling towards more radical options.

Economically, the continuing context was the decline of the Scottish manufacturing sector, in response to which the most notable report was that of the committee set up by the Scottish Council Development and Industry and chaired by Sir John Toothill (1961). The Conservative government set up the Scottish Development Department in 1962 (Levitt, 1996), and the Labour government which was elected in 1964 went further, with a Scottish national plan and the Highlands and Islands Development Board. The next Conservative government did not eschew this interventionism, and established a Scottish Economic Planning Department in 1973. All the extracts here address economic policy: none denies that the structure of government is related to economic success (although they draw vastly different conclusions from that).

So, while the UK parties' main responses to Scottish grievances were economic, they also responded explicitly on the constitution. Labour set up a Royal Commission on the Constitution in 1968, chaired by Lord Crowther and, when he died, by Lord Kilbrandon. The party remained firmly unionist, as is evident in its submission to the Commission (reproduced here): good government, it claimed, was best assured by reforming local government and by a strong UK welfare state. Labour nevertheless were in no doubt that Scottish culture was valuable and worth developing: they differed from the nationalists in asserting that culture was not a matter for politics. In this they were following a common tradition of liberalism and social democracy stretching back to the nineteenth century and right across Europe (Paterson, 1994). It could be found contemporaneously from such apparently surprising sources as the Saltire Society in its submission to Kilbrandon in 1972 (Royal Commission on the Constitution, 1972, pp. 32–6); it had been campaigning for Scottish culture since the 1930s. Nevertheless, individual Labour thinkers were open to nationalism, as the 1974 essay here by John Mackintosh shows (and as can be seen further in the collection of his essays edited by Henry Drucker (Drucker, 1982)). The reason why the political left was ambivalent about nationalism is explained here by Tom Nairn.

The Liberal party had better reason than the Labour government to claim that it had not been panicked by the SNP success, because it had a long record of advocating federalism. Its submission to Kilbrandon, reproduced here, summed this up clearly (and it has not essentially changed its position ever since). David Steel had written of the shortcomings of Scottish government shortly after he entered parliament in a by-election in 1965 (Steel, 1968), and in 1966 Russell Johnston had introduced to the House of Commons the first home rule Bill since 1927 (Parliamentary Debates, 1966). The Liberal party had an ally for its federalism in *The Scotsman* newspaper, which published a manifesto for Scottish government in 1968 on 3 February (p.8), 5 February (p. 6), 6 February (p. 8), and 7 February (p. 6).

Despite all this activity, however, it was the Conservative party which responded most creatively. On the one hand, as the article by Esmond Wright shows, they still had a subtle understanding of the UK in which Scottish nationalism could best be promoted through unionism: this has been called 'unionist nationalism' by Morton (1994). Wright's arguments were developed more fully elsewhere (Wright, 1970). Conservatives of this persuasion would have agreed with the journalist R. E. Dundas writing in the *Glasgow Herald* of 16 May 1968 (p. 8): 'there are great dangers in overestimating the political concessions necessary to placate Scottish feeling'.

On the other hand, the Conservatives also engaged in lively debate about precisely such political concessions. The Thistle group was established to press for home rule (Mitchell, 1996, p. 53). George Younger (a Conservative MP) welcomed the debate stimulated by the SNP victory at Hamilton (*The Scotsman*, 15 December 1967, p. 8). And, spectacularly, at the Scottish Conservative annual conference in 1968 – having been urged on by Younger and his colleagues – the UK party leader Edward Heath issued what later came to be known as the Declaration of Perth, extracts from which are given here. His main point was to endorse the idea of a directly elected Scottish assembly. The party set up a Scottish Constitutional Committee, chaired by former prime minister Sir Alec Douglas Home; it too recommended an elected assembly in its report (reprinted here). Further sympathy for this policy was expressed by Quintin Hogg (who, as Lord Hailsham, was to become an influential member of Margaret Thatcher's Cabinet): he argued for federalism in a pamphlet (Hogg, 1969) and in an article in a magazine published by the Scottish Council Development and Industry (Hogg, 1967). The Heath government of 1970–4 gave as the main reason for not acting on these promises that the Kilbrandon Commission had yet to report.

The publication of the Kilbrandon report in 1973 was a key moment in the whole three decades. It contained a mass of detailed argument and research, but the key legacy was from its scheme of legislative devolution, given here. On that was based not only the Labour government's reactions in the 1970s, but – even more closely – the 1997 Labour government's proposals which were endorsed in the referendum of 1997. At the time, however, few commentators expected much to come of the report (*The Scotsman*, 24 October, p. 11, and 1 November 1973, p. 11). Two of the members of the Commission produced a minority report which resembled the scheme advocated here by the Conservatives' Scottish Constitutional Committee: see Mitchell (1996).

The Claim of Scotland

H. J. Paton

From three extracts from *The Claim of Scotland*, by H. J. Paton (Allen and Unwin, 1968), originally in the *Glasgow Herald*, 26 February (p. 8), 27 February (p. 10) and 28 February (p. 10), 1968. Paton was an emeritus professor of philosophy at Oxford University, and had also lectured at Glasgow University. Paton refers his argument back to the Covenant of the late 1940s, which attracted some two million signatures in support of home rule, and to the Royal Commission on Scottish affairs of 1954, chaired by Lord Balfour, which added to the responsibilities of the Scottish Office.

The claim is that under the Crown and within the framework of the United Kingdom Scotland should have her own Parliament with genuine legislative authority in Scottish affairs. This reform, it has been contended, is necessary to secure good government in accordance with Scottish wishes and traditions and to promote the spiritual and economic welfare of the Scottish nation. It is also necessary in the interests of the United Kingdom, if the welfare of the whole depends upon the welfare of all its members.

Besides this major claim, there is a minor or secondary one, which is consequential. Since Scotsmen have a special concern with the government of their own country they should be given a clear opportunity to say what kind of government they prefer. This means that they should be allowed some sort of plebiscite or referendum.

. . .

It can hardly be said about the Scots, as it used to be said unfairly about the Irish, that they are unworthy, or incapable, of self-government. They have been far too successful in governing other people (including the English) for this to sound even plausible. Equally absurd would be the contention that Scotland is too poor and backward to enjoy the rights freely granted to other nations with strong English approval. Her claims to self-determination cannot be dismissed as weaker than those of such countries as Trinidad or Malta or Lesotho. Assumptions of this kind are not in need of refutation: to state them explicitly is to refute them. No less preposterous would be the view that Scotland is not a nation but merely a part of the English nation. She is, on the contrary, one of the oldest nations in Europe and has too long a history, and too great a reputation in the world, to be dismissed so lightly. In any case, whatever be the characteristics necessary to constitute a nation, the most fundamental is consciousness of nationality and this Scotland has never lost.

. . .

[A]gainst Scotland's claim for self-government . . . [o]ne argument . . . is this. If Scotland were given self-government her representation and influence in the British Parliament would have to be proportionately reduced. She has therefore to make a painful choice.

The choice would certainly be painful, but why should it be necessary? It would be reasonable enough to say that Scottish members should be excluded from voting on purely English affairs or – still better – that the English should have a regional Parliament or parliaments of their own. But Scotsmen, if they had some real control over their own affairs, would have no less interest than before in legislation affecting the United Kingdom as a whole – including such questions as defence and foreign policy and tariffs, to mention only the most obvious. To say that Scotland must lose her voice on all these matters in proportion to the amount of self-government she enjoys would be manifestly unfair.

. . .

It is sometimes argued that self-government for Scotland should be rejected because it would mean a further proliferation of bureaucracy with all its extravagance and waste. It is difficult to take such a contention seriously at a time when bureaucracy is encouraged to proliferate everywhere else with an almost tropical luxuriance. It is also hard to believe that any method of administration could be more wasteful and extravagant than the present ramshackle and top-heavy system, which no one could have invented deliberately. . . . Whatever may be the view of centralised officials anxious to smooth their tasks and add to their empire, a coherent system of administration in Edinburgh would probably require fewer men and less money; it would certainly be able to avoid the heart-breaking frustrations and delays and misunderstandings which do so much spiritual as well as economic harm. . . . Control would at least be less remote than it is; but the fundamental point is that the bureaucrats dealing with Scottish affairs would be exposed to democratic criticism and control as they can never be in a Westminster Parliament.

. . .

It is true that unless Scotland could trade with the rest of the world (including England) she would be in a difficult position; but there is nothing very exceptional about that. Nor can we take it for granted that without continual subsidies from England Scotland would totter to her doom – this may be the reverse of the truth.

As to 'help' in general, we can hardly assume that Scotland would be less prosperous and less contented if she could decide for herself where her roads and railways and steamers should run, which ports and airports should be developed, where her new factories should be located, and so on. Under the present system such things have in the last resort to be settled, in horrifying detail, by some unknown London officials who are primarily concerned with English interests and need never have seen the regions they control. This is the kind of 'help' we could well do without. It is one of the main sources of the present discontents.

. . .

What Scotland wants and needs is genuine, and not bogus, autonomy. If hope of this is continually deferred, if interference from London becomes ever more extensive and more arbitrary, and if as a result Scotland appears to be going downhill and to be losing her national identity and her national pride it is not surprising that some Scotsmen should begin to talk about independence. What is surprising is that this talk is so limited.

The high hopes raised by the signing of the Covenant in 1949 were smothered by well-tried methods of procrastination with the help of the Royal Commission [of 1954]. Since then London interference in Scottish affairs has steadily and insidiously increased; even the Scottish system of education is being knocked about to fit in with the latest innovations from the South. It is hardly surprising if the demand for independence has become stronger in Scotland, as also in Wales, and has won increasing support in parliamentary elections.

. . .

The case argued throughout this book is that the ideal solution would be to have a complete federal system like that of the USA where the separate States have equality in the Senate as well as full representation in Congress. If this is impossible, as so many think, the next best solution would be to set up subordinate national parliaments with real, and not illusory, control over their own affairs. If this, too is resolutely ruled out, what is left open to Scotsmen and Welshmen except to seek for independence?

There is a heavy burden of proof on those who assert that no matter what Scotland may desire she is not entitled to the independence freely acknowledged as the common right of all other nations in the world. The burden is all the greater since Scotland entered freely into the union with England and may reasonably claim that she has a further, and very special, right to leave it in equal freedom – a right certainly not weakened because the predominant partner has so often ignored the conditions of the union.

. . .

It is sometimes argued that an independent Scotland would have less influence on world affairs. This, too, is hardly plausible. At present she has no such influence – not even in matters that concern her deeply, such as the three-mile limit for territorial waters, where a tiny independent country like Iceland is able to defend her own interests. No one could argue seriously that Eire has less influence in world affairs than she had before she broke away. It may seem more plausible to say that an independent Scotland could not defend herself against external enemies. This argument might have had some weight in the past but today it applies to Scotland no more than it does to all independent European countries. We are all in the same boat and – if I may mix a metaphor – our safety depends on the American nuclear umbrella. Furthermore there is no reason whatever to suppose that an independent Scotland within the Commonwealth would be unable or unwilling to enter into the closest possible co-operation with England in all matters concerned with defence. It might even be hoped that the independence of Scotland could be a first step towards a genuine British federation or confederation or at least a close defensive alliance, which Ireland, too, might be willing to join on a footing of equality.

Perhaps the strongest argument for independence is that without a change of heart in England modest measures of self-government, even if they were permitted, could never cure the ills from which Scotland suffers. The Central Government would still be too strong, and English nationalism is so deeply engrained that the interests of Scotland would always be sacrificed to the real or imaginary interests of England.

The sad facts of history lend only too much support to this contention; and even today this habit of deriding all Scottish claims without any attempt to understand them is enough to make some Scotsmen despair of any solution short of independence. Is it too much to hope that our English brothers might at long last develop a truly British patriotism which would regard Britain as something more than an England possessed of a few recalcitrant provinces not yet completely assimilated?

. . .

Any kind of Scottish Parliament, provided it had some real power, would to my mind be better than none; for in it the voice of Scotland could no longer be muffled and smothered, and it would be impossible to maintain that nobody knew what Scotland really wanted. This by itself would be an immense gain.

WHY ENMITY AND CONFLICT?

Esmond Wright

From two articles in response to Paton's articles in the *Glasgow Herald*, 29 February (p. 10) and 1 March (p. 10), 1968. Wright had been elected Conservative MP at a by-election in the Glasgow Pollok constituency in 1967. He had been professor of modern history at Glasgow University, 1957–67.

Professor Paton is making a Claim; and he surveys Scottish history, the law, Parliament, bureaucracy, taxation, the Highlands, migration, broadcasting . . . the schools and the universities. Both as an ex-professor and as a politician I find much here to ponder, much to accept and much to reject.

. . .

He makes . . . some valid points. There is frustration in Parliament – even though, compared with anywhere else in Britain, Scotland's affairs get more time at Westminster in Committee or on the floor than do any other areas of the country; and, even on a day devoted to Scotland, quite a number of MPs will admit in confidence – but never in public – that by 7 pm in any debate all the major points are likely to have been made. There is the grip of bureaucracy – quite as substantial to the Wirral and to Wigan, however, as to West Lothian or the Western Isles. And there are the problems of the Highlands: though to them Edinburgh can seem quite as remote and bureaucratic as Westminster. Even if Scotland were independently governed, there would be a major problem of form and function of government to be tackled here. Indeed, Professor Paton skates over the real problems of the North too smoothly altogether. Not long ago – before Mrs Ewing won Hamilton – the Orkneys almost chose independence, not of London, but of St Andrew's House. One problem that Scottish secession would present would be that its success would encourage other secessions – as the events of 1861 did in the USA. If Scotland, why not Lerwick? If there were a Solway barrage would the future of the south-west be with Edinburgh or with the prosperity of Carlisle? Secession feeds on secession. We should consider the deliberate break-up of any structure in the full and desperate awareness that history has a momentum of its own, and events breed like events. States are not built in a day. But they can, these days, be rapidly disrupted.

. . .

I note the total absence of any reference to industry, except as something taken over by the wicked English. But the Scottish contribution to Britain (and the world) has been positive, from James Watt onwards. And if there are take-overs, they are too often take-overs by acceptance. Edinburgh and Dundee have for long invested in India and Latin America and Texas. Too few of the industrial barons have stayed at home. Even fewer have invested at home. And for this sober bit of calculation it is the Scots and not the English who should be blamed.

. . .

[T]here is all too little here, surprisingly little, of what is truly nationally distinctive in Scotland, its culture. The pre-occupation is with that institution that is all too easy to attack, the BBC. Yet the BBC – even the Scottish BBC – has rendered immense service to Scotland: to its music – utterly omitted here – and its poetry. There is an inadequate view of the distinct character and high commercial success of the Scottish press – when the English press is in difficulties. I find no reference to the Citizens' Theatre, to the Burrell Collection, to the S[cottish] N[ational] O[rchestra]. Is this not part of the claim of Scotland? Must all our claims, I repeat, be of enmity and conflict?

. . .

The truth rests in the fact that since 1707 we have built in these islands a unique political system unmatched elsewhere; a federal society of English, Scots, Welsh and Irish (of whom Professor Paton writes with some asperity) and nowadays many more, that is nevertheless a single centralised political system. This tiny congested island has enjoyed a standard of living to which its own natural resources in no way entitle it. It has lived by exporting its highly skilled products and these have for centuries included its brains – English as well as Scots brains have emigrated. That is what imperialism meant. It is unique and it has been successful.

Part of the depression of our days – one reason for *The Claim of Scotland* – is precisely because the United Kingdom is not quite so prosperous nor nearly as important as it used to be; there is frustration, with loss of empire, loss of status, loss of pride. But this is still a unique society, and we must change its political character only if we genuinely believe that the errors and weaknesses in it are of so essential a sort, so intrinsically related to our decline as a world Power, that they are the cause of our 'failure'. I do not believe this to be the case.

. . .

Indeed what needs saying is that we are all of us more closely related, rather than the reverse. The independence of Eire has not halted the Irish brain drain to Britain. To cut Scotland off from England precisely when both are seeking to enter Europe is absolute folly.

. . .

Nor is there evidence that a Scottish Parliament was in the past, or would be today, the force for liberation and drive, for stimulus and effort that we need. A modern Watt or Kelvin or Walter Scott would do more for us than a glorified Glasgow Council meeting in Parliament House. We are these days – in both countries – over-preoccupied with Government and the State, too much the slaves of a nationalism that is too easy, too emotional and too unreflective.

The Declaration of Perth

Edward Heath

From a speech on 18 May 1968 to the annual Scottish Conservative Party conference in Perth. Heath was leader of the UK Conservative Party, and became prime minister between 1970 and 1974.

Scotland has a long history, often gay, sometimes grave, but always characteristically Scottish. You are proud and rightly proud of your traditions. As the MacIntosh of MacIntosh said this morning, proud of your famous regiments. Proud of your sons who have contributed so much to Britain and to the world. The Conservative Party has always cherished our national traditions. We look to diversity to enrich our national character. The rich variety of our people which has proved to be the glory of our nation.

Yet in the modern fast-moving world – a world of mass industrialisation, mass communication and increasingly complex organisation – there is a constant pressure towards uniformity and centralisation. . . . In the United States power tends to move increasingly away from the States and towards the Federal Government. In Europe countries have combined together in the Common Market and pooled some of their powers in the Central Council of Ministers. . . . [P]eople today demand more efficient services – whether in traffic, health, housing or education. They demand to see the practice in whatever is the best area of the country applied everywhere. They want to see each problem dealt with by the most specialised group of experts. All this requires Government to become more centralised and to be organised on a larger scale.

Yet, as this happens people suddenly realise that those who take the decisions on these matters – decisions which affect their daily lives in so many different ways – have become more remote. People feel deeply and instinctively that they are taking little part in making or even influencing those decisions.

. . .

The British have always been proud of their pragmatic approach to these problems. Our lack of a written constitution has given us greater freedom and increased flexibility. In the past we have used this to great advantage to develop our institutions, to meet the changing needs of our society. In this, as in so many other fields, we Conservatives, who have never been doctrinaire, have taken the lead.

. . .

And so in this situation I turn again to our basic principles. We find there two important strands. The first is that we have long been the party of Union. We remain the party of Union. Our fundamental belief is in the destiny of the United Kingdom. This strand was reinforced by the Liberal Unionists who joined us in the 1880s and added the name of Unionist to our Party. They shared our view then that the role of the United Kingdom was that of a great imperial power with world wide responsibilities. Today Britain's power, relatively speaking, may be less. But many of her international responsibilities remain. We can still exert an influence for good in the councils of the world. And I, for one, firmly believe in the unity of Britain.

The second strand is our belief in the devolution of power. As Quintin Hogg wrote twenty years ago in his book on Conservative philosophy: 'Political liberty is nothing else but the diffusion of power. . . . If power is not to be abused, it must be spread as widely as possible throughout the community' [Hogg, 1947, p. 62].

. . .

It is right that Scotland, which has for so long had her own legal system, her own local authority organisation and her own arrangements in so many other spheres should give a lead in new developments in the way in which she is governed. . . . Much of the dissatisfaction evident everywhere is of course due to bad Labour government. A failure of both men and measures. . . . Yet even if there were no Labour Government today it would still be right for us to be considering the most suitable form of government to handle the problems of our troubled age.

. . .

Some people want Scotland to remain not only an individual nation but to become a separate country. A country with its own Parliament, its own armed forces, its own customs arrangements, its own seat in the United Nations. This is separatism. Of course I respect the right of those who hold such a view to propagate it. They point to other countries smaller in size and population who stand completely independent. But in the Western world these are the countries which are moving towards closer alignment with their neighbours, not away from them. In Western Europe these nations are prepared to surrender part of their individual sovereignty in order to become members of a larger economic community. Any movement for the complete independence of Scotland is running against the tide of history in Western Europe.

. . .

It is therefore natural that some minds should have turned towards a federal Parliamentary system for the United Kingdom. They have been attracted by the idea of a Scottish Parliament responsible for all Scottish domestic affairs. . . . But this would lead naturally to a Welsh parliament and thence to Westminster becoming a purely English parliament. Some further body would then be required to handle the defence and overseas affairs of the United Kingdom.

. . .

There are considerable advantages in the Stormont system [for Northern Ireland]. They include the easy access of Ministers and Members of Parliament to their constituencies; the ability of groups with special concerns to press their case on the spot; the development of close relationships between local authorities and Government Departments; moreover, the system provides a seedbed for initiative in operation and for diversity in administration. Yet before we rush to reproduce Stormont in Edinburgh, it is as well to remind ourselves that conditions in Northern Ireland are very different from those in Scotland. Ulster accepted home rule because at the time it represented the only practical method of retaining the Ulster connection with Britain. This has remained Ulster's predominant aim and therefore Stormont has been prepared consistently to follow the pattern set by Westminster. But this is not the purpose of bringing about changes in the machinery of government in Scotland.

And a further point of great importance. In any full federal system Scotland might have to bear her own financial burdens. The greater the Scottish control over expenditure, the more the people of Scotland would have to shoulder the responsibility of finding the money to meet it. This could penalise Scotland. The people of Scotland might have to draw upon their own resources to an extent that would place them under intolerable strain.

. . .

The form of Government we seek must have the following characteristics:

- First, it must keep the United Kingdom united. . . .
- Second, it must make an effective effort to improve the machinery of government as it affects the people of Scotland. Quicker decisions, more speedy reactions to people's needs, more up to date legislation . . .
- Third, it must allow the people of Scotland to play their part in making decisions on Scottish legislation in Scotland.

. . .

- Fourth, it must provide them with an increased opportunity to propose and discuss United Kingdom policy as it affects Scotland.

. . .

To achieve these objectives the machinery of government in Scotland must be reorganised so as to enable it to carry out five distinct functions. This reorganisation should:

- Establish in Scotland a new means of expressing Scottish opinion on all matters relating to Scotland.
- It should enable purely Scottish legislation to be handled at certain stages in Scotland.
- It should form a direct link with the Secretary of State for Scotland and the Scottish Ministers as well as with Parliament.
- It should provide co-ordination on those matters where it is required, including finance and capital expenditure, between the new local authorities which are likely to be set up as a result of the Report of the Scottish Royal Commission on Local Government [the Wheatley Commission] and the central government.
- It should create in Scotland individual institutions in the limited field where further administrative devolution is still possible.

. . .

We would propose . . . the creation of an elected Scottish Assembly, to sit in Scotland. What we have in mind is that this Scottish Assembly would be a single chamber, and would take part in legislation in conjunction with

Parliament. In addition it would have all the other functions I have described.

. . .

Of course a large number of questions require to be examined and answered in detail before such an Assembly could be decided upon. Among those things which would have to settled would be:

- the precise constitution of the Assembly;
- the method of election and the timing of the elections – not necessarily based on traditional patterns;
- the detailed powers of the Assembly;
- the procedure for the resolution of any conflicts which might arise between the Assembly and Westminster;
- the allocation of financial responsibilities between the Assembly and the new local authorities.

. . .

Such problems are not insurmountable: but they require careful and detailed consideration.

THE THREE DREAMS OF SCOTTISH NATIONALISM

Tom Nairn

From an essay in *Memoirs of a Modern Scotland*, edited by Karl Miller (Faber, 1970), pp. 34–54. Nairn has been one of the most influential writers on Scottish nationalism since the 1960s; his own position has shifted from the one outlined here to that illustrated by his essay in Part IV.

Modern Scottish Nationalism has led a fluctuating, intermittent existence since 1853. Now, quite suddenly, it has become a more serious political reality. In the past it has gone through many renaissances, followed by even more impressive and longer-lasting collapses into inertia; but the present upsurge looks likely to last longer than others, at least, and to produce more of a mark on history.

Seen from without – from London, or in the perspective of British politics – the change appears welcome for many reasons. Like the companion nationalism of the Welsh, it brings an element of novelty into the hopelessness and corruption of the post-imperial political scene. Obviously, fringe nationalisms will be good for the English, by forcing upon them a more painful reassessment of themselves than any they have yet undergone. The smug 'deep-sleep' Orwell spoke of – the fruit of the older and most successful of modern imperialisms – would be more disturbed by the loss of Wales or Scotland than ever it was by the loss of India or Africa. And at the moment, a particular attraction to many must seem the near-destruction of the Labour Party's power which would result from the permanent loss of their Scottish or Welsh strongholds. In the slow, festering decay of British state and society, they are the most important forces of disintegration to have appeared yet; they prefigure the dismemberment of the united British society which built up the imperial system itself. They are at once a product of the collapse of the system, and the sharpest possible comment on the advanced state of this collapse. What justice it would be, if the Wilson government which came to power to 'save the pound' ended by losing Wales and Scotland as well!

Externally a positive reaction to the humiliating agony of a long era, Scottish Nationalism has another inwardness. For the Scots themselves, it is the late reflorescence of a dream, the hope of an identity, to which they have clung, obscurely and stubbornly, across centuries of provincial stagnation. Such a dream – and still more so, the time of its reflorescence – have a meaning which is bound to be far from clear outside Scotland.

. . .

The now dominant dream of Scotland reborn should perhaps be seen as the third phase in the dream-psychology (which has very often been a dream-pathology) of Scottish history. It is deeply marked by both the great dreams that preceded it. Like them, its most important trait is a vast, impossible dissociation from the realities of history. The best short definition of Scottish history may be this: Scotland is the land where ideal has never, even for an instant, coincided with fact. Most nations have had moments of truth, at least. Scotland, never. The resultant chronic laceration of the Scots mind – most brilliantly conveyed to the world in Stevenson's fable of Jekyll and Hyde – is the thing which gives poignancy to the hope of a Scotland remade, when seen from within. Scottish autonomy must appear there as the healing of the secular wound which has informed – and most often poisoned – Scottish consciousness ever since the Union of 1707. The real drama of the situation lies in its potential tragedy. It is not at all evident that the forms of autonomy one can reasonably foresee – whether partial or total – could cure the disease. They might perpetuate it, crystallising the long central hopelessness of Scottish history within a framework of archaic bourgeois nationality.

But this is to anticipate. The logical place to begin is with the first tormented vision Scotland was subject to: the Reformation. . . . [T]here is no doubt that Scotland was one of the most radically and successfully Reformed countries of Europe. The movement, which went on vigorously and progressively for over 150 years, from the time of Knox to that of the Covenanters, corresponds to the revolutions which have left their stamp on the histories and national psychologies of other countries.

. . .

This religious revolution derived its power and character precisely from its historical isolation. In the dreadful, chronic anarchy and medieval poverty of Scotland, it represented the one great effort of the Scottish people towards a meaningful order of their own. The effort was separated by centuries from the material conditions which – in Weber's or Tawney's thesis – should have corresponded to it, the process of capital accumulation [see Marshall, 1992]. This meant that originally the Reformation movement was an absolute attempt at moral and religious order, isolated from the very conditions that would have made it an integral part of history – at once 'corrupting' it, and bestowing upon it a real historical sense. Just because it could not be the veiled ideology of a class, the Scottish Reformation was bound to be an abstract, millennial dream – in effect, a desperate effort at escape from history, rather than a logical chapter in its unfolding. The Scots wanted, and needed, Salvation in the most total sense imaginable. Scotland's Revolution gave it them neat.

. . .

The strange, truncated condition of Scotland after 1707 made it natural to search for effective substitutes for the lost national identity. The Kirk was indeed such a substitute. But because of its unwordliness and its limitations of bigotry, inevitably an unsatisfactory one in the long run. In the later eighteenth century, Scotland produced two contrasting movements of culture that tried to compensate for the loss in their different ways. Basically similar to developments elsewhere in Europe, they acquired a particular meaning from the Scottish dilemma.

One was of the Edinburgh Enlightenment associated with the names of David Hume and Adam Smith. This was, in effect, an escape from the peculiar destiny of Scotland, onto the plane of abstract reason (though possibly the taste for abstractions it revealed had something to do with the theological inheritance). There was a cutting edge to Hume's celebrated joke about wishing to be pardoned his Scotticisms, rather than his sins, when on his death-bed. The other movement was the same reaction to the Enlightenment as other cultures produced, towards feeling and the particular: Romanticism. It is difficult to exaggerate the importance of Romanticism for Scotland. While the Enlightenment was only an episode, Romanticism entered her soul.

Here was the second of the dreams still implanted in the subsoil of Scottish consciousness. European history shows a general relationship between Romanticism and the nationalism of the nineteenth century, not entirely unlike that between the Reformation and capitalism . . . But, again, Scotland was a drastic exception to whatever generalities hold in this field. There, the new freedom of expression and the discovery of a folk-culture could scarcely be the precursors or the supports of a new nation in the making (as in Italy, Hungary, Germany), nor the accompaniment of triumphant nationality (as in England and America). The Scottish nationality was dead. Scotland was once more severed from those real conditions which should have lent meaning to her culture. No revolution against the humiliations of the Union, no Scottish 1848, was to furnish a historical counterpoint to Robert Burns and Sir Walter Scott. The romantic consciousness too, therefore, could only be an absolute dream to the Scots. Unable to function as ideology, as moving spirit of history, it too was bound to become a possessing demon. Elsewhere, the revelation of the romantic past and the soul of the people informed some real future – in the Scottish limbo, they *were* the nation's reality. Romanticism provided – as the Enlightenment could not, for all its brilliance – a surrogate identity.

. . .

A most exact historical sense can therefore be given to the assertion that Scotland is peculiarly haunted by the past. She is doubly dominated by her dead generations. At bottom there is the bedrock of Calvinism, the iron, abstract moralism of a people that distrusts this world and itself; then, overlaying this, the sentimental shadow-appropriation of this world and itself through romantic fantasy.

. . .

From this fertile soil has grown the myth-consciousness of modern Scotland, expressed in her nationalism. Nationalism is her third dream. It is basically a dream of redemption. For the Scots, national existence must represent that magic, whole reality of which they have been cheated by history – in it, their maimed past will be redeemed, in more vivid colours than a history can ever provide.

. . .

Scotland's myths of identity are articulated sufficiently to suit everyone. Though ministers of the Kirk, lawyers, lairds, tycoons and educationalists all have their own contrasting angles on the Geist, the principle articulation is between two poles. Nationalist ideology draws all its real force from one or the other. On the one hand, there is the popular – or populist – complex of ideas, which coincides enough with the foreign image of the Scots to need little elaboration here. Sporranry, alcoholism, and the ludicrous appropriation of the remains of Scotland's Celtic fringe as a national symbol, have been celebrated in a million emetic ballads. It is an image further blackened by a sickening militarism, the relic of Scotland's special role in the building up of British imperialism. Yet any judgement on this aspect of Scottish national consciousness ought to be softened by the recognition that these are the pathetic symbols of an inarticulate people unable to forge valid correlates of their different experience: the peculiar crudity of tartanry only corresponds to the peculiarly intense alienation of the Scots on this level. On the other hand, apparently (and very self-consciously!) remote from this, but part of the same machinery, there is the national consciousness of the intelligentsia. This is best seen as a sort of ethereal tartanry. Based upon rejecting the trash-image of Scotland, it aims to substitute something purer, but whose function will be the same: in effect, to seize the *real* soul of the land, beyond its blood-stained philistinism, beyond the Industrial Revolution ('This towering pulpit of the Golden Calf'), beyond the Kirk and its progeny.

. . .

Inevitably, Nationalist politics are built upon this web of accreted myth-consciousness. No more striking illustration of this can be found than the common myth of Scottish Left-ness. Useful as a North Atlantic Cuba would be, the conviction that this is Scotland's destiny rests on particularly shifting ground. Scotland is certainly a more egalitarian country than England, and in some ways a more violent one. It does not follow that she is a more revolutionary one.

Scotland's gritty sense of equality derives from the old theocracy, not from Jacobinism or Bolshevism. It is double-edged, like every other aspect of that heritage. It stands for the democracy of souls before the All Mighty, rather than an explosive, popular effort to *do* anything. It is extremely touchy, but passive. This passivity is intimately linked to something even more dangerous. According to the rabid forms of Protestantism that got the upper hand in Scotland, the democracy of souls is an uneasy one. Souls may be either saved or damned, and which way one goes is by far the most important question of life on earth. Regrettably, there is no rational way of resolving the problem, so that argument about it is necessarily sectarian, and endless. The only solution is by fiat, from above, by an Authority that selects the Elect from the ranks of the damned. Hence, a kind of masochism, a craving for discipline, in fact, accompanies this Scottish sense of equality. . . .

Scottish Nationalism is not in the least inherently 'Left'. It belongs squarely within a category quite familiar in the history of the world outside Scotland: bourgeois nationalism. This is, in fact, implied by the majority of Nationalist propagandists, in their favourite argument: why not Scotland? They compare the case of Scotland to those of the many new nations and nationalities which have emerged since 1945, every one of them blessed with a seat at the United Nations. Surely Scotland's 'claim' is as good as any of theirs?

Claim to *what*? This is the question that the Nationalist myth mentality appears largely consecrated to evading, with the assistance of all hands. The

right to be free, territorial self-control, even the idea of nationality itself –
these are not timeless truths, but the products of a certain logic in the
historical process. . . . Nations and nationalisms are aspects of the bourgeois epoch of world history. Within this epoch it has (or in most cases, has
had) two sorts of justification as a historical force. Firstly, as a necessary
means of escape from feudal or other primitive systems that were an
impossible barrier to economic and social progress. In this sense, nationalism was a precondition of the formation of modern society, and such a
vital one that bourgeois civilisation has on the whole remained cast in its
mould; it is only now beginning to break away from it. Secondly – mainly in
the twentieth century – nationalism has served as an analogous instrument
for non-European societies to escape from another system which for them
constituted an equally insuperable barrier to development: western imperialism. . . . [I]n both cases nationalism had a double positive function:
externally, as a means of sweeping away archaic or predatory social forms,
and internally, as a means of mobilising populations for socio-economic
development.

Where is Scottish Nationalism located in this perspective? In its present
form, nowhere. That is, a tragic dream comparable to the other dreams of
Scotland's history precisely in its remoteness from those real conditions
which could give it the historical significance it implicitly claims. Any
reasonable political judgement on Scottish Nationalism must take into
account both this remoteness, and its meaning in terms of Scottish history.

True to their nature, the Scots usually voice their nationalism in a very
moral manner. Nowhere more so than in placing themselves within the
great twentieth-century anti-imperialist movement of national liberation.
There can therefore be no harm in pointing out some of the moral truths
which *do*, in fact, attach to the position of their country in the history of
the world.

First of all, Scotland is not a colony, a semi-colony, a pseudo-colony, a
near-colony, a neo-colony or any kind of colony of the English. She is a
junior but (as these things go) highly successful partner in the general
business enterprise of Anglo-Scots imperialism. Now that this business is
evidently on its last legs, it may be quite reasonable for the Scots to want
out. But there is really no point in disguising this desire with heroic ikonry.
After all, when the going was good for imperialism, the world heard very
little of the Scots' longing for independence. . . .

Admittedly, Scotland – along with the English North-East and South-
West – has also long been the victim of the unequal development
characteristic of advanced capitalism. Such areas are characterised by
higher, chronic rates of unemployment, poorer housing, high emigration,

and generally lag behind the favoured zones of growth (like the English South-East, or the Paris conurbation). It has been recognised that one way – perhaps a necessary way – of countering this tendency is to give more power over their own affairs to these regions. . . .

But this is to confer upon Scotland's problems a status quite different from the one enshrined in the Nationalist mythology. It makes the purpose of 'independence' into a minor administrative problem. Autonomy becomes an antidote for some of the worst damage done by the reckless past evolution of the capitalist system. Looked at in this perspective, regional nationalisms could have usefulness to the system second only to its principal support through times of crisis: the Labour Party. There is some formal analogy between such regional distortions of development within capitalism, and the world problem of 'underdevelopment'; but there is such a difference of scale and quality that is really absurd to try and read the same political meanings into the two situations.

. . .

This study has not dealt with the tired legalistic arguments for independence, re-heated and served up in every Home Rule debate for the past 100 years. Anyone concerned with these fantasms . . . will find a good summary of them in H. J. Paton's recent *The Claim of Scotland*. Nor has it dealt with that other major obsession of the Nationalist mind: the totally Pickwickian 'economic problem' of whether Scotland would be 'viable' and could survive 'on her own' – as if she was some kind of small shopkeeper, in fact, not part of an international economic order. It has concentrated, instead, on certain aspects of Scottish history which may explain the larger depths of feeling, the structural (often half-conscious) attitudes of Nationalist psychology.

The objection that any such attempt always meets is that things are left out of it, that it fails to embrace the variety and richness of a society. In the case of Scotland, the objection is especially strong, both because of the intellectuals' revulsion against Kirk and tartan (which leads them to stress some other aspect of the country as all-important) and because of the actual variety of society there. But the point of the analysis is not to embrace and explain everything, or even to touch upon everything important. It is simply to outline the *dominant* cultural tradition: the lasting complex of attitudes derived from the historical mainstream, which asserts itself as the central reference-point, the matrix, in the system of communication that is a culture. This reference-point does not obliterate everything else, or seek to do so. Yet everything else is compelled to define its own cultural existence in relation to it, whether this relation is subordination or the utmost conscious hostility. It is the central language or idiom, whose terms everyone must begin from.

. . .

It seems to me difficult to deny that the tradition considered here, deriving from Calvinism and Romanticism, is still a 'dominant' one in this sense, in Scotland. Indeed, it is a singularly dominant and obsessive one, quite unmistakably present in most facets of her national culture. This particularly strong hegemony is clearly related to Scotland's provincial character, to the abstraction of her culture from history in the last two centuries, and the consequent stagnation and in-growing nature of what was left. The whole problem is here. A fossilised and recessive culture is the product of Scotland's long half-life. And while this means that the country badly needs a more whole life again, so that new ferments can put an end to this stagnation, the fossilised cultural language is itself a major barrier to such wholeness. Nationalism merely ignores the problem, and this ignorance is the precise measure of its own provinciality. The belief that a bourgeois parliament and an army will cure the disease is the apex of lumpen-provinciality, the most extreme form of parochialism. As if half Europe didn't testify to the contrary!

The point of a successfully dominant tradition like the one I have tried to outline is not that it obliterates all difference and contrary tendencies – but rather, that it renders them ineffective and secondary.

. . .

In this land, it is also true that the spirit of the old Scots grim man has been constantly challenged, that the Kirk and our miserable tartan-waistcoated bourgeoisie have never had things all their own way. But the pity is, that they don't have to have things all their own way. I do not want to forget, or belittle, the popular folk tradition that has always underlain the sermons and the nostalgia. But – in the perspective of this discussion – the point is that (unfortunately) it has been forced to remain a minor, subordinate tradition of protest. I do not want to turn aside either from Scotland's native tradition of working-class protest, from John Maclean, Clydeside radicalism, or the communist tradition of the miners. But again, one is compelled to admit their lack of success, in the long battle, their failure to destroy or seriously change the character of the enemy.

It is perhaps even more important today to point out the danger to the very survival of such dissenting currents which Nationalism represents. For Nationalism appeals powerfully both to popular folk tradition and to the working class. Its essence is exactly a kind of phoney, apparently radical populism, which looks all the more radical because of its unfamiliarity in British politics. Populism unites the whole 'people' behind the image of the nation, which is everyone's birthright, everyone's property. But in fact, where it does this on the basis of a social and cultural structure like Scotland's, it really conscripts the rebels and the dissenting classes behind their old enemies. The Edinburgh baillie and the shipyard worker can both be joined in praise of Nationalism; but the nation and its culture belong to the former, not to the latter, and the triumph of a merely populist nationalism will signify a greatly strengthened grip of the real ruling class.

. . .

We can only escape from our unreality, our historical dreamland, through a dream which places Scotland in the living mainstream of the history of our time. And this is not in the dusty mansion of SNP rhetoric – it has nothing to do with it. In the same years in which nationalism again became a force in Scotland, the western world was shaken by the first tremors of a new social revolution, from San Francisco to Prague. I for one am enough of a nationalist, and have enough faith in the students and young workers of Glasgow and Edinburgh, to believe that these forces are also present in them. I will not admit that the great dreams of May 1968 are foreign to us, that the great words on the Sorbonne walls would not be at home on the walls of Aberdeen or St Andrews, or that Linwood and Dundee could not be Flins and Nantes. Nor will I admit that, faced with a choice between the spirit of the Mouvement du 22 Mars and Mrs Ewing, we owe it to 'Scotland' to choose the latter. On the contrary, in a country poisoned by stale authoritarianism, the universal revolt of youth against authoritarianism should have a quite special sense and value.

. . .

Of course, one might object that the dichotomy is too sharply drawn. In any case, a nationalist triumph – even SNP-style – must bring a certain amount of social upheaval and change, and the liberation of new ideas and forces. But this doesn't lessen the choice one bit. For obviously the time to start fighting for the new ideas, with the new forces, is now, not then.

THE GOVERNMENT OF SCOTLAND

Labour Party in Scotland

Part of a submission which the Labour Party in Scotland made to the Royal Commission on the Constitution (Kilbrandon Commission). It was published by the party in 1970.

– INTRODUCTION –

In this evidence we shall argue that the best interests of Scotland will be served by radical changes in local government structure – such that local democracy as it now exists can be strengthened and extended over greater areas – and by changes in the Scottish Office and other Government procedures so that decisions made by existing authorities are more open and more comprehensible. We have considered long and carefully the possibility of a separate Parliament, Assembly, Council or some other elected authority with executive or legislative powers covering the whole of Scotland, and we feel strongly that any such body – whilst superficially attractive as a short-term palliative to our problems – would be divisive and would inevitably create an unfavourable environment for the methods of government which we require.

As socialists, we have traditionally fought to bring more power to the people. A central tenet of our faith is, and always has been, that every community should have the powers to control decisions which affect its life. No other party has campaigned as we have to extend the franchise, to support elected representatives in their local efforts, to improve egalitarian education, to bring democracy to industry, and to build a society which is based upon co-operation and community. Labour *is* the Party of the local community, and in many ways our very existence is due to the efforts of local leaders and their struggles to build a cogent structure of self-government in which every citizen can play his part.

Democratic socialism has always held that those decisions which can best be taken in a local community should be based there. But democratic socialism has also held that the eventual key to man's ability to control his environment and co-exist with others must lie in finding an *international* perspective to his problems. In short, as democratic socialists, we believe both in strong local communities *and* in the development of an international order.

. . .

The position of Scottish government within the present structure of the United Kingdom is unique. Scotland's interests are looked after by machinery which involves Scottish Office and civil servants at all levels of policy making and discussion, within UK Ministries and at Cabinet level. The Scottish Grand Committee of the House of Commons has more respect and larger experience than any other similar group, and to this has been recently added a Select Committee on Scottish Affairs.

It is hardly surprising that the representatives of English regions of similar proportion and size often envy us both this machinery and the results it can produce for Scotland. We enjoy this favourable administrative situation partly because Scotland is not a region but a member nation of the United Kingdom, and also because it is recognised that Scotland has economic and social problems which require the special attention which such a structure makes possible.

. . .

– The Case against Separatism –

The major factor determining how far it is possible and desirable to increase domestic scrutiny over decision-taking on Scottish affairs is the impact on Scotland following changes in the internal cohesion of the United Kingdom and particularly the cohesion of the United Kingdom economy. Conflict can and does occur in designing machinery of government between the needs of efficiency and the requirements for democratic public accountability.

The economic case for decision-taking at the United Kingdom level and against fragmentation of economic planning powers is overwhelming. Technological, financial and marketing factors would all be distorted if policies were evolved for Scotland which were not harmonious and compatible with economic policy for the United Kingdom as a whole. In fact, the present trend of economic management is moving towards greater integration – towards a harmony of the United Kingdom economy with others through such agreements as the General Agreement on Trade and Tariffs, the Kennedy Round, bilateral trade agreements, bilateral production pacts and even possible entry into the EEC.

On these grounds alone a separate Scotland is unacceptable to us. Maximum benefits to Scotland will only come if the United Kingdom economy is planned as a whole. An economy of over 5 million with more than its fair share of older industries and far more than its share of urban and social problems is not a healthy economic base in this modern world.

. . .

– THE NEED FOR DEVOLUTION –

Having said all of this, it is not our purpose in this evidence to suggest that no changes in the present machinery of Government are necessary. Quite apart from the setting up of the Commission on the Constitution, the reform of government in general is now benefiting from a vital public debate.

There are a number of reasons why this is so. First, as we have indicated, tremendous changes are taking place in the structure of UK government. Since 1964 reform . . . of Parliament, the law, the civil service, trade unions and the nationalised industries has begun to take place. Second, a new and welcome enlightenment of the power of ordinary people to control events is now occurring; this sometimes means peaceful demonstrations in the street, but far more often it means that people simply do not believe – until they see the evidence – the claims of government to have advanced their causes. In Scotland this has meant, unfortunately, that there is a gap between what actually has been achieved and what people think has been achieved. Thus a desire for change may rest upon inadequate information and appreciation. But, third, perhaps the most important present manifestation of desire for new initiatives has come from the debates surrounding the work of two Royal Commissions on Local Government Reform [Wheatley in Scotland and Redcliffe-Maud in England and Wales]. The evidence submitted to those bodies, and their eventual reports, undoubtedly created fresh interest in and awareness of the need for radical reform of local democratic structures.

Democracy is not just an exercise in head-counting. A healthy and progressive democracy is most complex; it must involve the representation of minorities; it must allow for leadership and trust – even at times when a simple majority would not automatically and immediately follow; it must devise institutions which are themselves representative, and which are clearly seen to be so; and it must create machinery whereby decisions can be fashioned to fit the needs both of the individuals who are primarily concerned and of the whole community at large. Democracy requires equality, but democratic institutions must be flexible enough to recognise and represent the deep and important cultural and social differences which might exist amongst the people being governed.

Labour's policy for Scotland has evolved against this intellectual back-cloth. We have supported measures which can nurture and sustain the traditions, the strong sense of community, and the strong feeling of national identity which exists in Scotland. . . . That is why we have held to our view that cultural and economic needs must be distinguished. . . .

The motivation of today's pressure for greater devolution is complex. But we believe that much of it can be traced quickly and directly to a perfectly natural reaction against the pace of change in modern economic institutions. This reaction we oppose. The rest arises from the development of a greater consciousness that economic and administrative efficiency – whilst crucial in themselves – are insufficient to create a satisfactory society. Democracy is about collective decision making as well as efficient use of resources; it is about accountability and understanding as well as economic progress.

– ECONOMIC PLANNING –

One considerable step in devolution which has taken place since 1964 has been the setting up, throughout the UK, of Economic Planning Boards and Councils. The creation of the Scottish Economic Planning Council has enabled local authorities, industrial, trade union and other leaders to play a larger part in shaping economic policy for Scotland. The position of the Secretary of State as Chairman of the Council enables direct channels of communication to be opened up between these outside interests, the Scottish Office and the Cabinet.

. . .

[W]e favour an approach which increases the influence of the Planning Council without according it executive 'powers' – these would in any case in practice be curtailed by the need to agree common policies applicable to all of the UK. Our proposals are as follows:

1. Representative institutions should be encouraged to submit matters for consideration by the Council, which could itself set up a small Agenda Committee which would sift such suggestions and table them for discussion in addition to those brought forward by either the Secretary of State or the main sub-committees of the Council.
2. The Council should have powers to commission studies on matters affecting the economic development of Scotland. To this end it should

have a small expert secretariat of its own and have its own research budget. This would help to distinguish the Planning Council from the Scottish Office and enable some of the more speculative proposals to be publicised and explored, entirely without Government commitment.
3. The work of the Planning Council should be more widely publicised, with its agenda and minutes put widely into circulation amongst the institutions represented on the Council.

. . .

– Local Government Reform –

The Scottish Council of the Labour Party firmly believes that the reform of local government presents the best and most immediate opportunity for further devolution of power to Scotland, and for a parallel strengthening of Scottish local democracy. In our view the reform of local government is long overdue, and the consequent inability of present structures to meet modern needs has contributed enormously to the wider call for devolution in recent years. Local government is, therefore, the most appropriate field in which to build greater public control over our environment.

. . .

– MPs and the Grand Committee –

[T]he people of Scotland already possess a legislative and executive instrument which serves them better than they think and which is capable of as much single-minded concentration upon Scottish interests as is compatible with the continued functioning of a genuine United Kingdom Parliament. The legislative and executive instrument is composed of the Scottish Office, the Scottish Ministers of State, and the total of 71 Members of Parliament elected for Scottish constituencies. Of course, it is true that legislation is passed at Westminster, but, as we see it, Parliament at Westminster serves the Scot for purposes of passing legislation at least as well as it serves the English.

. . .

In our view, while there should be ample scope for purely Scottish measures and for the more occasional pioneering effort, we think that much legislation affecting Scotland should continue to take the form of Great Britain measures and would expect that the Scottish interest in those measures will be taken proper care of by Scottish ministers and Members.

If it is objected against such a course that the Scot will always be in too small a minority at Westminster properly to protect the Scottish interest, we would say that legislative differences are almost always Party differences and that Scots like others will normally divide on Party lines.

. . .

Some recent Parliamentary developments point the way to . . . greater powers of scrutiny, and it seems to us that Scottish MPs and Scottish people can benefit from these no less than can non-Scots. Among these developments, we refer particularly to the setting up of the Office of the Parliamentary Commissioner, or Ombudsman, which extends and refines the ability of Parliament and the MP to probe and rectify possible injustices. Second, the increased number of House of Commons Select Committees, including the Select Committee for Scottish Affairs, provides added means whereby public services and government functions can be examined with a thoroughness that would have been quite impracticable without this Parliamentary instrument.

. . .

[W]hether or not the Scottish Grand Committee should meet in Edinburgh, either during or outside Parliamentary sessions, for us the most important consideration is the likely effect upon the unity of the United Kingdom government. What we fear and would oppose is any move that was likely to cause a widening breach between the Scottish people and the rest of the British people. There is a risk that Edinburgh sittings of the Scottish Grand Committee could lead to a reduction of Scottish time and facilities at Westminster, and if those fears and that risk are guarded against, we think that Edinburgh sittings of the Scottish Grand Committee could be tried. We remain open-minded to the possibilities of further non-divisive steps in devolution in the longer term future if these appear to be necessary and practicable after Scottish local government reform has been implemented and tested.

Forms and Consequences of Federalism

Scottish Liberal Party

Part of a submission which the Scottish Liberal Party made to the Royal Commission on the Constitution (Kilbrandon Commission). It was published by the party in 1970.

– Federalism in other countries –

There are many different kinds of federal systems practised in many countries all over the world from Switzerland to the United States, from Canada, to Germany, to Australia. It is noteworthy that whilst resisting federalism at home, successive British governments have fathered federal systems in their principal former colonial dependencies. It is obviously impractical for the Scottish Liberal Party to give detailed evidence on the operation of federalism elsewhere, but we would most strongly urge the Commission to make such comparative studies.

. . .

– Use of referendum –

Federalism as a form of constitutional government has always been invoked in other parts of the world as a method of linking together separate sovereign states or colonies. In arguing for the creation of federalism in the United Kingdom, we are arguing for the devolution of an existing unitary state, and while we would certainly argue that this would strengthen rather than weaken its cohesion, it remains true that we are approaching federalism from a new standpoint and this inevitably creates certain difficulties. Where two or three states wish to form a federation they meet and decide which powers are to be given to the new central federal government and which powers are to remain with the original governments. This is not possible in the United Kingdom as there are no proper agencies through which the nations could act. Initiative must, therefore, come from the existing Westminster Parliament . . . We know that referenda have not been a customary method of ascertaining opinion in the United Kingdom . . . and . . . we feel their use should be confined to constitutional issues but on such issues their use to establish initially the real feelings of the peoples of the United Kingdom would be invaluable.

. . .

– Scottish Liberal Party's views –

The Scottish Liberal Party's views on a Federal structure were embodied in the Bill put forward by Russell Johnston MP in 1966. This set out our proposals on how such a system should be operated with regard to Scotland and its relationship with the UK parliament. . . . [It] proposed a Scottish parliament and government with power both to legislate for Scotland in matters not reserved to the UK parliament and to levy taxes in Scotland other than customs and excise duties. A Joint Exchequer Board would agree Scotland's contribution to the UK government expenditure (defence, foreign office etc.) and Scotland's share of UK customs and excise revenue. The chief subjects reserved to the UK parliament were: the Crown; peace and war; foreign affairs; defence; customs and excise, and 'the maintenance of the currency and such economic policy as is agreed to affect both countries'. The division of powers could be changed by agreement between the Scottish and UK parliaments. The Scots representatives at Westminster would remain, but would not vote on domestic non-Scottish matters.

– A POSSIBLE FEDERAL CONSTITUTION –

The report of the Scottish Liberal Party's Structure of Government Committee outlines possible Federal and Scottish constitutions expanding on the proposals in [Johnston's] Scottish Self Government Bill . . . The Federal parliament would have two chambers – a directly elected Assembly of approximately 315 members and a Senate of 32 indirectly elected from the Federal Assembly and the National Parliaments.

– Scottish Parliament –

The Scottish Parliament would comprise a single directly-elected Chamber of about 142 members. It would be competent to legislate for all matters not specifically delegated to the Federal parliament and to levy, collect and appropriate all taxes, other than customs and excise and associated duties and National Insurance and associated contributions.

– Federal Parliament –

The Federal Assembly would have delegated responsibility for, broadly, defence and foreign affairs. It would also debate federal economic policy.

The Federal Senate would, initially, apportion assets and debts among the National Governments. It would have delegated responsibility for:

1. matters of common interest (e.g. those within the scope of common policies of the European Community);
2. parity of the currency and standardisation of weights, measures etc;
3. determination of scales of National Insurance and scales of social security and associated benefits;
4. levying and collection of customs and excise and associated duties;
5. determination of apportionments from the Federal Treasury and to National Treasuries; and
6. appropriations from the Federal Treasury to finance Federal Senate responsibilities.

The Federal Senate is envisaged as, in effect, a Committee of the leading National Ministries and opposition spokesmen, which would deal with the detailed Federal economic policy, while the Federal Assembly would debate its general principles.

A UK Federal Court would be established with two judges from each UK nation. It would decide in doubtful questions arising from the Act setting up the Federation and would also act as a final UK court of appeal on civil rights – a Declaration of Rights being envisaged as part of the Act setting up the Federation. There would be a further right of appeal to the Council of Europe.

– Possibility of a Phased Federalism –

If, however, your Commission is unwilling to contemplate recommending the adoption of a federal constitution forthwith we ask you carefully to consider the possibilities of a phased federalism. This falls short of our aims, but would certainly be a considerable improvement on the present situation, would be relatively easy to implement and would create a situation and indeed a climate in which movement towards full federalism would be simplified. We confine the gradualist suggestion to Scotland but clearly similar proposals could be worked out for England and Wales. Northern Ireland might require special treatment.

– Scottish Parliament to control St Andrew's House –

The existing administrative responsibilities of the Scottish Office are: Law, Education, Agriculture, Forestry and Fisheries, Health and Welfare, Police, Fire, Prisons etc, Housing, Local Government, Transport (roads) and Power (electricity). We would suggest that these be brought under the control of an elected Scottish parliament chosen, to avoid complicated electoral machinery, from the existing constituencies, so that each constituency would elect two MPs, one to Edinburgh and one to Westminster. This Scottish Parliament should also be given control over: Transport (railways, airports and ports), Power (gas, coal and oil), Public Building and Works, Industrial Development, University Education, Culture and Sport. Arrangements would have to be made for the closest co-operation between Edinburgh and Westminster Governments over such common matters as railways, nuclear energy and industrial training.

. . .

– Powers of First Stage Scottish Parliament –

The main difference between this first stage of devolution and our federal policy is that the Scottish government would simply allocate annually . . . the total amount of UK government expenditure on Scotland which would otherwise be spent piecemeal and controlled item by item in London. . . . The normal electoral pressure of the seventy-one Scottish seats at Westminster would continue to ensure a 'fair' share of public expenditure in Scotland. Within this, policies and priorities in expenditure would be wholly determined in Scotland by a government responsible to a Scottish Parliament.

The Scottish government and parliament would also have the power to make direct representations to the UK government on any matter not within their executive control. This parliament and government would be established by a 'Government of Scotland Act'. In the event of the Scottish Parliament wishing a change in their constitutional position they would be empowered to petition the Westminster parliament for alterations to either the Government of Scotland Act or the Act of Union. Such a petition would require to be debated by both the House of Commons and the House of Lords within three months of its presentation. In this way the Scottish Parliament would not only have democratic control over a Scottish government, but would act as a powerful political focus in Scotland and as an effective instrument for constitutional advance. The Scottish parliament would be free to press for full federal or even separate sovereign status. The Scottish parliament in addition to holding debates and questioning its ministers would also assume full power over Scottish legislation. The Scottish Grand Committee would be abolished and the UK parliament would have no power to extend its legislation to Scotland in those fields over which the Scottish parliament was sovereign.

The Westminster Parliament would be unaffected except that the seventy-one Scottish MPs would no longer be allowed to participate or vote on purely English or Welsh affairs and the English and Welsh in turn would be freed from the marionette compulsion to vote on the Report Stages of Scottish Bills.

An Assembly

Scottish Constitutional Committee of the Conservative Party

From *Scotland's Government* (1970) report of the Scottish Constitutional Committee, which had been set up by Edward Heath in 1968, and which was chaired by Sir Alec Douglas Home, former prime minister: see Mitchell (1990, pp. 58–60). Douglas Home was MP for Kinross and West Perthshire.

We feel that it is appropriate to repeat one of the main principles laid down by the Balfour Royal Commission on Scottish affairs (1954, p. 12):

> Scotland's needs and points of view should be known and brought into account at all stages in the formulation and execution of policy, that is to say, when policy is being considered, when policy is decided and when policy is announced.

We agree with this statement.

Consequently, we have tried to ensure not only a more effective Scottish say over Scottish affairs but also to enable Government and Parliament fully to be aware of Scotland's interests and needs. Our aim has been to find a solution to Scotland's problems which would combine administrative efficiency with a greater participation by the Scottish people in matters of concern to Scotland.

We have tried to indicate how some improvements can be made in this direction by strengthening the machinery at the disposal of the Secretary of State and the other Scottish Ministers. Such progress would be enhanced by conferring new responsibilities on enlarged local authorities. Lord Wheatley's Royal Commission has recommended a possible pattern for the future based upon Regional and 'second-tier' District authorities.

. . .

– A Scottish Assembly –

If local government reform were to proceed on the lines recommended in the Wheatley Report there would be two sets of persons chosen by the

Scottish electors to represent them. Members of Parliament would continue to be sent to Westminster after election on the present constituency basis, while Regional and District councillors would be elected from other constituencies yet to be defined.

Between the Members of Parliament and the Regional councillors and the administrative services which they would provide there would remain an important field of service to the Scottish nation. Public discussion of policy is desirable at a variety of local levels, as well as in Parliament. One of the questions which we were set to answer was whether it could take place with advantage on an all-Scotland basis.

– Types of Assembly –

The case for an assembly depends on the functions which it could usefully perform. Two alternatives and variants of them have been subjected to a very detailed investigation. We considered:

1. an assembly which is advisory, consultative and inquisitory; and
2. an assembly which has, in addition, legislative powers.

– The Case for an Assembly –

It is all too evident that the Scottish people in general do not know nearly enough about how their affairs are conducted. Extensive publicity might help to remedy this situation, but an increased involvement in the process of decision making would do more. A valid Scottish point of view may fail to make an impact on Parliament in time – that is, before legislation is drafted and put into the shape of a Bill. Parliament has not always appreciated peculiarly Scottish requirements or particular aspects of Scottish Law. Lack of knowledge in Scotland about what is already being done on Scotland's behalf combined with experiences which appear to support the charge of neglect by Whitehall add up to a considerable sum of frustration.

On the evidence, we find that there is a case for doing more of Scotland's business in public and in Scotland; and our task has been to decide how best this goal could be achieved.

– A Consultative Assembly –

One way of reaching this end would be to bring together elected representatives drawn from the new local authorities and some independent persons in order to focus, to harmonise and to present a Scottish point of view on all aspects of government which affect Scotland. Such an assembly would meet for certain purposes:

1. to co-ordinate Regional views on contemporary issues and help to form Scottish opinion;
2. to meet the Scottish Ministers, in order to review and to consult upon the state of the nation;
3. to express an opinion at a preliminary stage on legislative and financial proposals concerning Scotland;
4. to question the Scottish Ministers on the implications of national and local decisions;
5. to comment on the Scottish estimates; and
6. to debate matters of concern to Scotland.

The sittings of such a body would be held in public.

An objection to this type of assembly is that it could only 'talk'. But talk is in fact a very large part of Parliament's activities. Indeed, 'parleying' was the origin of Parliament. The right to discuss should by no means be disparaged, particularly when it can contribute to the spread of knowledge and understanding. Such a body would go a long way towards creating an informed Scottish opinion. It would give to Scottish Ministers the benefit of local experience, knowledge and opinion and provide for a full expression of Scottish points of view before decisions were taken either in Edinburgh or in London. An assembly of this kind could be elected directly or indirectly from the constituencies to be formed for the new local government authorities.

– AN ASSEMBLY WITH LEGISLATIVE POWERS –

The question then arises as to whether an assembly limited to such a role would meet the need, or whether some legislative function ought to be added. An assembly with legislative powers would need to be directly elected.

At present parliament passes three main types of public legislation:

1. measures affecting the United Kingdom (or Great Britain) as a whole;
2. measures affecting all of the United Kingdom (or Great Britain) but requiring special clauses to make them applicable to Scotland; and
3. measures applying to Scotland alone.

Under existing arrangements there are Bills in category 3 which are certified by the Speaker of the House of Commons as exclusively Scottish measures. These Bills are, in effect, already separated from the mainstream of United Kingdom legislation and are considered by the Scottish Grand Committee and the Scottish Standing Committee.

It would be an extension of current Parliamentary practice to send these Bills, certified by the Speaker of the House of Commons as exclusively Scottish Bills, to a Scottish Assembly. Such Bills could be passed through the main legislative stages of Second Reading and Committee and Report stages in Edinburgh, the Third Reading and all stages in the House of Lords being reserved for Westminster, in order to preserve the essential principle of the sovereignty of Parliament. . . . It would also be appropriate for a Scottish assembly to handle Bills relating to Scottish Law. . . . In addition, it should be possible to arrange for the assembly to assist in the consideration of private legislation proposals and statutory instruments.

The effects of such changes would be to transfer much of the work of the Scottish Grand Committee and the Scottish Standing Committee to an elected body in Scotland, while retaining the final say with Parliament. Such arrangements would help substantially to relieve the congested Westminster time-table and free Scottish Members of Parliament from the excessive amount of work at present laid upon them.

. . .

There are two ways in which Scottish Bills might be devolved. The first would be automatically to transfer all Scottish Bills certified as exclusively Scottish, so that their main stages could be taken in Edinburgh. The second would be that Parliament, on a Government motion, should decide which Bills it would wish to keep for debate in Westminster and which should be sent to the assembly. We think that Parliament may well prefer the second of these alternatives.

. . .

We are convinced that the present number of Scottish members of Parliament in the House of Commons (seventy-one) should not be reduced. . . . As the assembly would constitute in effect a chamber of Parliament, all its members should be directly elected. The elections of the assembly should take place at the same time as those of Members of Parliament.

. . .

– THE SCOTTISH MINISTERS –

An important question which arises in connection with an assembly concerns its relations with the Secretary of State for Scotland and the other Scottish Ministers. Unless there is to be confusion and therefore bad government, the duties of the Queen's Ministers must be precisely defined. We consider it to be essential that the Secretary of State and the other Scottish Ministers continue to be the Scottish Executive. It is, moreover, necessary for the Government of the day to have the opportunity to pass its programme of legislation into the law of the land. This can only be done if the responsibility of the Secretary of State and the other Scottish Ministers is clear and undiluted. This principle is fundamental to our recommendation of an Assembly.

– [DIFFICULTIES] –

The possibility of friction between the assembly and the Secretary of State has to be faced. There will doubtless be occasions when a Bill will be rejected on Second Reading or amended in ways which are not acceptable. The Secretary of State would then have the ordinary parliamentary remedies. He could take the Bill back and modify it, introduce a new Bill, drop the Bill altogether or introduce it in Parliament. A study of the list of Scottish legislation suggests that such happenings would be very rare. In the main this consists of legislation which is not unduly controversial. We believe that should the members of an assembly try to be factious and to block Scottish legislation the electors would soon take steps to remedy the situation. Finally, it is reasonable to assume that Scotsmen are responsible citizens.

The possibility of a single political party becoming permanently entrenched as a majority in the assembly has been mentioned to us. An analysis of Scottish Parliamentary representation in the last seventy years does not support this fear.

. . .

– ADVANTAGES –

An assembly would provide a parliamentary forum in Scotland for the promotion of Scottish legislation and for the public discussion of Scottish affairs. It would add to the time available for dealing with Scottish business and at the same time help to relieve congestion at Westminster. It would provide an opportunity for contact and partnership between local politics and national politics in ways which have not been possible up to now. It would make the administration responsive to an elected body in Scotland, at a time when greater power is likely to be placed in the hands of officials. It would contribute to the improvement of government generally. It would enable persons of ability and experience, whose commitments in Scotland make it impossible for them to fulfil the duties of a Member of Parliament, to make their contribution to Scottish public life through a chamber meeting in Scotland. We would hope that a number of members of the new local authorities would feel it advantageous also to stand for election to the assembly. We believe that the assembly will fill a void in the framework of Scottish institutions and provide a necessary forum for Scottish discussion of Scottish affairs.

– TITLE –

Because it has a Scottish flavour and in order to avoid confusion with ecclesiastical bodies which periodically comment on Scottish public affairs, we propose that the Scottish legislative assembly should be styled 'The Scottish Convention'.

– CONCLUSION –

Throughout our deliberations we have been very conscious that Scotland's problem is but one part of a much wider debate over how to reconcile local interests with the wider political and administrative machinery which is necessary for efficiency and prosperity in the modern world. There are many features of Scotland's life – the Church, the Law, the Secretaryship of State, the Scottish Office and the evolving practice of Scottish legislation in Parliament – which provide a natural basis for parliamentary devolution.

It is clear that such a devolutionary plan would need to have regard to the new pattern of local government, following consideration of and action on the Wheatley Commission's Report.

In our proposals we have insisted on certain principles:

1. that the sovereignty of Parliament should be preserved;
2. that the Union should be maintained; and
3. that the process of change should be consistent with the evolution of existing Parliamentary practice.

Within these proposals we sought a solution which will give the Scottish people greater opportunity to express their opinion in a more effective way in Scotland. We believe that a Scottish Convention will go far to remove existing grievances and frustrations. The Convention will ensure that Scotland's needs and points of view will be taken fully into account.

A Scheme of Legislative Devolution

Royal Commission on the Constitution

The report of the Kilbrandon Commission was published in 1973 (Cmnd 5460). The extract reproduced here (from paragraphs 1125 to 1148) is the part of it which had the greatest influence on subsequent debate.

– General Description of the Scheme –

In this scheme responsibility for legislating on specifically defined matters would be transferred to a Scottish or Welsh legislature consisting of the Sovereign and a directly elected assembly. Executive authority in relation to the transferred matters would be exercised by Ministers appointed by the Crown from among the members of the assembly. . . .

At the outset all existing legislation of the United Kingdom Parliament applying to Scotland and Wales would continue to apply. Thereafter any amending or new legislation on transferred matters would ordinarily be enacted by the Scottish or Welsh legislature. Parliament and the central government would continue to be responsible for matters not transferred, and for the international aspects of matters which were transferred. Parliament would retain ultimate legislative authority in all matters, but it would be a convention that in the ordinary course this power would not be used to legislate for Scotland or Wales on a transferred matter without the agreement of the Scottish or Welsh Government. The power would, however, be available for use at any time without agreement in exceptional circumstances. The United Kingdom Government would also have power, for use in exceptional circumstances, to determine, with the approval of Parliament, that a Bill passed by the assembly should not be submitted for the Royal Assent.

Although in essence the scheme is similar to that which was provided for Northern Ireland under the Government of Ireland Act 1920, there are a number of important differences. The functions proposed for transfer are less extensive, and only prescribed functions would be transferred. The assembly would be much larger than the old Northern Ireland House of Commons; it would be elected by proportional representation for a fixed term of four years, and there would be no second chamber. The financial arrangements would be very different.

– TRANSFERRED MATTERS –

Legislative responsibility would generally be transferred to the assembly for whole subject matters; exceptionally, responsibility for some subjects might be divided between Parliament and the assembly along lines laid down by statute.

The matters transferred to the Scottish assembly would be mainly, but not exclusively, those for which the Secretary of State for Scotland or the Lord Advocate now has executive responsibility, either exclusively or together with other Ministers. They are in the fields of the environment, education, health, social services, home affairs, legal matters, and agriculture, fisheries and food. Scottish Office matters which would not be transferred are electricity supply and some functions in the field of agriculture, fisheries and food, where responsibility for price support measures and other grants and subsidies would remain with Parliament, while responsibility for some other functions of international concern, such as animal and plant health, would be divided.

. . .

[W]e are not in a position to reach firm conclusions about the precise range of the matters to be transferred under any scheme of devolution, since this would require more detailed enquiry and consultation than it would have been appropriate for us to undertake. With this reservation, the matters suggested as being suitable for transfer to both Scottish and Welsh legislative assemblies are as follows: local government, town and country planning, new towns, housing, building control, water supply and sewerage, ancient monuments and historic buildings, roads (including the construction, use and licensing of vehicles), road passenger transport, harbours, other environmental services (e.g. prevention of pollution, coast protection and flood prevention), education (probably excluding universities), youth and community services, sport and recreation, arts and culture (including the Welsh and Gaelic languages), social work services (including, for Scotland, probation and after-care), health, miscellaneous regulatory functions (including matters such as betting, gaming and lotteries, obscene publications, shop hours and liquor licensing), agriculture, fisheries and food (with the exceptions noted in the above paragraph), forestry, crown estates, and tourism.

The following additional matters might be transferred to the Scottish assembly only: police, fire services, criminal policy and administration, prisons, administration of justice, legal matters, including law reform,

Highlands and Islands development (including crofting), and sea transport.

The assemblies would not have legislative or executive powers in other matters, except perhaps in some narrowly defined fields; they might, for example, be given limited powers in relation to some aspects of consumer protection, railways, road freight, civil aviation and broadcasting. In their debates the assemblies would in no way be confined by the limitations on the range of matters transferred to them. As the voices of their respective nations, they would provide the means whereby the needs of Scotland or Wales could be viewed as a whole and expressed to the central government and its agencies.

– FINANCIAL ARRANGEMENTS –

The assemblies would be allowed the greatest financial scope consistent with the political and economic unity of the United Kingdom. . . . [T]he chief object of any scheme would be to give the Scottish and Welsh Governments maximum freedom in expenditure. Each would have its fair share of United Kingdom resources and freedom to allocate expenditure on the transferred services according to its own chosen priorities.

The main features of the scheme proposed are set out in the following paragraphs in Scottish terms. The same arrangements would apply to Wales.

The scheme would require an exchequer board, acting in relation to both countries and independent of the Scottish, Welsh and United Kingdom Governments. The annual Scottish budget, which would be timed to fit in with the central government's Public Expenditure Survey, would be drawn up by the Scottish Government in accordance with its own policies and standards of provision, and would be submitted to the exchequer board. Taking into account the representations of both the Scottish Government and the United Kingdom Treasury, the board would recommend what Scotland's total expenditure should be. The Scottish Government could then in the ordinary course count on having revenues up to that amount. If its revenues consisted wholly of grants from United Kingdom funds, the total amount granted would be the same as the total expenditure recommended by the board. If the Scottish Government was entitled to a share of United Kingdom taxes, the grant would equal the board's total less Scotland's share of the yield from those taxes. If it possessed not only shared taxes but also devolved taxes, and was therefore able to alter the level of taxation within Scotland, the grant would equal the board's total less the Scottish yield from the shared taxes and less the yield which the devolved taxes would produce in Scotland if levied at the rates applying in other parts of the United Kingdom. In this case Scotland's total revenues would be less than the board's total if it levied rates lower than elsewhere, and more than the board's total if it levied rates higher than elsewhere. . . .

The total expenditure recommended by the board might be rather more or rather less than the previous year's expenditure, allowing for normal increases in costs, but in no circumstances would it be below a level adequate to finance all the transferred services.

In determining the Scottish Government's total expenditure the board would pay regard to the demand which that expenditure would make on real resources; subject to this its main object would be to furnish Scotland with sufficient money in total to finance United Kingdom standards in all the transferred services. These standards would be fixed by the board every five years after an examination for the relevant services in all parts of the United Kingdom; the cost of providing them would be calculated in terms of total expenditure per head of population. The cost of providing them in Scotland would allow for special Scottish conditions.

The sole purpose of the standards would be to calculate the total money and resources to be allocated to Scotland; the Scottish Government would not be obliged to adopt the individual standards in practice. It could instead choose to distribute its total expenditure in a different way, providing higher standards in some services, offset by lower standard in others. At the end of five years the exchequer board would redefine United Kingdom standards by reference to the standards actually being provided in the various parts of the United Kingdom (including Scotland) at that time; and, correspondingly, it would re-compute their cost, thus arriving at a new figure of Scottish expenditure per head, which, making due allowance for normal increases in costs, would serve as a yardstick for the next five years. The board's general policy, over the five-year period, would be to move Scotland on to its proper standard of expenditure as quickly as current economic and financial circumstances allowed.

– THE ASSEMBLY –

The Scottish or Welsh assembly would be a single-chamber body of about 100 members directly elected for a first term of four years by the single transferable vote system of proportional representation, using as far as possible multi-member constituencies obtained by grouping parliamentary constituencies. Consideration might be given to the exceptional use of the alternative vote system in single-member constituencies in the sparsely populated areas of the Scottish Highlands and Islands, where geography would make multi-member constituencies impracticable. All matters relating to the franchise and elections to the assembly (but not elections to local authorities in Scotland and Wales) would be reserved to Parliament.

It would be for the Scottish and Welsh people to decide on names for their assemblies. The term Convention seems to find some favour in Scotland, and Senate has been suggested for Wales.

Dual membership of Parliament would be permissible, and indeed some common membership might be desirable. Peers would not be debarred from membership of the assembly as they are from membership of the House of Commons; nor, in Scotland, would Ministers of the Church of Scotland.

– THE EXECUTIVE –

There would be no Governor. The functions of the Crown would where necessary be performed by Royal Commissioners appointed for that purpose.

The devolved powers would be exercised by Ministers appointed by the Crown and drawn from members of the assembly. A Cabinet system of government would operate, with the doctrines of Cabinet and Ministerial responsibility applying in broadly the same way as Westminster. It would follow that one of the Ministers, usually the leader of the majority party, would be chief Minister. The specific designation would be a matter for the assembly to determine; we suggest 'the Scottish (or Welsh) Premier' as a possibility.

While the Westminster legislation establishing the assembly would provide for the initial appointment of Ministers and for the establishment of their departments, it would thereafter would be for the assembly itself to decide what arrangements should be made.

There would be separate Scottish and Welsh civil services. In each case facilities for interchange would be desirable with both the United Kingdom and local government services.

– REPRESENTATION IN PARLIAMENT –

Scotland and Wales would continue to be represented in Parliament. Their representation in proportion would be the same as that of England, subject to any allowance which might be found appropriate for special geographical conditions. The probable effect would be to reduce Scotland's representation from 71 to about 57 and that of Wales from 36 to about 31.

– Representation in the Central Government –

As most of the executive responsibilities of the Secretaries of State for Scotland and Wales would have been transferred to the new assemblies and governments, the offices of Secretary of State would disappear. But it would still be appropriate for Scotland and Wales each to have a Minister with the special responsibility of representing the interests of that country in the Cabinet, much as the Home Secretary for many years used to represent the interests of Northern Ireland. This representative role would be somewhat wider than it was for Northern Ireland, since a wider range of functions would be retained at Westminster. The Ministers would be available to discharge other duties, provided that they were not duties which might clash with their special responsibilities for looking after the interests of Scotland or Wales.

The New Appeal of Nationalism

John P. Mackintosh

From an article in the *New Statesman*, 27 September 1974 (pp. 408–12).
John Mackintosh had been Labour MP for Berwickshire and East Lothian
from 1966 until February 1974, when he lost the seat to the Conservatives.
He regained it in October 1974 (the election about which he was writing
here). He had been professor of politics at Strathclyde University (1965–6),
and he became part-time professor of politics at Edinburgh University from
1977 until his death in 1978.

As the reporters and commentators flock up to Scotland to observe the
political situation, one fact strikes them all. Only the Scottish National
Party (SNP) has a sense of dynamism, only it is talking about the number of
votes and seats it will gain. Both the Labour and Conservative Parties may
hope to win one or two constituencies by tactical voting; that is as a result of
their main opponent suffering most from third party intervention but, as
regards their total vote, the objective for all the other parties is to see if they
can hold what they have already got against the SNP challenge.

How has this come about when only eight or ten years ago the
Nationalists were a bit of a joke and if anyone thought seriously about
nationalism as an idea they often found it either ridiculous or positively
distasteful? Part of this old reaction sprang from the situation in Britain and
part from the recent history of nationalism. The word has had such varied
connotations. In early nineteenth-century Europe, nationalism meant the
claim of subject peoples such as the Poles or Czechs to govern themselves
and to speak their own language in their schools and offices. It meant the
right of Greeks to be free of Turkish dominance and Italians to come
together and rid themselves of petty foreign tyrants. In recent years, African
nationalism was entirely respectable for much the same reasons. As
colonialism drew to an end, new African states had to be built up with
their own sense of national identity, nationalism was coupled with
democracy and self-determination and was far more acceptable than the
only other source of cohesion which was tribalism.

But for most people in Britain in recent years nationalism has had a bad
taste because it has been associated with authoritarian and aggressive
governments and with nasty claims to racial and cultural superiority. In
the 1950s and 1960s, there was a general preference for internationalism and
for larger political units with the specific objective of reducing the fear and

suspicion of foreigners that underlies xenophobia and also of preventing single states with previous records of aggression from acting in this way again. Also, as far as domestic nationalists were concerned, they had had the freedom of the ballot box for a century so they could not argue that they were being suppressed. If the people of Scotland or Wales had wanted a different regime, they would have acted accordingly at election time.

As a result of this rejection, nationalists were not in the mainstream of politics. They tended to be vernacular poets like Hugh MacDiarmid who listed his hobby in *Who's Who* as 'Anglophobia', to be Welsh language specialists, Princes Street Highlanders, oddities who thought there was some point in stealing the stone of Scone from Westminster Abbey and people who objected to the title Queen Elizabeth II because the first Queen Elizabeth had been Queen of England before the union of the crowns.

Yet, though many Scots regarded these nationalists of the 1950s and early 1960s as cranks, this does not mean that these same people did not feel a certain consciousness of being Scottish as well as British. Edinburgh is a quasi-capital city different in kind from Bristol or Newcastle. Scots who go to live and work in the South of England feel they are in a foreign country (as do English exiled north of the Border) and, apart from the language problem, Scots often say they feel more at home in Copenhagen or Oslo than in London. And even in the most British of Scots, the hackles could be raised. I recall being told by a former editor of the *New Statesman* that all Welsh were thieves and feeling a little annoyed but then positively angry when he gave it as a serious opinion that there could be no talent in Scotland, for anyone of ability was bound to have left to take a job in London.

This pervasive Scottish consciousness arises from the existence, ever since 1707, of some of the traditional carriers of nationality, the institutions which have kept such feelings alive in parts of Europe which have endured centuries of alien domination. First, Scotland has retained its own Presbyterian Church with its General Assembly in Edinburgh, the nearest approach to a Scottish Parliament. Churchgoing is still much more common in Scotland, the total attendance rate being about 33 per cent, and the General Assembly is commented on in the media, especially when it deals with social and semi-political issues. Scotland has also kept its own educational system and though it is hard to detect any special philosophy or practice in the actual teaching, the atmosphere at Scottish schools and universities is markedly different from that of English public or grammar schools and Oxbridge. Indeed it is this difference of experience that chiefly marks out the real Scotsman from the Anglo-Scot whose connection is just hereditary. It was the tendency of the Scottish aristocracy to send their sons to English schools and universities that cut them off from their Scottish roots and it is this that gives the Tory MPs in Scotland their air of unreality. They are part of an English-based ruling class even if their stately homes are in the north and the other chaps at Eton insisted on calling them 'Jock' or 'Alec'.

A third indigenous institution has been the local government system, culminating in a series of administrative departments which since 1939 have been known as St Andrew's House where the bulk of the senior civil servants are drawn from the Scottish universities. The Treaty of Union left a separate legal system with its courts of appeal and high court in Edinburgh, thus retaining in the city a judicial bench and a faculty of advocates. Although appeals can go to the House of Lords, for practical purposes the legal system and its personnel are exclusively Scottish.

There are other classic aids to national feeling which do not exist or are derisive in their effect. Language, for example, is not a factor as only some 60,000 out of five million speak Gaelic. The dialect of Robert Burns is very much a south-west Lowland dialect and quite different from that of the industrial central belt or Aberdeenshire. Race, likewise, has not left any clear-cut Scottish characteristic so that Celtic strains are evident in the north-west, Orkney and Shetland have Norse remnants, the nineteenth century Irish influx into the Clyde has left its mark while the Borders and the east coast are Anglo-Saxon in origin. But the uniting influence of common systems of education, local government, law and religion [has] imbued all those who have been to school, lived and worked in the country with a sense of being Scottish; with perhaps an incomplete but none the less definite element of national identity.

At the same time, these Scots have also had a British dimension in which, for over two centuries, they have taken reasonable pride. The original motive for accepting the Treaty of Union was the difficulty of running two economic policies under one executive and the relative poverty of Scotland. The prosperity which came some decades after the union gave the British connection a positive aspect. And though many Highlanders were forced overseas by the landlords' clearances, the Scots took a pride in and heavily populated the Empire. There were also opportunities in England and to be British was to be part of a great country which led the world in industrialisation, had a high standard of life, enjoyed the most stable and effective form of parliamentary democracy and had a praise-worthy record in international affairs.

. . .

When the Scottish National Party began to make some impact in the 1950s it did not draw its members or its leadership either from the landed elements or from the organised working class. Those who moved towards nationalism came mainly from professional groups and the lower middle class, people who had not hitherto taken any very active interest in politics. Starting from a low or almost negligible level, the SNP then proceeded to double its support at every general election. And the bulk of this support came not for specific reasons, not because voters wanted anything as precise as a Scottish Parliament or the revenues from North Sea Oil (though both of these appeals have helped). The support came because a series of events in the world and in the United Kingdom made the British side of the dual nationality less and less attractive till finally considerable numbers, for the first time for 200 years, began to doubt whether it was worth preserving at all.

– Sense of Failure –

The decline in the self-esteem and self-confidence of the British is something with which we are all familiar. There was the evident slide from being a world power during the war and even in the post-war years to the level of the major European power. Britain had so many Commonwealth and overseas interests that Anthony Eden could not see the country relegated to the status of a mere European power in 1958 when the Common Market was formed. Soon after, we were asking for permission to join, only to be rebuffed. Then the question was whether Britain would be a liability to the new Europe; we sank behind France and Germany as European powers and now Chancellor Schmidt says he is too busy to waste his time on 'the misery of England and Italy'.

And the process of the decline has come home to people as Britain has sought to achieve the same growth levels as the EEC powers and has failed. One balance of payments crisis has followed another, economic targets have been missed and now the forecasts are that Britain in the 1980s will have fallen behind till her standard of living is no higher than that of Greece or Spain.

A once strong imperial power, Britain has not merely abandoned almost all of its colonies but failed where the Israelis later succeeded in an invasion of Suez in 1956. A handful of white Rhodesians defied the Government in the late 1960s and it seemed as if all Britain could do was recapture the island of Anguilla from some non-existent Mafia elements. In general a gloom hangs over the country, a sense of failure. In England, this has led to a lack of faith in both major political parties and a massive swing in

[February] 1974 to the Liberals, and this despite the nagging doubt that they have no answer to the country's problems, that their chief merit is that they have not yet had the opportunity to fail in office.

In Scotland, there is no such problem. With the dual nationality, there is a simple alternative if the pride in being British wanes; just be Scottish. It is an 'opt out' solution which allows each person to imagine the kind of alternative to the disappointment of being British which he or she wants. For businessmen, such as Sir Hugh Fraser, an independent Scotland would be less trade union dominated than the UK. For others, self-government would mean no balance of payments problem and therefore more rapid growth and lower taxation. For internationalists, Scotland could at least take her place in the European Community after the English had insisted on burying their collective heads in the sand. For those who dislike EEC policies, Scotland could stand on its own like Norway, proud and unsullied outside any such amorphous conglomerations. For the extreme Left, Scotland could achieve socialism easier than an England dominated by the multinationals and the City of London. In general, there is a sense of untapped energy and unused human resources; at least this is an available and cheering alternative which has not been tried and found wanting.

– WHY THE SNP PROSPERS –

It is in the light of the rise of these sentiments that the Scottish policies of the established parties must be considered. For years the Labour Party has had only one idea about Scotland and that is to press on with a vigorous regional policy. Willie Ross, Labour's Scottish spokesman, has had one speech devoted to this subject, give or take a few statistics, which he has used for over ten years. From time to time, regional policy is revamped with new incentives and new boundaries for their application. The form of the incentives are varied from grants to tax relief, from advance factories to regional employment premiums. But the SNP continues to prosper. The explanation is simple. If Britain was confident and booming, there would be little need for a regional policy; and if the economy is stagnant, all the financial incentives in the world will not move non-existent new firms from the Midlands to Scotland.

In any case, the economic side of the regional problem is overdone. The real difficulty is the Clyde Valley conurbation. If it is taken out of the statistics, the Scottish figures for incomes, employment, health and housing are right on the average for the UK. It is the greater Glasgow area, with two and a half million people, that is the problem and it does not seem to respond to regional policies because of the antiquated industrial structure and the reluctance of businessmen to go there. But even if regional policy succeeded and Scottish wages rose from the present ninety-six per cent of the UK average to equality, or if unemployment fell from one and a half times the UK percentage to the same level, this would not necessarily mean that the Scots became pleased and happy to be British. Such a sentiment depends much more on the overall atmosphere in the United Kingdom.

– THE ASSEMBLY PALLIATIVE –

The same problem arises over the latest palliative, a Scottish Assembly. In many people's view, the best model, if democratic local government in Britain is to have any real scope, is the big region or state like the German Länder or the American states, with a subordinate second tier of local councils. But the idea that the SNP fires are fuelled by the Scots' desire for a subordinate assembly is to miss the point. When people are asked: 'What is needed to diminish your dissatisfaction with the current political system?' 20 per cent in Scotland and 9 per cent in Wales say 'more devolution' (Kilbrandon Report figures). But this is because the Nationalist parties have been active promoting this proposal. If the questioner in England points to a map, explains what the local region would comprise and then asks: 'Would you be happier if people like you had more say in the affairs of this region?', the response in favour is not markedly different and the average 'level of agreement' exceeds the percentage in favour in Wales:

Total	Scotland	Wales	Yorkshire	North West	South East
61%	73%	57%	60%	69%	57%

The explanation is that people express their general discontent with Britain's record in recent years in a variety of ways and majorities will endorse more power for central or for local government; they will say 'yes' to more party loyalty and to more independence on the part of MPs, to more power for Parliament and more referenda. It is quite possible that a Scottish Assembly (or one for East Anglia or the South West of England) might produce livelier and more effective local government. But the reason why respondents will say 'yes' to a variety of often contradictory changes in the machinery of government is that they feel a general sense of disappointment with the results of British government in recent years.

There is no evidence that the creation of a Scottish Assembly with limited powers over health, housing and education would alter this general sense of dissatisfaction. The SNP have manoeuvred the other parties into a position where they had to assent to this proposal or appear to be totally insensitive to the situation in Scotland. And the Nationalists are also in the very advantageous position that if an Assembly is created and is reasonably successful, they can say: 'We forced them to do it and think how much better it would be if it was a sovereign parliament'. If it makes no difference or is a disappointment, they can say: 'But of course, we always said that anything short of real independence would be a farce'. And all the time, the wind in their sails has little to do with anger over too few advance factories or lack of this or that form of Scottish Assembly, it is due to the decline in the pull of 'Being British'.

Yet the pull still exists for many. The one line of attack that the SNP dislike is emphasis on separatism – that they intend to set up a Scottish Republic like Eire with its own army and navy and diplomatic representatives and with customs posts at the English Border. They shy away from this as they want somehow to suggest that independence is possible without losing all aspects of being British.

The residual hold of this aspect of the dual nationality takes several forms. Principally, there is the reasonable point that Scotland is one of the poorer areas of the UK and, despite endless SNP statistics, seemed to be getting a subsidy (as poorer areas should) from the richer parts of the UK. The Labour government went to endless trouble to demonstrate this in the Scottish budget it produced in the late 1960s. It is here that North Sea oil has had such an impact. Many voters recoil from the cruder SNP claims that it is 'Scotland's oil' and that an independent Scotland could behave like a Gulf sheikhdom. A recent ORC poll found that when the statement was made 'The oil in the North Sea should be used to benefit all of Britain and not just Scotland' 60 per cent of respondents agreed. But the oil does diminish the feeling that Scotland could not afford to be a separate state (though 46 per cent still agreed with this sentiment in mid-1974) [see Kellas, 1986, p. 138]. So the oil has weakened Scots fears on economic grounds of ceasing to be British. And no one has done more to ram this point home than [prominent Labour MP] Denis Healey with his repeated remarks that once North Sea oil starts to flow the position of the British economy will be transformed.

– LEADERSHIP WORRY –

A second fear about losing the broader base from which the Scots have operated since 1707 is that, on its own, the country might become too parochial and introverted. Who would run an independent Scotland? Perhaps because Edinburgh has not been a political capital, no governing class or group has emerged in Scotland. The Scottish MPs are not major figures in Scottish life and have contributed less than their numbers might have suggested to British politics. Only one or perhaps two of the Secretaries of State since the war would have made the cabinet had there been no need for that post and its tenure by a Scottish MP. So, would there be effective leadership in an independent Scotland or would there be a long, isolationist period while English firms were told to leave and only Scottish history and literature was taught in the schools?

This worry has tended to decline, in part because the performance of British leaders has been so unimpressive in recent years. Could anything Scotland do be worse than the recent conduct of British foreign policies that has filled our friends abroad with a mixture of despair and disgust? It may take a little while for an impressive leadership to appear but Eire has now its Conor Cruise O'Briens and its Garret Fitzgeralds and the more successful the SNP is the more its numbers are augmented by reasonable, able people, who simply want some hope for the future.

Then the vocal sections who have turned against growth, power stations and motorways on austerity grounds also hope for much from greater independence. They feel that Scotland could, like Norway, remain a bastion of a quieter, more rural, more traditional, form of society, escaping the pressures of modern life and their tendency to dehydrate and package all the essentials of civilised life.

– POINT OF CONVERSION –

For all these reasons a point comes at different times with different individuals when they suddenly wonder if this nationalist idea which they have first ignored and then belittled does not make some sense after all. . . . So nationalism is making many converts in many places for many reasons. It is the answer to so many of the present discontents. One must hand it to the SNP that their challenge is the central issue of this election in Scotland. They have forced the other parties to fight on ground chosen by the SNP: namely, what can these parties do for Scotland? And anything that they suggest will always be inadequate, be it more regional economic advantages or assemblies or a percentage of oil revenues; it will all be inadequate so long as there is no proper pride in being British. Only one thing will halt or reverse the onward march of the SNP and that is a period of government in London which is really successful so that it ends with a satisfied electorate eager to vote positively for a party that has once again restored the feeling that Britain is a successful, worthwhile country to belong to for those who do have other places where they can go and other traditions and titles to which they can turn.

Part II: The Devolution Years, 1974–83

Introduction

The debates in the second half of the 1970s were influenced by the responses to the Kilbrandon report, by the electoral success of the SNP – winning eleven seats and 30 per cent of the vote in the second general election of 1974 – and by the precarious position of the Labour government between 1974 and 1979.

The government adopted some of the main elements of Kilbrandon's scheme of legislative devolution: its proposals were issued in the 1975 white paper *Our Changing Democracy*, the main points of which are summarised here. The allocation of responsibility was broadly the same as proposed in Kilbrandon, but – after a supplementary statement in 1976 – there were to be no independent taxation powers. The supplementary statement also added in some further powers in relation to the Scottish Development Agency. Most of the Labour movement eventually acquiesced in this reluctantly, although not without an attempt between the two 1974 elections to maintain the opposition that had been expressed in the party's submission to Kilbrandon (Part I): see Vernon Bogdanor's article here. The London leadership forced the pace because they feared that a failure to promise a Scottish assembly could lead to the SNP's destroying Labour in Scotland. Some parts of the movement were enthusiastic, notably the STUC (evidenced in its reaction to Kilbrandon, included here: see also Aitken (1997)). John Mackintosh continued to articulate what came to be known as the 'maximalist' position, going significantly beyond the government's proposals to include in an Assembly's remit, for example, significant economic powers, some access to the oil revenues from the North Sea, responsibility for the universities, and autonomy within the devolved areas (so that the London government could over-ride the Assembly only in extreme cases and by a difficult route involving legislation at Westminster): the nature of his case is illustrated in his 1975 pamphlet here. Maximalism, at that time, had supporters across the political spectrum – for example, the Conservative MP Alex Fletcher writing in *The Times* on 12 August 1975 (p. 12). But the government adopted its more cautious approach to ensure that the majority in the party would not follow Tam Dalyell and others in their outright opposition: by the end of the decade, Dalyell's 1977 book (an extract from which is given here) became the main text for the opponents of devolution.

These internal rifts, and the government's tiny majority at Westminster, caused great difficulties for the Bill which eventually emerged from the white paper; after one failed attempt to legislate for Scotland and Wales together, a separate Scotland Act struggled onto the statute book in 1978. Dalyell articulated his opposition relentlessly and eloquently, notably on three topics which resonated with the wider electorate. Devolution, he claimed, would erode the powers of local government, which itself had been reorganised in 1975; this argument echoed Labour's submission to Kilbrandon (Part I). As a result of this fear, most local councillors were at best sceptical (Clarke, 1976). It would also, he said, put Scottish MPs at Westminster in the anomalous position of being able to vote on English domestic policy while these same topics were devolved to a separate body in Scotland. The Conservative MP Enoch Powell christened this 'the West Lothian Question' after Dalyell's constituency (Parliamentary Debates, 1977). And Dalyell predicted that devolution would lead to the break-up of the UK.

Labour MPs who agreed with Dalyell's critique but who did not want to embarrass their government resorted to the tactic of proposing a referendum (Buchan, 1975). It was difficult for supporters of a Scottish assembly to reject this: if devolution was about democracy, then why not trust the people to take the final decision? Nationalists had, in any case, long argued for a referendum on this issue, to pre-empt (they believed) a Westminster veto: this proposal is found in H. J. Paton's article in Part I and in the Scottish Liberal Party's submission to Kilbrandon. The referendum was complicated by a requirement – forced on the government by Labour MPs – that at least 40 per cent of the whole electorate vote in favour before the assembly could be set up. In the event, this threshold was not crossed when the referendum was held in 1979: on a turnout of 64 per cent, 52 per cent voted in favour (Bochel et al., 1981). It might nevertheless have yielded a clear majority for devolution had it not been for three other significant factors. The government's popularity declined sharply after 1977, and so it was no longer as persuasive with voters as it might have been: this point is analysed by Vernon Bogdanor here in his assessment of the vote. The Liberal party slid away as allies, wanting to distance themselves from the government which they had briefly supported in 1977 partly in order to secure an assembly: they had begun to find opposition to devolution among their supporters in Scotland (Steel, 1976; Grimond, 1979). The third influential factor was the complete reversal of the Conservative position, from Heath's and Douglas Home's sympathy in the late 1960s to Margaret Thatcher's hostility from 1976 onwards. The reasons are summed up in the 1978 article by Teddy Taylor MP reproduced here. They were also reiterated a year after the referendum in an interview with Alec Douglas Home himself (also here).

Many supporters of devolution regarded this Conservative shift as a betrayal. This sense is evident in the 1976 speech here by Conservative MP Alick Buchanan-Smith, who had resigned a fortnight earlier from the post of shadow Secretary of State for Scotland in protest at Thatcher's new opposition to the government's scheme of devolution. The accusation of betrayal was made most often against Home: a fortnight before the vote, he made a speech in which he argued for a No vote in order that a better scheme of devolution could be produced. (The sole extant portion of this is given here.) Home criticised the government's proposals because the assembly would have no tax-raising powers, would be too large, would create conflict with Westminster, would be anomalous because of the West Lothian Question, and would not be chosen by a proportional electoral system. He genuinely believed that a postponment would lead to a better scheme: the specific occasion for his remarks was a speech on the previous day by the prime minister, James Callaghan, arguing that this referendum was Scotland's last chance to achieve an assembly. That Home was not being disingenuous is shown further by the extracts here from the pamphlet by two of his senior colleagues in the Conservative party, Francis Pym and Leon Brittan (1978). Pym had been advocating an all-party conference to agree a scheme, and the pamphlet was a draft of the Conservative submission to such a discussion. The remarkable feature of it, in the light of the intransigent opposition to devolution which Thatcher had adopted, is its open-mindedness. It reasonably discusses all the main options apart from independence, and acknowledges the case that can be made for a scheme not far removed from the Labour government's. If the referendum had in fact given clearer endorsement of devolution than it did, then – on the evidence of the analysis by Pym and Brittan and of Home's speech – it is likely that the new Conservative government might have taken the issue much more seriously than it did. As it was, in his interview Home foresaw the Thatcherite intransigence lasting for at least a decade.

Developing alongside this debacle was something quite different and recently unprecedented – an association of radicalism and home rule that, by the late 1980s, was to embrace most of the Scottish left. An early statement of this position is given here, by Isobel Lindsay, from an influential collection called *The Radical Approach*. One of the reasons why this radical current could survive was that it kept its distance from Labour's devolution proposals, even though supporting it in the referendum as the only scheme on offer: see Stephen Maxwell's critique of John Mackintosh here. The radical position gained its sustenance, not from the Labour movement, but from a wholesale shift towards nationalism in Scottish intellectual culture; it had also appeared in the collection of essays edited by the Labour politician Gordon Brown (1975). This radical current is noted in the essay here by the historian Christopher Harvie, who was then in the Labour party but who joined the SNP a decade later.

The ambiguity of the referendum result ensured that the Thatcher government did not have to set the assembly up. But it also ensured that the issue would not go away, as Vernon Bogdanor forecast in his 1979 essay reproduced here. Constitutional change remained necessary, according to commentators such as Bogdanor, because the UK was too centralised. Politically weak though Labour and the SNP were until late in the 1980s, its leaders in Scotland shared this view, as can be seen in the interview here with John Smith, who had piloted the legislation for a Scottish assembly through Westminster. He had always been an optimist: he had not been among those who had expected little to come of the Kilbrandon report (Smith, 1973). He welcomed the Labour party's maintaining its position after 1979. In the statement on devolution to which he refers (Labour Party, 1981), the party had affirmed that a majority had voted Yes in the referendum, that an assembly could have protected Scotland from Thatcher, and that it could strengthen democracy. It also envisaged the possibility that any future proposals could incorporate some tax-raising powers. Smith also, notably, recognised that another referendum would be needed, and that, next time, it should take place before the detailed legislation was presented to Westminster. But it would be sixteen years – and, sadly, after Smith's death – before the party would again be in a position to do anything about that.

SCOTTISH GOVERNMENT

Scottish Trades Union Congress

From the 1974 annual report of the STUC (pp. 157–61).

Since its foundation Congress has on various occasions debated proposals in favour of Scottish Government or in favour of further devolution of power from Westminster to Scotland. . . . [F]or the first twenty years of its existence Congress on many occasions discussed the question of home rule and in fact Congress for some time lent support to the Scottish Home Rule Association. From the 1930s onwards the concern of Congress has been to advocate the further devolution of responsibility from Westminster to the Scottish Office.

. . .

At the 1968 Congress two motions were remitted to the General Council for further consideration. The first motion proposed by the National Union of Mineworkers: Scottish Area was as follows:

That this Congress, recognising the desire of the Scottish people for a Scottish Parliament, calls upon the Government to introduce legislation to establish a Parliament for Scotland, the ultimate form and powers of which should be determined by the Scottish electorate.

The second motion proposed by the Amalgamated Union of Engineering Workers was as follows:

That this Congress views with concern the rise of nationalism in Scotland. We are justly proud of our Scottish heritage and traditions but feel that any attempt to secure total devolution, i.e. complete separation, would lead directly to a lowering of the living standards of the Scottish people. This Congress believes that an economically viable and socially secure Scotland can only be achieved (a) within the economic framework of Great Britain and (b) if pay and conditions of Scottish workers are no less favourable than those in other parts of Great Britain, and are secured wherever possible by national joint negotiating machinery covering Scotland, England and Wales.

The General Council established a working party which reported to the

1969 Congress. . . . The main conclusions of the Working Party submitted to the 1969 Congress were:

1. that the complete political and economic sovereignty of Scotland would represent a retrograde step which would set back substantially the hopes and expectations of the Scottish people; and
2. that there should be advantage in providing a Scottish legislative assembly which would rectify the present political and administrative deficiencies in Scotland.

. . .

The conclusions of the working party were accepted by Congress and in due course the General Council submitted detailed evidence to the Royal Commission [on the Constitution] and followed this up by giving oral evidence. . . . The General Council gave full consideration to the Royal Commission's report and in January 1974 issued the following submission:

1. The General Council argued strongly in both the written and oral evidence to the Commission that the people of Scotland should have a greater say in the decision making process. The Commission, however, disagreed on the nature of the assembly, the majority proposing a legislative assembly and those dissenting that the assembly be administrative in character.
2. Although the General Council's oral evidence for an elected Scottish Assembly did not include legislative powers, they nevertheless believe that the basic concept of the Commission's recommendations for an elected legislative assembly are both sensible and realistic. The actual legislative powers which would be exercised by such an assembly would not in themselves be extensive. Most importantly, however, the massive administrative responsibility at present in the hands of the Secretary of State for Scotland and St Andrew's House would become the direct responsibility of the elected assembly.
3. The General Council accept the proposition of the Commission that the Assembly should not be restricted to discussing those matters over which it had direct control. The UK Parliament would still retain the responsibilities for matters such as economic policy and it would be essential that the elected Scottish Assembly put its views to Parliament on vital economic issues pertaining to Scotland.
4. The General Council tentatively favours the suggestion to establish an Exchequer Board to consider the financial arrangements for the

Scottish Assembly. It is, however, difficult to see how such a Board could be truly independent of the United Kingdom Government and the method by which the Budget for a Scottish Assembly is decided would need very close scrutiny.

5. The economic problems presently experienced in Scotland are of such magnitude and complexity that they are not capable of solution within a purely Scottish context. The solution of these problems depends largely on the concentration of UK resources on the needs of those parts of the UK suffering from disproportionately low levels of economic development. Scotland's economic needs are clearly most likely to be met if the UK economy is planned to ensure maximum capital investment and that such an investment programme take account of the need:

a. to promote maximum assistance to Scotland's emerging industries;

b. to ensure new industrial development in areas of high unemployment and declining job opportunity in our traditional industries.

It is equally essential that the importance of these traditional industries to the economies of both Scotland and the UK is recognised and appropriate measures taken to support them.

6. The Assembly, having little power to raise revenue, will obviously have to depend for its finance on the Exchequer Board. There must be no mere allocation of finance on any calculation based on population. The development of North Sea oil, for example, will demand high expenditures on infrastructural development which could well inhibit equally desirable developments elsewhere. The resources made available by the Board must be based on the Assembly's estimate of the problems they face and the measures they propose to meet them. Presumably, any attempt to assess Scotland's needs or its economic performance could best be made if the Assembly were to ensure the production of an annual Scottish budget.

7. In their evidence to the Royal Commission, the General Council stressed the need for the retention of the post of Secretary of State for Scotland. However, on balance they accept the Commission's proposition that the actual post of Secretary of State would disappear but a minister of Cabinet standing would be retained with responsibility for Scotland. It is suggested that the minister might have additional responsibilities. This the General Council would not oppose, providing that due regard is paid to his responsibilities to Scotland.

8. The Commission propose the introduction of proportional representation for the Scottish Assembly. The General Council doubt the

unilateral application of proportional representation to the Scottish Assembly in a situation in which elections to the UK Parliament and to the new Regional and District Authorities are still to be based on the single vote.

9. The General Council still favour their proposition that the election to the Assembly be co-terminal with the elections to the UK Parliament. . . . They would, however, agree that the proposed four yearly period of office could be introduced and reviewed in the light of experience. Obviously there will be many aspects of both election and work of the Assembly which will need re-evaluation.

10. The General Council are, however, quite definite in rejecting any proposal to reduce the number of Scottish constituencies sending MPs to the UK Parliament as the result of the Royal Commission's recommendations. They accept that changes will inevitably take place arising from the recommendations of the Boundaries Commission. There will still be large areas of Scottish affairs controlled by the UK Parliament and adequate representation is, therefore, essential. They see no basic contradiction between the concept of an elected Assembly and seventy-one MPs from Scottish constituencies on the floor of the House of Commons.

A Parliament for Scotland

John P. Mackintosh

Mackintosh always operated between academic study and practical politics. The earlier piece by him (Part I) is an example of the analytical mode, this one of the practical. It was published by Berwickshire and East Lothian Labour Party in 1975.

There are the strongest positive reasons why all those who are democrats and who are left of centre in British politics should support the creation of a Scottish Parliament with powers to legislate on those internal matters which affect Scotland alone and with powers then to execute these policies.

Some have accepted the need for this kind of devolution out of fear that unless action is taken along these lines, the Scottish National Party will gain even more than the 30 per cent of the vote and the eleven (out of seventy-one) Scottish seats which it secured in the general election of October 1974. . . . [T]he electoral threat from the SNP is real and there are no good reasons for thinking it has diminished or will diminish. But there are also much more satisfying motives for carrying through an effective measure of devolution and these motives would be as strong or stronger even if the SNP had never come into existence.

The first of these motives is the old desire for democratic self-government which underlay the formation of the Labour Party; the idea that the people should, through their representatives, take the major decisions affecting their lives. There is, in fact, less self-government and more government by the bureaucracy in Scotland than elsewhere in the UK. To begin with, all over Britain, successive governments have been doing so much more in industry, in welfare, in land use planning and in the management of local government than they used to before the last war, let alone before 1914. As a result, Parliament is far less effective in scrutinising all these various activities of government and, in practice, many policy decisions, as well as the application of policies to difficult cases, are in the hands of civil servants.

In the case of Scotland, this is worse or has gone further because Scotland has some different institutions requiring the application of modified or special policies. These special needs give more scope to Scottish civil servants because they can get on with the job of governing the country from Edinburgh while Scottish MPs are down in London with less time available for gathering evidence, pressing the minister and enforcing a degree of accountability. People in England often forget that Scotland has, since 1707, retained some of the separate institutions that help to perpetuate a sense of national identity. Scotland has its own legal system based on Roman law with its own courts and legal profession. There is a separate educational system and the older Scottish Universities have quite a different atmosphere either from Oxbridge or from the English redbrick universities. Then there has always been a somewhat distinct pattern of local government and the highly distinct Scottish Presbyterian Church with its annual General Assembly in Edinburgh. As a result, Scotland has to have its own laws on such subjects as education, housing, planning, social work, land holding, divorce or industrial tribunals.

This ought to mean that Scottish MPs have a special job to do controlling the Scottish Office and watching over its actions. In reality, the Scottish Grand Committee allows one two-and-a-half-hour debate a year on some of these special topics. All major Scottish Bills are taken on the floor of the House. But there are no separate cabinet ministers on Scottish health or education and therefore no special Question Time for each of these subjects. Thus, though Scottish MPs work hard, the Scottish Office has a far freer hand than English ministries each with its own minister and forty or fifty English MPs living on their doorstep and watching their every move.

So there is the democratic case for special machinery and this must mean a form of representative government which can exercise control over the Scottish Office. There are further aspects of this case. The civil servants are honourable, patriotic men doing their best, but they know that they must not embarrass their minister or the UK cabinet. As a result, when special Scottish institutions or problems suggest a particular solution, this can only be adopted if it is also applicable to England or at least will not lead to invidious comparisons. For instance, the private sector in the Health Service could have been abolished in Scotland quite easily so that all available energy and enthusiasm went into the Health Service but this was impossible because of the size and influence of the private sector in the South-East of England. The Highlands and Island Development Board would have been set up far more easily had the Treasury not fought the proposal tooth and nail on the grounds that if this was done for one problem area in the UK, every other problem area would soon be demanding similar treatment.

Another part of the case for special time and treatment (and therefore for special institutions) is simply that as Scotland often requires special laws and since the parliamentary time table is always crowded, many things are not done at all. English divorce law was reformed in 1969 but the Scots Law – which causes just as much misery in its present form as the unreformed

English law – has remained unreformed and Scots MPs are told that they must wait till one of them wins a place in the lottery for a private member's bill. There is a great impatience with the old Scottish licensing laws. A Committee under Dr Clayson was set up in 1971 which recommended reforms in 1973 but nothing can be done because there is no parliamentary time available (or so some Scottish Ministers say). The Law Commission of distinguished Scots lawyers have been working for years to bring Scottish Law up to date, to make it relevant to modern conditions, but not one of its proposals has been enacted for lack of parliamentary time.

A final aspect of this democratic case for a Scottish Parliament is that such an institution would give a focus or rallying point for all those involved in Scottish affairs. To take education as an example, at present the Scottish Universities look to the UK University Grants Committee on matters of policy. Scottish education is not only headless but its control is fragmented between the staff of Training Colleges, Scottish Office civil servants, the Inspectorate and some leading teachers. But there is no political point of decision-making which would draw these groups together and make them face the options in a Scottish context. As a result it is not clear who does control Scottish education, the major issues go by default, there is no sense of leadership and in practice the only thing left is to tag along behind the decisions of the English Department. It was frustration over this situation that played a major part in the recent strike of Scottish teachers. (To be fair, the same factors on rare occasions allow Scotland to take the lead, as happened over the Scottish Social Work Act [in 1968].)

In addition to the democratic argument, all those on the left in politics have good reasons for wanting a Scottish Parliament. The most obvious is that throughout the period since the war (with the possible exception of the years 1955–7), there would have been an anti-conservative – normally purely Labour – majority in contrast to the position in Westminster where the Conservatives have been in power for seventeen of the thirty post-war years.

Nor is this surprising, for Scotland has more than its share of the problems which bring left-wing governments to power and which only left-wing governments can solve. The class system is more evident and more ingrained in Scotland. There is more slum housing than anywhere in England while the problems of the Clyde Valley are so deep rooted and complex that it ranks among the worst areas of urban deprivation in western Europe. As a result, the Conservative Party in Scotland is a weak, unhappy remnant yet it is constantly bolstered up by the majorities in the UK Parliament imposing a Conservative Secretary of State and administration on Scotland when the voters north of the Border actually returned a

Labour majority. Would it not be desirable to have a government which did represent the Scottish people dealing with those problems that are peculiar to Scotland while a different government which represented overall UK election results looked after overall UK matters such as defence, foreign affairs and national economic policy?

Some in the Labour Party may think it selfish of the Scots to want to be governed at the Scottish level by the kind of majority they actually elect, while the UK as a whole has bouts of Conservatism. But it is also in the interest of the Party throughout the country that this should happen. One of the weaknesses of the British political system is that if a party is out of office in Westminster (as Labour was for thirteen years at a stretch) it loses all contact with government at that level. It has no opportunity to try out its policies and to retain that important stimulus and challenge, the actual contact with reality. What made the German Social Democratic Party so successful when it came to office after decades in the wilderness was that its leaders had been in power all through this time in certain states of the federation and knew exactly what they wanted to do and could hope to achieve.

. . .

To this, some will reply that the case for decentralisation has been made but not to units with some nationalist feeling because such feelings are inherently undesirable and to appease them will only whet the appetite for more concessions till total separation becomes inevitable.

The answer to the first part of this objection is to look at the character of the feeling that Scotland as a unit has claims for a measure of internal self-government. . . . Always about two thirds or more of the electorate want more political power devolved to Scotland and not only are the SNP a minority in this group but a minority of SNP voters actually want their party's full policy of independence.

The reason appears when the nationalist sentiments that have been mentioned are considered over the period since the Union. In practice, the Scots have developed a dual nationality; they are both Scottish and British. Some of the institutions that matter are peculiar to Scotland and create a sense of identity while others – such as the tradition of parliamentary democracy – are purely British. . . . The kind of sentiment that wants more control in Scotland over Scottish affairs is not necessarily or even usually anti-English nor have the people holding these views any of the nastier characteristics of the aggressive or exclusive nationalists that have done so much damage in recent history. This was well revealed by the way the SNP found that the selfish and materialist slogan 'It's Scotland's Oil' was not a winner. The ORC survey on Scottish attitudes carried out in 1974 found that the statement 'the oil in the North Sea should be used to benefit all of Britain and not just Scotland' was accepted by 60 per cent of all electors and even by 36 per cent of SNP voters [see Kellas, 1986, p. 138]. The same point was revealed in a rather different way by the referendum on British Membership of the European Community. The SNP urged the case for 'a tactical "No" vote' but found that on an issue affecting the whole of Britain, the Scots could not be persuaded to see the issues solely from a Scottish tactical angle; they realised that the question was addressed to Britain as a whole and answered it in these terms.

Thus to carry through a measure of devolution is to meet the expressed desires of a large majority of Scottish voters and there are the sentiments in existence to back up or give strength to such a policy. But these sentiments exist together with a desire by the bulk of the electorate to remain British; they do not conceal a rabid and exclusive separatism nor are they a half way house towards such opinions. This is the answer to those who say 'devolve – perhaps but never to a unit with anything that has a national tradition'. It is also the answer to the 'slippery slope' argument. To go beyond devolution towards total independence would be to move from a change desired by two-thirds of the electors towards a very different policy desired by only some 17 per cent of voters (the ORC survey) [see Kellas, 1986, p. 148].

As for the further point that once a Scottish Parliament was established every failure would be attributed to inadequate powers and more and more demands would be made and concessions won till independence became the next logical step, the only answer is that this has not happened in any part of the developed world where federalism or a devolved system of government has been tried. Indeed, in all decentralised patterns of government where the people have been satisfied with the degree of local autonomy they enjoy, they have become much more pragmatic and have often asked or allowed the central government to resume certain nation-wide policy-making or executive powers either in the interest of greater uniformity or in order to benefit from central government financial aid.

All the evidence from other countries shows that once a generous degree of decentralisation has been conceded, the virtues of remaining part of a larger unit became much clearer. In terms of this analysis, once the Scots are free to determine those issues that are purely Scottish, they can then also freely express the British side of their dual nationality through Westminster.

The Devolution of the Intellectuals

Christopher Harvie

Originally appeared in the *New Statesman*, 28 November 1975 (pp. 665–6). Harvie is a historian who was then working for the Open University. He was active in the Labour Party at this time.

A subjective impression will do for a start. Increasingly, as I read through the Scottish papers, I feel as if I've just come off the Holyhead boat at Dun Laoghaire and am reading the *Irish Times* en route to Connolly Station, entering a strange and intriguing political world in which the affairs of Westminster appear as if viewed through the wrong end of a telescope. Different issues and different polarities have taken over, a dance to the music of nationalism in which principles and opinions are changed with a frequency and panache only otherwise to be found in *The Charterhouse of Parma*. Westminster alignments appear useless as guides to opinion in Scottish affairs: on the eve of the devolution White Paper – and the expected parliamentary backlash – a specifically Scottish politics now exists whose preoccupations are steadily diverging from those of the body which will, in the last analysis, have to decide on home rule. How much, I wonder gloomily, turning to the English papers, is this apparent in the South?

Ignorance about the current evolution of Scottish politics is the most plausible explanation of the behaviour of the cabinet's Right wing. Distress at growing class polarisation in British politics ought logically to have led Messrs [Reginald] Prentice, [Roy] Jenkins and [Anthony] Crosland and Mrs [Shirley] Williams to endorse devolution, at least as a diversionary exercise; instead they have chosen to oppose it. This is understandable, given that their departments have few, if any, Scottish responsibilities, and that they themselves are not renowned for a social vision extending beyond Oxford (or, on a clear day, Grimsby). Moreover, as seen from Westminster, there appears nothing new or even particularly threatening about the Scottish agitation. The eleven Nationalist MPs have scarcely set Westminster ablaze; Mr Donald Stewart [SNP leader] is no Parnell. Polls showing sweeping Scots majorities in favour of devolution have been commonplace since the 1930s to no positive effect. So time and a crowded session, the dependable anaesthetics, can be allowed to do their work, and the Scots can be mollified with some shuffling around of oil revenues.

This scenario obviously appeals to Labour's mandarinate, and Mrs Thatcher is believed to concur, so from the Westminster point of view the indefinite deferment of devolution appears a real and inviting possibility. In Scotland, too, devolution is by no means regarded as a pushover: the punters reckon the odds in its favour as about 60: 40. But the alternative is not Unionism. If devolution is not passed Labour stands to lose enough votes to the SNP to give the Nationalists anything up to fifty Scottish seats. With a majority of seats (thirty-six) in Scotland, the SNP would then, in terms of its constitution, withdraw from Westminster and set up its own Constituent Assembly and government, as Sinn Fein did in Ireland in 1918. There will then be only two ways out for an English government – concession or occupation. It is not a situation any government should attempt to gamble on: the only precedent is a tragic one.

The illusion probably still exists that the whole issue is a bluff that can be called: that some political formula can be worked out which (a) exposes the fact that only a small minority of Scots actually want independence, and then (b) having done so, quietly pigeon-holes any concession towards devolution in view of its constitutional complexity. Dicey's ghost still shambles through Westminster, wailing against federalism. Certainly, Scottish bluffs were successfully called in the past: the Convention movement, which secured massive endorsement for home rule between 1949 and 1951, was ignored to death; the Nationalist revival of the later 1960s ended up aground in the shallows of its own unsophisticated populism. But that easy answer no longer applies: the momentum of Scottish politics is no longer dependent on the behaviour of Westminster. Above all, the classes which were once the guarantors of the Union have got the devolutionist bit between their teeth. If devolution is refused, they are more likely to opt for independence than Unionism.

Oil alone has not accomplished this: it has simply acted as a catalyst in the transformation of existing relationships and tendencies into a new national politics, not a movement but a range of preoccupations which absorb nationalist and home-ruler alike. Scotland's economic problems, endemic since the inter-war depression, have been qualitatively worsened by uneven regional development and the need to create an infrastructure for an industry whose stay may only be temporary. And, alongside all this, the old national institutions of church, law and education, which the Union guaranteed, struggle to preserve their identity in the age of multinational corporation and the EEC bureaucrat.

The agenda of specifically Scottish problems is crowded, but the critical change is one of consciousness. Such concerns are not only being articulated by the traditional upholders of nationalism but by the intelligentsia as a whole. This intellectual Zionism, the preoccupation of the 'lads o' pairts' with their own territory, is almost totally new. If anything characterised post-Union (or for that matter post-Reformation) Scottish culture it was its essentially schizoid quality. The 'red' Dr Jekyll part of the intelligentsia – Hume, Carlyle, Geddes, Reith – was cosmopolitan, self-avowedly 'enlightened' and, given a chance, authoritarian, expanding into and exploiting greater and more bountiful fields than their own country could provide. Back home, in his kailyard, lurked Hyde, demotic, parochial and 'black' reactionary, keeper of Tom Nairn's 'great Tartan monster', reader of the *Sunday Post*. 'Red' and 'black' Scotland depended on each other: Jekyll remitted money and prestige; Hyde kept the place distinctive, ensured that the ladder of social promotion was kept open, that the social stratification of the English governing class was not imposed. Nationalist agitation, of a very hygienic sort, ensured that the Scots, red and black together, would control the rate of their own assimilation to the greater world. Whatever might befall the crofters of the North or the Lanarkshire miners, or the majority of Glasgow families who lived for most of this century in one- or two-roomed houses, Jekyll would always have the empire as his oyster, while Hyde would keep his less fortunate compatriots content with religion, football and whisky.

The fortunes – or lack of them – of nationalism have largely been bound up with the relations between the red Scots and the Empire. Traditional nationalists have always held that Scotland was England's first colony: it would be nearer the truth to claim the red Scots as the more decisive members of the imperial partnership, from their first colonial ventures in seventeenth-century Ireland to the liquidation of the Empire by Macmillan and Macleod in the 1960s. They provided the Empire with its Bibles and opium, its steamers and railway engines, its non-commissioned officers: engineers, bankers, clerks and missionaries. This success was largely due to Scots distinctiveness, to the relative excellence and accessibility of secondary and higher education: in the 1860s one Scot in every 1,000 went to University, one Englishman in every 5,800. Yet by depriving the country of the resident intelligentsia which, in nineteenth-century Europe, acted as the focus of nationalism, the red Scots yielded place to the antiquarian tartanry of black Scotland, the pseudo-patriotism of a non-nation.

Difficult though it is to discover tendencies in the drunkard's progress of twentieth-century history, 'real' nationalism appears to have made most headway when the opportunities for red Scots were curtailed. During the inter-war depression the birth of political nationalism was essentially 'the revolt of the MAs'. It produced a poet and ideologist of genius (though scarcely a political leader) in Hugh MacDiarmid, and, on the eve of the

Second World War, had all but converted the Labour Party to the principle of home rule.

Significantly, this was the achievement of a pressure group of London-based expatriates, which included Naomi Mitchison, Ritchie Calder and A. S. Neill. The war checked this démarche. The heavy industries boomed, government was centralised and expanded: the way to the South was open again. For about fifteen years the old pattern survived, until economic collapse, imperial withdrawal and competition from a modernised English educational system brought the world of the red Scots rapidly to an end.

As a result of this, Scotland seems to have been trying to pack into the last decade and a half the cultural evolution of a comparable small European state over the last two centuries, with salutary if rather alarming results. The complacent conservatism which characterised middle-class Scottish culture seems almost completely to have disappeared. The old Scottish institutions are admitted to be in dissolution; the hold of the churches has been broken; law is seen more as a restrictive practice than a national ornament; education is badly in need of reform. Political nationalism is no more prepossessing as an ideology than it was, but there is no longer a British or imperial alternative. The intelligentsia can only now create a tolerable, convivial community in its own country.

This was the situation before the oil bonanza was in prospect. Oil has simply brought matters to a crisis. It has, for the first time, transformed Scotland from being a beneficiary of imperialism to being its victim. This poses a peculiarly ironic dilemma for the red Scots. If they maintain their traditional loyalty to the Union they will end up being exploited by an alien elite – oilmen, Whitehall and Brussels bureaucrats, and what have you. If they maintain their traditional elitism they must emerge as the leaders of nationalism. In present circumstances there's little doubt about which course will be taken. The real disquiet, among those of us who want a rational transition to home rule within a federal Britain, must now concern the ability of the English political elite – Jenkins, Crosland et al. – to recognise and compromise with the new Scottish politics.

Our Changing Democracy

This is the summary contained in the Labour government's white paper *Our Changing Democracy*, Part II (pp. 4–7) (1975, Cmnd 6348).

Political and economic unity has been maintained and deepened throughout Great Britain for over two and a half centuries, giving its countries a common history, heritage and way of life richer than any of them could have enjoyed on its own.

The Government are firmly committed to maintaining this unity. It is a powerful and constructive force shaping the daily lives of us all; and those who advocate destroying the United Kingdom, for the sake of a real or imaginary short-term gain to some, brush aside the long-term loss to all. The Government reject entirely the idea of separation for Scotland and Wales and the break-up of the United Kingdom, and believe that the vast majority of Scottish and Welsh people endorse this rejection. As the Government made clear in the White Paper of September 1974 (*Democracy and Devolution: Proposals for Scotland and Wales*, Cmnd 5732), they agree wholeheartedly with the Kilbrandon Commission in rejecting also federalism within the United Kingdom.

Unity however is not uniformity. Within the United Kingdom Scotland and Wales have kept their own identities with distinctive elements of tradition, culture and institutions. Respect for these diversities has strengthened the Union far more than an imposed conformity could have done.

This respect underlies the long tradition of decentralisation of Scottish government – that is, the practice whereby large areas of government work for Scotland are carried out not in London but in Edinburgh under Ministers answerable to Parliament at Westminster but nevertheless distinctively Scottish. In 1964 the Government extended this system to Wales; and its scope in both countries has recently been widened by the transfer of new responsibilities in the industrial field to the two Secretaries of State.

Decentralisation remains a useful means of ensuring that administration in Scotland and Wales is founded on an understanding of the needs and wishes of these countries; the Government will continue to use it and indeed in some respects to extend it . . .

The Government believe however that something more is needed – the creation of elected as well as administrative institutions distinctive to

Scotland and Wales. This is what devolution means. There will be new democratic bodies, directly chosen and answerable to the Scottish and Welsh people for very wide fields of government.

The central task on which the Government have concentrated in developing the devolution schemes is to define those areas of activity where decisions affect primarily people living in Scotland and Wales. It would plainly be wrong to devolve to the Scottish and Welsh Assemblies powers over activities which substantially affect people elsewhere, or the well being of the United Kingdom generally. The need is to achieve balance – to reconcile unity and diversity in a stronger and better system, offering more achievement and satisfaction to the parts while improving the efficiency and stability of the whole. In working this out the Government have observed the principles which flow from acceptance of the essential unity of the United Kingdom. They have also kept in mind the need for a consistent and coherent pattern of government, which will be clear and understandable to the people who work in it and the public whom they serve. The objective throughout has been the long-term advantage of the people of Scotland and Wales within the United Kingdom.

Under the Government's proposals, the Assemblies will control policies and spending priorities over a very wide field, including for example most aspects of local government, health, personal social services, education, housing, physical planning, the environment and roads, and many aspects of transport. They will have a very large block grant from the Exchequer and some power to supplement it from local taxation, and they will have the fullest possible freedom to decide how the money should be spent among the services they control. The Scottish Assembly will also be able to make new laws or amend present ones in these matters, and it will be responsible for most aspects of the distinctive private and criminal law of Scotland.

All these powers will enable the new Scottish and Welsh administrations to bring far-reaching influence to bear on the whole physical and social environment of their countries. That influence, together with the huge spending power which they will control, will enable them to have a very marked effect also on their economic environment.

The new powers will not however be conferred at the expense of the benefits which flow from the political and economic unity of the United Kingdom. Political unity means The Queen in Parliament, representing all the people, must remain sovereign over their affairs; and that the Government of the day must bear the main responsibility to Parliament for protecting and furthering the interests of all. In particular, the Government must be able to do whatever is needed for national security; they must conduct international relations, including those flowing from our membership of the European

Community; and they must maintain the national framework of law and order, guaranteeing the basic rights of the citizen throughout the United Kingdom.

Economic unity plainly means that the Government must manage the nation's external economic relations – the balance of payments, the exchange rate, external assets and liabilities, and economic trading and other arrangements with other countries. But the principle reaches much further. The Government must be able to manage demand in the economy as a whole – to control national taxation, total public expenditure and the supply of money and credit. The Government must be able to regulate the framework of trade, so as to maintain a fair competitive balance for industry and commerce everywhere. Within the wider common market which the European Community is developing we already enjoy a common market throughout the United Kingdom, and any new and artificial barriers within that long-established market could be seriously damaging. And the Government must also keep the task of devising national policies to benefit particular parts of the United Kingdom, and of distributing resources among them according to relative need. This last point is the cardinal fact about our whole system of allocating public expenditure. Resources are distributed not according to where they come from but according to where they are needed. This applies between geographical areas just as much as between individuals.

People are less and less ready to tolerate extremes of wealth and poverty alongside one another in our society. Unplanned economic forces, changes in world demand and the discovery of new natural resources can bring fortune or misfortune to large areas, and over the centuries almost every part of the United Kingdom has experienced this ebb and flow. In recent times successive Governments have increasingly sought to reduce inequalities; the fact that Scotland and Wales are at present classified in their entirety as assisted areas is evidence of this. So, too, is the fact that under successive Governments Scotland and Wales have continued to benefit from levels of public expenditure per head significantly higher than the United Kingdom average. If these had been financed entirely by Scotland and Wales, their taxpayers would have had to pay much more.

Regional policies have been formulated and implemented for Great Britain as a whole, so that priorities can be judged and the resources of the whole country deployed to help solve problems as they arise anywhere within it. Relative need can be assessed only by taking an overall view, and this must be the responsibility of the Government. It would not be practicable even to leave particular areas to draw up their own schemes of economic support and assistance within an overall allocation, since divergences could easily distort competition in ways incompatible with a unified economy.

The Assemblies will have great economic influence . . . The Scottish administration will control the Highlands and Islands Development Board. In addition, the arrangements for the Scottish and Welsh Development Agencies . . . will give the Assemblies an important role in relation to the work of these new bodies, which are intended to give a fresh stimulus to industrial and environmental regeneration. At the same time the transfer of manpower functions – crucial to economic development – to the Secretaries of State for Scotland and for Wales . . . will add an important new dimension to the decision making in the economic field carried out in Scotland and Wales.

. . .

Arrangements will be needed for extensive but flexible consultation on many subjects and at all levels, political and official. Through these the Government and the devolved administrations will keep one another informed and will work together as closely as possible. Interests will sometimes differ, and give and take will be needed. But the Government see no reason to fear that the long-standing spirit of partnership within the United Kingdom will be lost; indeed, they believe that it will be enhanced. They look forward to working out effective two-way consultation arrangements with the devolved administrations as soon as possible, and to operating them constructively over the years.

At the same time the Government cannot shed their responsibility for the interests of the United Kingdom as a whole. They must ensure that they and their successors remain able to act freely and promptly in those interests. Reserve powers are therefore built into the devolution proposals to enable the Government of the day to intervene, subject to the approval of Parliament, in actions by the devolved administrations which the Government judge seriously harmful. It is impossible to predict what situations might lead to the use of these powers, and it is largely for this reason that the Government propose to provide them rather than attempt to deal specifically in the Act with every possible eventuality. Their use should not therefore be regarded as a last resort implying a serious confrontation. But if the schemes of devolution fulfil their objectives, the necessity to use reserve powers should not arise frequently and need not be a source of conflict. The future of us all turns to a great extent upon harmonious co-operation between all the people of the United Kingdom and their elected representatives, whether in Parliament or in the Assemblies.

NATIONALISM, COMMUNITY AND DEMOCRACY

Isobel Lindsay

From *The Radical Approach*, edited by Gavin Kennedy (Palingenesis Press, 1976, pp. 21–6), a collection of essays by people in and near to the SNP. Lindsay was (and is) a lecturer in sociology at Strathclyde University and was a vice-chair of the SNP.

One of the most striking things about the conventional political debate is what it has not been about. Many of the fundamental developments in our society have gone almost without comment by mainstream politicians of right or left. Our only legacy has been a sterile, highly ritualised debate about the marginal redistribution of the spoils. There has been an almost total failure to come to terms with the social and political problems generated by the development of highly centralised, advanced industrial societies whether of East or West or to question the purposes and limitations of economic growth. The development of the nationalist movement in Scotland and elsewhere is not a quaint aberration or a simple campaign for economic betterment; it is concerned with how a modern society can fulfil the social, emotional and material needs of its citizens.

. . .

– NATIONALISM –

The debate on Scottish independence has been clouded by the confused thinking which surrounds the concept of nationalism. It is often regarded as something which must be either morally good or morally bad in itself rather than something which, in its broadest sense of attachment to a territorial and/or cultural community, is morally neutral. To define nationalism in abstract as either good or bad is rather like saying that the sex drive in abstract is good or bad whether it be rape or between consenting adults. The sentiments which attach people to place and to kin are of fundamental importance to any highly socialised animal with a complex culture. This attachment serves two purposes. It helps to create an overriding loyalty to balance the inevitable conflicts and tensions which will arise when people live in proximity to each other. More important, even the simplest culture cannot survive without continuity and stability. If, to reduce it to absurdity, we had no particular territorial or group attachments and we all led an individualistic, nomadic existence, it would be virtually impossible to pass on knowledge and values in any systematic way. Therefore, whether you call it tribalism, nationalism, patriotism, this sentiment is not atavistic. Its absence in a modern society is not a sign of emancipation. It is, on the contrary, quite fundamental to what we are.

Having said that nationalism per se is a morally neutral concept, one must point out that there is an important and valid distinction between nationalism and imperialism although the former can degenerate into the latter. Attachment to one's own community in no way implies any desire or necessity to deprive others of similar rights. It is, in fact, quite in keeping with a preparedness to defend the rights of others to self-determination within their own territory. Imperialism, on the other hand, arises from the desire of one territorial or ideological group to impose its will on another. It may be done in the name of nationalism, religion, capitalism, socialism or whatever but it does not follow that nationalism, religion, capitalism or socialism must of themselves be imperialist.

Nationalism is neither geographically nor culturally static. Changing circumstances may forge new identities and new groupings although the emotional need for continuity and stability is likely to ensure that attachments do not change rapidly. Nationalism can also at different times and in different situations be a centralising or a decentralising force. For example, in the United States 'nationalism' is associated with the Federal Government as opposed to State or lower level community political power. In this century, however, nationalism has probably been more significant as a decentralising force, most notably in the case of the nationalist movements breaking down the former centralised imperialist empires, and, of course, what we now see emerging is the growth of decentralising nationalism or regionalism in the highly developed industrialised societies. These centralised advanced societies are beginning to face an internal challenge and it is groups with a long-established political/cultural identity which are spear-heading this challenge. The problems which give rise to it, however, have wider relevance and the success of the more culturally distinctive areas may very well stimulate others.

. . .

– CULTURE –

Perhaps the most central [idea] of all is the concept of 'culture' – the intricate, complex, pervasive and distinctive way in which societies have evolved and individuals are socialised into them and take identity and meaning from them. It was fashionable not so very many years ago deliberately to destroy established cultures for the sake of 'emancipation' or creed or greed. It is still being done but it has become less fashionable to proclaim it. The plight of many of the indigenous peoples of North and South America, of Africa, of Australasia has become the subject of sympathetic media treatment. These show in extreme form the demoralisation, the disorientation, the loss of personal identity which results. But those who readily condemn the dramatic examples are often remarkably slow to draw any lessons of relevance to our own society. Of course, we do not have such extreme cases (although the Gaelic-speaking communities could offer many examples from the not too distant past) but the same processes have been in operation. . . .

If there is something of a class stereotype in the attitudes of the Scots to the English, then it is because the Scots as a nation – middle as well as working class – have experienced something akin to what the lower classes experience as a sub-group in the larger society. Our language or dialect was rejected as inferior and the centres of power and influence increasingly moved outwith the country. With the growth of centralised media the people who dominated entertainment and current affairs were certainly not Scots. If you wanted to be considered really successful you had to go South, if you wanted to get something done, all too often you had to go cap in hand to London. Scotland was the poor relation, the dependent, the small and weak partner. The cumulative effect of this has been to produce in the Scots a sense of being, in Norman MacCaig's words, 'a failed nation'.

It is, of course, twentieth-century developments which more than any other period have produced this effect. The cultural impact of the loss of political independence was comparatively slight in earlier periods when the role of central government was a very limited one, when economic activity was more localised in control and communications not highly centralised. But to lack political independence in the modern situation has a much more important cultural impact. It not only deprives us of a powerful tool of protection and reform which can be used to counteract economic and cultural centralism, it also deprives us of the political expression of national identity and in that sense is a diminution of the latter.

Ultimately it is hard to envisage a situation in which a high degree of political and/or cultural centralism will not have a debilitating effect on the peripheries. The vicarious identification with a more dominant culture may carry with it a heavy social cost.

. . .

– POWER –

If there is one factor which exposes the total inadequacies of mainstream Socialist and Conservative thinking, it is their failure to come to terms with the problems of power in contemporary society. On the socialist side we still have the Marxist legacy, excusable in Marx given the particular circumstances of his own time, of assuming private legal ownership to be synonymous with power and further assuming that the transfer from private legal ownership to public legal ownership, will, of itself, constitute major social change. . . .

If you try to redefine the class struggle in terms of the distribution of power rather than the legal relationship to property (and what is property if not simply one form of power), as Ralf Dahrendorf did in his book *Classes and Class Conflict in Industrial Society* (1959), you produce a model in many respects more applicable to our own society and certainly one which can more readily explain the centre/periphery conflict.

One of the other faults in the discussion of class conflict by the mainstream left is the assumption that conflict in the society is at root one-dimensional, that it is really about the wealthy and the poor and that other conflicts are simply confusions, digressions, 'false consciousness'. And yet if you look, say, at the planning decisions in our cities which have had such a major effect on people's lives, is this simply to do with the relationship between the rich and the poor? If you look at the problems which arise in most industries, will there ever not be real conflicts about the pace of change, about differentials, about the right of some people to tell others what to do irrespective of whether the industry is privately or publicly owned? Of course, the relative distribution of wealth and the degree of power derived from private wealth will be a major issue in most societies, but if it is to be understood, it must be seen in the total context of social conflict not as a unique factor which in some sense causes everything else.

Within the traditions of British socialism there was a strand more conscious of these other dimensions. Romantic socialists like William Morris and Guild Socialists like G. D. H. Cole were most concerned with the problems of community and culture and centralised power – in Cole's phrase the problems of 'democracy face to face with hugeness' [1950]. But this attempt to develop a 'community' socialism was totally swamped in the face of conventional statism. If you believe that the object of radical politics is to ensure the delivery of a comparable quantity of goods to the citizens of a state, then it may be that the crude, centralised statist solution has something to commend it although in reality the distribution of goods too often goes hand in hand with the distribution of power and prestige, whatever the formal aims of public policy. However, if you feel that in working towards a more egalitarian society the distribution of power and status must stand along with the distribution of goods as a central importance in political policy, then the solutions must be decentralising ones. Whatever the large centralised state can achieve in terms of redistribution of wealth (probably not very much), it is almost impossible by definition that it can fulfil any major power and status redistribution unless it destroys itself. At best it may change the nature of the elite groups. To achieve this more fundamental egalitarianism you must radically disperse the points of power and initiative and communication in society.

Little reference has been made to the Conservative position because, in modern UK politics, Conservatives have made so little attempt to think out any consistent position at all. Interestingly, unlike their counterparts in some other countries, British Conservatives have not at all been critical of big business nor have they been notably the champions of local or regional 'rights' against the centre. Their rhetoric has been heavily weighted with attacks on state power although their actions in office have belied this. Their philosophical base has been shoddy and inconsistent; growing centralisation in the private sector is not criticised and their policy priority appears to be that of transferring a few powers from the powerful public sector to the powerful/privileged private sector. Many American conservatives are critical of big business as well as big government. It is not moving power sideways that matters most; it is in reducing the size of the political units that the best hope of social and political democratisation now lies.

– Community –

. . .

We use the word community in two senses – to indicate a geographical area with interacting social institutions and in the other subjective usage, a feeling of belonging, a sense of special identification with a particular grouping of people. Both are of great importance; both have been substantially ignored as matters of political interest. The size and shape of our communities has major economic and social implications and Scotland has just about the worst of all worlds in its (expensive) extremes of rural depopulation and urban congestion. In city redevelopment we have created huge, unpopular, aesthetically unattractive, single-class ghettos and most of it 'just happened'. We still find politicians discussing problems of crime and punishment as if these could be divorced from the nature of the community, from the weakening of one of the most powerful controlling factors of all – knowing and being known.

Human beings will normally seek 'community' in its subjective sense. The point at issue is not whether they will seek it but in what form will they seek it and whether they will achieve it. . . . Political decision-making in its broadest sense provides a socially creative channel through which people can work out their priorities, their values, their goals and they can act in some respects as a collectivity. A political unit can provide a goal for collective achievement, something which has greater continuity through time than any individual. It may reinforce community at the same time as requiring community to provide its coherence.

The question of the basis on which political units should be determined must ultimately rest on value judgements. If you believe that people should be participants rather than voyeurs, that variety is an important factor in stimulating creativity, then you will favour trying to keep as much decision-making as possible close to those whom it will most effect. But the other factor with which you must work is that political units should where possible reflect community identification and this may be determined by historical experience, by cultural differences, by differing interests. It is remarkable that the feeling of being Scottish should have remained. We ought to have become North British but being awkward and unreasonable, we didn't. For the people who live in Scotland, Scotland is a meaningful aggregate and we want to achieve the political expression of this national identity. We are even bold enough to think that we might make not such a bad job of it as our present masters. What the ultimate pattern of decision-making within Scotland will be is a choice for the post-independence situation but the thinking which leads to self-government is likely to be the thinking which will lead to a vigorous local and industrial democracy.

. . .

Speech to Parliament

Alick Buchanan-Smith

Speech on the second reading of the Scotland and Wales Bill (14 December 1976: Hansard, fifth series, vol. 922, columns 1290–5), the government's first attempt to translate into legislation the principles contained in the white paper *Our Changing Democracy*. Buchanan-Smith was Conservative MP for North Angus and Mearns.

. . .

There are many other people in Scotland apart from the nationalists who believe that we require an improvement in government in Scotland.

. . .

In matters affecting the constitution we are playing for very high stakes indeed. We are not dealing merely with the future of Scotland and Wales. We are dealing with the future of the United Kingdom. I could not endorse more fully what was said yesterday by [Margaret Thatcher] – namely, that we want a stable and lasting solution. In working for that solution we must take account of the feelings and aspirations of the people in Scotland and Wales.

Although I appreciated what was said by [Teddy Taylor] in his opening remarks, I believe that this is not just a bread-and-butter matter, not just a matter involving material considerations, but that there are important things to be considered, such as national identity and the aspirations felt in various parts of the United Kingdom, not just in Scotland alone.

Although we are playing for high stakes in these deliberations, the subject in hand is important not only for Parliament but for the great national parties in this country. We must demonstrate in what we do and say in the House that we are sensitive and that we can show our sensitivity towards individual parts of the United Kingdom that make up the whole. If we take that course, we shall truly show that we believe in the integrity and unity of the whole nation.

I agree with the Secretary of State for Scotland that time is no longer on our side, although that may at one time have been the case. I remind my colleagues that we in the Conservative Party have now been discussing these matters for about ten years. The Labour Party has come to these matters more recently. However, I welcome the fact that the Labour Government have at least been prepared to bring forward a measure for consideration at this time.

It is right to criticise the provisions of the Bill, as [Margaret Thatcher] did yesterday. I, too, have my doubts about some of the detailed provisions. I have doubts about how some of the responsibilities are divided between the United Kingdom Parliament and the Assembly in Edinburgh. I should like to see many of those responsibilities more clear-cut because that would lead to less risk of conflict.

I am also concerned about some of the problems of resolving those conflicts, and some of them derive from the fact that there is a dual Executive [in the Assembly and in the Secretary of State for Scotland]. I am also worried on the subject of cost – a point dealt with by [Teddy Taylor] earlier in the debate. However, I agreed with [Reginald Maudling] that if we are to keep the United Kingdom united, we must at the same time put the matters of costs into perspective.

What concerns me is that so far it has been left to Opposition Back Benchers to speak of our party's commitment and belief in devolution and of an Assembly in Scotland. It is true that this matter has been spelt out outside the House [in the proposals of the Scottish Constitutional Committee]. . . . It is a way of devolving government for the United Kingdom, I believe that it has a great deal to be said for it, and I hope that we shall hear more from the Opposition benches about the benefits of that solution. It maintains the link with the United Kingdom Parliament, it provides continuing machinery that will seek to resolve conflict when conflict arises, and it avoids a second Executive.

Let me say to those who seek to pour scorn on the matter that the Kilbrandon Committee did not pour scorn on the proposal, but treated it as a sensible and practical alternative. The Kilbrandon Committee rejected the proposal, but it regarded it as one way of trying to deal with the problems of devolution in the United Kingdom.

I emphasise to my hon. Friends that simply to criticise the Government's proposals without spelling out any alternative will not do. Of course there will be conflicts in our proposals, just as there are conflicts under the present system. In fact, the present conflicts have given fire to the desire for devolution in Scotland.

Having listened to the criticisms of [Margaret Thatcher] yesterday I was tempted to say, just as [John Mackintosh] said, that, if these criticisms are so valid, perhaps the Government proposals do not go far enough. If we are not prepared to consider some framework of devolution, as the Government are trying to do with this Bill, then perhaps we should not dismiss out of hand the idea of some federal solution which might cope effectively and adequately with the conflict to which [Margaret Thatcher] referred yesterday. That is not necessarily the right thing to do, but if we are exposing some of the risks, we must face up to the consequences, consider them constructively, and then either accept or reject them.

Be that as it may, the worst course of all is to do nothing. Opinion in Scotland cannot be ignored. This is not something which will just go away. If we in the House appear to frustrate the genuine aspirations of the Scottish people, this is the very thing which turns moderates into extremists. Scotland is not a country of extremists – Socialist, nationalist, or anything else. It is up to us in this debate to ensure that we do not turn moderates in to extremists.

. . .

A vote against the Bill – I say this in particular to my right hon. and hon. Friends from south of the border – will be misunderstood by many of the people in Scotland if we are to remain true to our commitment to an Assembly for Scotland. The Prime Minister has promised to consider constructive amendments in committee. If we were unsuccessful in Committee, there would still be Third Reading. But at this stage we should get the debate going.

. . .

The Union to which we all rightly pay allegiance will not be preserved and strengthened by us ignoring the aspirations of one party to that Union; the Union will not be preserved and strengthened by denying the opportunity to discuss one possible way of meeting those aspirations; and the Union will not be preserved and strengthened if we ignore the views of the majority of Scottish MPs on a matter so deeply affecting Scotland.

On the other hand, I believe that the Union will be preserved and strengthened if we in this House can recognise and react to the fact that the majority of those in Scotland who want more say in the running of their own affairs want it to be within the framework of the United Kingdom. By doing that in a proper way we destroy the very attractions of narrow nationalism of which [Eric Heffer] spoke.

For nearly ten years I have campaigned within my party and in Scotland for what is embodied in the principle of the Bill – an Assembly for Scotland within the United Kingdom. I do not intend to change my position now.

THE SLIDE TO INDEPENDENCE

Tam Dalyell

From *Devolution: the End of Britain?* (Jonathan Cape, 1977, pp. 228–67). Dalyell was Labour MP for West Lothian.

To their credit, supporters of the SNP have always had a far more realistic and far-sighted attitude towards the establishment of an Assembly in Edinburgh than their pro-devolution opponents: they have campaigned for devolution on the very reasonable grounds that the Assembly, in itself an uneasy compromise, would be unworkable, and that the resulting frustration and sense of grievance on the part of its members would inevitably push them into demanding a still greater degree of autonomy for Scotland and, eventually, complete independence from the United Kingdom. Far from satisfying nationalist aspirations, an Assembly with limited powers – not least in the crucial area of finance – would only create new problems and aggravate old grievances. Ironically enough, its very existence would bring about the situation it was designed to avoid.

As a subordinate Parliament in a unitary state, the Edinburgh Assembly would soon find itself in an impossible position. . . . [I]t would remain financially dependent on Westminster; and despite the Government's neat, theoretical distinction between 'devolved' and 'reserved' areas of legislation, it would in fact be impossible to separate specifically 'Scottish' issues from those affecting the United Kingdom as a whole. Conflict between West-minster and the new Assembly would be inevitable, particularly if the governments in London and Edinburgh were of different political persua-sion; members of the Assembly, from all points on the political spectrum, would be more than human if, having once tasted power, they did not come to resent the limitations imposed upon them and to demand greater power for themselves. It's hard to believe that many of those who blithely advocate the setting up of a Scottish Assembly cannot have thought out the full implications of such a step. A Parliament is, by definition, a very different kind of institution from a local authority or even a Regional authority, and inevitably arouses far greater expectations both in its members and those who vote for it: an unworkable and essentially frustrated Assembly is a recipe for disaster. It is to the impracticability of the proposed Assembly and its potentially fraught relationship with Westminster that we must now turn.

– THE ASSEMBLY IS A CONSTITUTIONAL IMPOSSIBILITY –

A fundamental error on the part of those who advocate an Edinburgh Assembly – whether out of self-interest, political expediency or a genuine belief that to do so is to align oneself with the mainstream of enlightened thought – is the assumption that it is possible to establish a subordinate legislative assembly in a unitary Parliamentary state like Britain: and that an Assembly in Edinburgh can be thought of in much the same way as existing elected bodies such as local councils or Regional authorities.

The truth of the matter is that the proposed Assembly represents an unsatisfactory and impracticable half-way house in a unitary state which is doomed to failure. Clearly if the United Kingdom is to remain in existence Scottish and Welsh voters must continue to be represented at Westminster – and we shall be examining the formidable and often farcical problems this will raise later in this chapter. If drastic changes are called for – and I do not believe that they are – then the establishment of Scottish and Welsh Assemblies must have one of two different results: either Britain becomes a Federal state, with a written Constitution setting out the powers and scope of the Assemblies and Parliament, as the Liberals suggest, or – and this is the long-term aim of the SNP and Plaid Cymru – the United Kingdom is dismantled, Scottish and Welsh voters are no longer represented at Westminster, and Scotland and Wales take their place as fully independent nations. To assume that there is a realistic third alternative is to inhabit the realm of fantasy.

But why, it may reasonably be asked, should Britain not become a Federal state? After all, West Germany – whose post-war economic record is so enviable by British standards – is a Federal state. And why should Britain not have a written Constitution, in common with the United States and most West European countries?

. . .

In general terms, one should always be cautious about the feasibility of transplanting a system which has worked well in one country into the different conditions of another.

More specifically, the German system is fundamentally different from a British scenario in which only Scotland and Wales would be comparable Federal states. To pursue the German analogy, it is as if Schleswig-Holstein and Baden-Württemberg were alone to have their own subordinate state legislatures, while at the same time being over-represented in a Bonn Parliament which was responsible for the government of the rest of the

Federal Republic. This would be intolerable to other Germans, particularly if the Schleswig-Holstein and Baden-Württemberg representatives determined the complexion of the Government in Bonn, and were able to deal with matters for which they were not responsible in their own provinces.

Second, the German states were for the main part ancient kingdoms, like Bavaria, or margravates or Hanse cities, with a proud separate history. Only Nord Rhein-Westfalen is an artificial new land. The Scottish and the Welsh situations are perhaps broadly comparable: the English position is not. Because England is so much more heavily populated than Scotland or Wales, the Federation would be completely out of balance, nor is there any identifiable demand for subordinate Parliaments in Norwich for East Anglia, Winchester for Wessex, Birmingham for Mercia, Manchester for Lancastria or Newcastle for Northumbria – all areas which, in terms of population, are comparable with Scotland or Wales.

. . .

The sine qua non of a Federal system is a written Constitution. In the absence of a written Constitution and a Supreme Court, which would interpret such a Constitution, a Federal state would find itself enmeshed in interminable internal difficulties, and disputes as to the frontiers of power. Now there is no reason why Britain should not in theory have a written Constitution. In practice, it would mean altering our way of government far beyond the confines of the Scotland and Wales Bill. And even if such a radical change were to take place – for which there is little obvious demand in England – would it really solve the problem of Scotland and Wales? The SNP demand nation-status, with all the trappings of a separate army, navy, air force and diplomatic representation which accompany nation-status. Exactly the same factors which would help to make any devolution settlement unstable would operate in the case of a Federal solution. For a Federal solution to work, there would have to be a unanimous desire to want to make it work. And it is this that is manifestly lacking in the Scotland of the 1970s.

Nor is it possible to pretend – as so many politicians would understandably like to – that an Assembly in Edinburgh would be little more than a glorified county council and that its establishment need cause no alarm to anyone on either side of the Border. . . . An elected Assembly with legislative power is neither more nor less than a Parliament; it is not a local authority. Local authorities, whatever their size, have no power to make or alter the laws they apply; they take decisions at a purely administrative level within the limits laid down by the law, which is not made by them, but by

Parliament. Nor do the local authorities attract the feelings of patriotism and emotion invested in a Parliament, which acts as a focus of national pride. An Assembly of the kind proposed for Edinburgh, whatever the limitations on its power and whatever its innate implausibility, is a very different kettle of fish from even the grandest local authority. It is both misleading and unrealistic to pretend otherwise.

. . .

Money is at the root of the problem. It has been suggested that the Westminster Parliament should grant the Scottish Assembly an annual block grant, the size of which would be decided in London; it would then be up to the Edinburgh Assembly to decide how the money should be spent in those areas which had been devolved to it. Financial dependence is humiliating and frustrating at the best of times, and especially for those with great expectations; and if there isn't enough to go round it's natural enough to blame whoever holds the purse strings. The obvious answer is to allow the dependent to make his own money and pay his own way – in other words, for the Assembly to raise its own taxes inside Scotland; but . . . this is easier said than done.

. . .

[I]t has hitherto proved impossible to suggest an acceptable form of revenue-raising for the Assembly. For three years now, able Ministers and ingenious civil servants have racked their brains to discover one, and they have all failed – not for want of the necessary expertise, but because there is simply no way of raising revenue for a subordinate Parliament within a unitary state which is acceptable to a sensitive and democratic electorate. The result is that the Assembly will be totally dependent on its annual block grant; and however skilfully and persuasively the Scottish Executive may present its case to the Prime Minister and the Chancellor of the Exchequer in London, the size of the grant will be determined by the United Kingdom Treasury and endorsed by the United Kingdom Cabinet.

. . .

[F]or all the government claims about the Scots having freedom of choice, the Assembly's room to manoeuvre would be extremely limited, particularly in these tight economic times. Assembly members would naturally come to resent their dependence on Westminster. Not only would they complain about the size of the grant, and blame their inability to push through their electoral promises on the parsimony of London; they would also resent the fact that their ability to decide how the money should be spent would in fact be extremely limited, particularly in the early years when hopes were at their highest (most Government programmes, from roads to school buildings, are decided years rather than months in advance). However first hand the knowledge of its members about the problems of Scotland, the Assembly's scope for making any early changes or improvements on the way money is spent in those areas for which responsibility has been devolved to it would be extremely marginal.

Not only would Scottish politicians and those who elect them feel frustrated and resentful: ironically the chances are that Scotland would end up worse off than it is at present. Despite the age-old belief that the Scots are England's poor relations, the Scots – rightly or wrongly – receive more than their share of United Kingdom public expenditure at present. For every £100 of public expenditure at present, someone in Scotland currently receives £119, someone on Humberside £87. And for as long as Westminster and Whitehall feel fully responsible for Scotland, public expenditure will continue to be allocated on a basis of both political judgement and need. But if the Scots had their own Assembly, Government Ministers in London would come under tremendous pressure – particularly from those areas of England whose need is as great as that of Scotland – to make sure that the Scots do not get more than their fair share of the cake when the annual haggling over the size of the block grant comes round.

. . .

– Legislative Confusion –

Financial lack of clout is not the only disappointment in store for the newly elected Assemblymen. As we have seen, the Assembly is by its very nature an uneasy hybrid which is unlikely to satisfy anybody and the diversion of powers between Westminster and the High School [the proposed home of the Assembly in Edinburgh] offers little hope of its being a success. It is, in effect, being suggested that the Edinburgh Government should carry into effect – and produce secondary legislation for – legislation originated by the Government in London, which may well be of a totally different complexion. The problem is aggravated by the fact that the Edinburgh Government would be responsible for administering many of the social services without being in a position to control or even influence the economic policies which would produce the resources to fund these services. Here again, some of the social services would be the responsibility of Westminster, while others – such as housing – would be controlled from Edinburgh: an artificial distinction which completely ignores the fact that one cannot differentiate between 'Scottish' and national issues and the perennial interaction between the two.

. . .

– Scots MPs at Westminster –

. . . What exactly will [the role of the Scottish MPs at Westminster] be? To what extent could they involve themselves in Scottish affairs which – theoretically at least – were the concern of the Assembly? How many MPs should Scotland have at Westminster? What should be the role of the Secretary of State and what should his relationship be with the Chief Executive of the Scottish Assembly?

. . .

We would have the absurd situation in which Scottish and Welsh MPs could continue to legislate on subjects which had been devolved to the Assemblies in their own countries. They would not be responsible to their own constituents for such legislation, nor would they be answerable to the English voters who would be affected by it.

. . .

Scottish and Welsh interference in purely English affairs would be strongly resented, particularly since the participation of these MPs could well be decisive in deciding whether such legislation was introduced or not. Scottish and Welsh MPs could furthermore decide the political complexion of the Parliament at Westminster: to add insult to injury, this could happen after an election which had in part been decided on the issue of how autonomous the Edinburgh and Cardiff Assemblies should be.

. . .

– THE ROLE OF THE JUDICIAL COMMITTEE –

Everything we have said so far points to inevitable and all too frequent clashes between Westminster and the Edinburgh Assembly over the division of responsibilities between them. How could these conflicts be resolved?

Perhaps the only tenable answer to this problem is to set up a Judicial Committee of the Privy Council. Such a proposal seems entirely reasonable at first glance: who is better equipped than the judiciary to give a disinterested opinion? To counter the inevitable, if unfair, argument that Her Majesty's judges are divorced from the realities of life, the Judicial Committee should also include Privy Councillors with years of political experience behind them. However, the presence of judges on the Judicial Committee would bestow on it legitimacy, and a reputation for impartiality, in the public mind.

To expect judges from the English High Court and Senators from the College of Justice in Scotland to settle demarcation disputes between the High School and Westminster raises some very fundamental issues. The strength of the British judicial system lies partly in its record of uninvolvement in party politics, something for which it has been much admired in the rest of the world: yet it is now suggested that judges should become involved in trying to resolve arguments over the most delicate and sensitive matters of political power – and any dispute which comes before the Committee is bound to be one which arouses extremely strong feelings.

. . .

– THE ROLE OF THE SECRETARY OF STATE –

. . .

The role of the Secretary of State would be an extremely tricky one as far as his relations with his Parliamentary and Ministerial colleagues in London and with the Edinburgh Assembly were concerned. The mind boggles at what would happen if a future incumbent had the curmudgeonly qualities of some of his recent predecessors. The 1974 Labour Party election manifesto faithfully promised that, should an Assembly be created, the Secretary of State would still remain in the Cabinet: the chances are that he would become less and less acceptable both in Scotland and to his Labour Party colleagues.

In Scotland itself, the Secretary of State would come to be regarded as a kind of High Commissioner in London, whose responsibilities and obligations could all too easily conflict with those of the Chief Executive. Prime Ministers inevitably like to conduct really crucial business themselves: any Scottish Chief Executive worth his salt would want to negotiate directly with 10 Downing Street and would resent being upstaged or by-passed by the Secretary of State. The prestige of the Secretary of State would inevitably be reduced in Scotland. Until now, he has always been a central figure in Scottish life, with a 'dignified' – in the sense in which Bagehot used the word – as well as a purely political role. Much of this would now be assumed by the Chief Executive.

Equally, the Secretary of State would carry far less political clout into the Cabinet. His colleagues would soon discover that it made more sense for them to discuss basic economics and social issues, whether theoretically devolved or not, with the Chief Executive and his Cabinet. The Secretary of State for Scotland would be under pressure to surrender his seat in the Cabinet to the holder of another portfolio, or it might be decided to reduce the size of the Cabinet. No longer would Scotland be represented at the Tuesday and Thursday Cabinet meetings: and even if the Secretary remained in the Cabinet on sufferance or as political window-dressing, he would be largely ineffective.

Relations between the Chief Executive and the Cabinet in London might theoretically be easier if both Governments were from the same political party or of the same ideological complexion. This might not in fact be the case, particularly if the setting up of the Assembly had been accompanied by bitterness and recriminations: and prickly, contentious issues like the distribution of oil revenues would present problems however theoretically amicable relations might be. Relations are unlikely to be exactly cosy even if both administrations are formed by colleagues of the same party.

. . .

– Devolution and Local Government –

A fundamental misapprehension on the part of those who favour the setting up of Scottish and Welsh Assemblies is that devolution is the same thing as decentralisation. . . . . 'Decentralisation' and 'participation' are of course fashionable political panaceas at the moment and to some extent, rightly so: yet it is extremely unlikely that devolution would in fact have the desired effect at all. The government of Scotland and Wales would become more, rather than less, centralised and regional and local government would be the losers: and since . . . different parts of Scotland have different requirements, local needs would be less sensitively treated than they are at present.

. . .

One of the great fallacies of the whole devolution debate is the superficially seductive but mistaken assumption that all governmental decisions are likely to be that much better for having been taken at as local a level as possible. Of course it is important that local affairs should be dealt with at a local level. . . . On the other hand, in a highly complex and increasingly integrated industrial economy it is essential that decisions of national importance – the management of the economy, foreign affairs and so forth – should be taken at a national level: in other words, by the Government in London. To emasculate Scottish local government in order to centralise the running of local government on Edinburgh would be in no one's interests.

. . .

[T]he [1975] reorganisation of local government in Scotland has made the effective political control and direction of local authorities more feasible. . . . Abolition of the Regions seems to offer a neat solution to those pro-devolutionists who are sensitive to the charge of over-government. But District authorities could not be expected to assume responsibility for the functions of the Regions, which would have to be transferred to the Assembly – in other words, to the state. In fact, it would spell the beginning of the end for local democracy and local government in Scotland.

THE TROUBLE WITH JOHN P. MACKINTOSH

Stephen Maxwell

From *Q* (no. 24 18 March 1977, p. 5), a vaguely nationalist magazine which was published monthly between October 1975 and August 1977. Maxwell was SNP press officer and an elected councillor for Lothian Region.

. . .

The source of John Mackintosh's ambivalence is most clearly revealed in his own considered contributions to the Scottish debate. These are at once superbly lucid and hopelessly flawed in their assessment of Scottish nationalism. Although John Mackintosh has been ahead of opinion in both England and Scotland in interpreting Scottish developments, his interpretations have usually been couched in terms which are familiar and reassuring to conventional wisdom. In the shock of SNP's Hamilton by-election victory, John Mackintosh warned Labour's social democrats through the *Socialist Commentary* that the result was not a fluke nor merely a mid-term protest against the economic failures of the Labour Government [Mackintosh, 1967]. Behind all this, he revealed was the 'elusive feeling that modern government is too complex, too remote'. He recommended that the Secretary of State for Scotland should exercise more leadership in electoral matters, that the extent of administrative devolution to Scotland should be more vigorously publicised and that a Scottish council or parliament should be set up to undertake the major local government functions and some of the central government duties devolved to the Scottish Office.

With some modest amendments these remained the chief elements of John Mackintosh's diagnosis and of his prognosis until 1974. In *The Devolution of Power* published in 1968, he joined his analysis of Scottish developments to a general account of the weaknesses of British government. He repeated his warning that nationalism was not purely, or even mainly, about economic deprivation. Many of the voters who supported the SNP belonged to a generation which had known only prosperity. Their concern was more with the quality of life and with their capacity to influence a system of government which too often presented itself as remote, indifferent and hopelessly complex. As part of a scheme of elected regional councils throughout the United Kingdom, he recommended the creation of Scottish and Welsh assemblies, in the Scottish case with additional powers over the legal system, the courts and other Home Office functions. Even in *The Government and Politics of Britain* published in 1974, Mackintosh attributed nationalism to dissatisfaction with remote bureaucracy and with the poor economic performance of London governments.

Mackintosh's consistency in analysing Scottish nationalism as a precocious reaction, or overreaction, to general defects of the British system has been matched by his consistency in denying it the status of a genuine Nationalism. To Mackintosh, Scottish nationalism has been 'neo-nationalism', a response to problems Britain shares with other highly developed political systems, but sharpened by Britain's peculiar post-war economic history and by a residual sense of Scottish identity preserved in the traditional Scottish institutions of law, church, education and local government.

– CULTURAL FAILINGS –

The reason for Mackintosh's refusal to admit Scottish nationalism to the company of the classic European nationalist movements appears to be his belief that it lacks a foundation of cultural nationalism. One must be cautious here for Mackintosh has never claimed to be a cultural historian and his references to Scottish culture – or to culture of any sort – are invariably brief. If, however, he intends to draw attention to the lack of a literary-cultural base for contemporary Scottish nationalism of the sort which sustained the nationalist movements of the nineteenth century, he is undoubtedly correct. (The nature of the relationship between the literary nationalism of the 1920s and 1930s in Scotland and contemporary political nationalism is a complex question so far almost untouched by Scottish historians.) And in the absence of a vital literary nationalism, Mackintosh is right to refuse to be impressed by whatever claims might be made for Scotland's traditional institutions as untapped reservoirs of cultural energy.

Yet his implicit definitions of culture may be too restrictive. Cultural identity need not depend on literary culture alone. It can draw sustenance from other areas of culture, from social institutions or even, as the case of Switzerland demonstrates, from distinctive political ethos or distinctive political institutions.

As a political intellectual John Mackintosh might be expected to be alert to the possibility of just such an alternative cultural base for Scottish nationalism. Indeed, in an article in the *New Statesman* at the beginning of last year ['Labour and Scotland', 16 January 1976, pp. 55–6] he hints at the emergence of a distinctive Scottish political culture. What blocks John

Mackintosh's vision is a quite explicit belief that the Scots have a dual identity – that they are both Scots and British – and that this is demonstrated above all in their political attitudes.

His pamphlet *A Parliament for Scotland* published in 1976 by his East Lothian Constituency Association includes one of Mackintosh's rare attempts to argue this thesis. He identifies the Parliamentary tradition as 'purely British', and cites in support the rejection by a majority of the Scottish public of the 'It's Scotland's Oil' slogan in favour of sharing with the rest of Britain and SNP's failure to persuade Scotland to cast a tactical 'No' vote in the EEC referendum. He concludes by quoting opinion polls showing a large majority in favour of Scotland remaining part of the United Kingdom.

Such flimsy evidence will appear less than convincing to those whose political formation and commitments are less directly British than those of John Mackintosh. He offers no defence against the obvious response that these attitudes are the residue of a rapidly wasting sense of British identity. Even a brief excursion into Scottish cultural history would suggest to him that his British political identity would draw little support from the general culture. If such a hybrid as British culture ever existed it was surely only in the nineteenth century through such Anglo-Scottish figures as the Mills, Macaulay, Carlyle and Ruskin, before it guttered to an inglorious end with Robertson Nicoll and *The British Weekly*.

Equally lacking from Mackintosh's assessment is a developed appreciation of the historical conditions making for a revived sense of Scottish identity. On rare occasions he has hinted at the possibility that the parallel decline of traditional Scottish inhibitions and the prestige of British political institutions has released an ambition to establish new – or rediscover old – reference points for Scotland. In a *New Statesman* article in 1974 called 'The New Appeal of Nationalism' he acknowledged that Scots might feel more at home in Oslo or Copenhagen than in London and recounts how, when invited to comment at a European conference on the shameless special pleading of a British Minister, he declined with the words: 'I am from Scotland and I must disassociate myself from all that you have just heard'. But he concludes the article by reasserting, if less confidently than usual, Britain's claim. 'Only one thing will halt or reverse the onward march of the SNP – a period of government in London which is really successful so that it ends with a satisfied electorate eager to vote positively for a country that once again restored the feeling that Britain is a successful, worthwhile country to belong to. . .'. The absence of any suspicion that such long-term, and irreversible, changes as the abandonment of Empire might be the crucial factors, not short-term changes in governmental performance, is entirely characteristic.

Even if Mackintosh is right in arguing for the dominance of a British identity, that identity would not necessarily provide a secure base for the continuation of the United Kingdom. The Scandinavian example demonstrates that some sense of common identity, even common political identity, can co-exist with constitutional separation.

– TRUDEAU –

Mackintosh's intellectual position in a Britain facing the problems of Scottish and Welsh nationalism perhaps bears comparison with that of Pierre Trudeau facing the challenge of Quebec separatism. Like Trudeau, Mackintosh represented a new reformist element in his immediate provincial context. Mr Trudeau believed that Quebecers should adapt themselves to the role of French Canadians, Mackintosh believes that Scots have a dual Scottish British identity. As Trudeau sought to reform Federal attitudes to accommodate Quebec's non-separatist ambitions, so Mackintosh has laboured nobly to instruct English political opinion in the new Scottish realities as he saw them. As Trudeau began by patronising the Quebec separatists as narrow-minded chauvinists only to learn that they had as keen a sense of the international context in which both Quebec and Canada must operate as he himself, so John Mackintosh once scorned the Nationalists as political kailyarders only to learn that even if they were not familiar faces at Königswinter conferences and the other gathering places of the new self-regarding European élite, they had their own perhaps more catholic view of Scotland's international links.

The comparison takes added point from the fact that it is not long since Mackintosh was prepared to cite Quebec's role in Canada as a reassuring example of the viability of Federal systems. Perhaps over the next few years Mackintosh and Trudeau will be witnesses of a practical demonstration that in an interdependent world of multinational corporations and international competition for natural resources, neither the economic nor the cultural survival of small societies can be secured within the political limits imposed by the classic Federal division of powers.

Why it must be 'No' when Assembly is put to the Vote

Teddy Taylor

From the *Glasgow Herald* (19 May 1978, p. 6). Taylor was Conservative MP for Glasgow Cathcart and shadow Secretary of State for Scotland.

. . .

Last Friday the Scottish Conservative conference voted overwhelmingly to oppose the [Devolution] Bill in the referendum. As most of the material written in the press to date has been extolling the benefits of the assembly plan, it might be helpful to explain why Scottish Conservatives, including a considerable number who support the principle of devolution, have come to the conclusion that the assembly proposed by the Government will do Scotland no good at all and could do a great deal of harm.

What is the case for a 'No' vote?

First, there is the question of cost. The proposed assembly will cost the taxpayer a considerable additional burden. The Government's estimate last year was that, apart from the cost of providing the assembly building, the assembly will cost an extra £13m a year, perhaps a small amount by Government standards, but not insignificant at a time when cutbacks in spending have resulted in curbs in essential services like home helps, and school crossing patrol attendants.

Secondly, there is the additional bureaucracy. The official estimate is that an additional 1,000 staff will be required – largely in the Civil Service – and it would be an unusual precedent if this estimate was not exceeded.

The third inevitable consequence of the assembly would be to add to the complexity of Government. With the prospect of Euro-elections in June, 1979, it would mean that each elector would have three legislators instead of one. The average constituency is to have two Scottish assemblymen and some will have three. And this top-heavy legislative structure is to be on top of our local government structure with regional and district councillors, not forgetting the community councillors. There is not only the danger of Scotland becoming the most over-governed country in the world, but of having vital decisions further delayed as each tier has to be consulted.

A fourth danger will be that the role of Scottish MPs in Westminster will become an untenable one. Our MPs from Scotland will have the full right to vote on English home affairs, but not on Scottish ones. It means that our Glasgow MPs will be able to decide on the future of educational policy in Birmingham, Manchester and Wigan but not on the policy to be applied in Perth or Dundee. But it's not just our members of Parliament. The position of the Secretary of State in the Cabinet – where the basic economic decisions are made affecting Scotland – will be immensely weakened and his practical role north of the Border will be reduced to that of a kind of colonial governor-general. And Scotland cannot afford to have its lone voice in the Cabinet weakened in any way.

Next comes the problem of the possibility of clashes between Edinburgh and London. If we are to have governments of separate parties in power in the assembly and in Westminster, there is no doubt that the normal course of politics will drive them into conflict. The problem would be reduced if the demarcation of responsibility was clear, but the Bill provides no such clear divisions. For example, the appointment of the members of the S[cottish] D[evelopment] A[gency] board will be a matter for the assembly, but the economic guidelines they will work to will be determined by Westminster. It's a recipe for conflict – a conflict which could well arise even if there was not the possibility of the Scottish and United Kingdom governments being of a different political complexion.

The sixth objection is that the assembly could damage the economy and job prospects for the simple reason that the constitutional framework would be unstable and would not last. Even those who supported the assembly in Parliament freely admitted that the assembly was not a logical stopping point constitutionally, but would lead to something else – some think federalism, some think separation, and others consider that it will somehow collapse. The setting up of an assembly to pass laws and administer services without the power to raise any taxes and without any economic powers will inevitably create frustration. In short, there is a logical argument for not going so far on devolution and an argument for going a lot further. Constitutional uncertainty is the enemy of industrial confidence – as the people of Quebec are finding out to their cost – and it is little wonder that industry and commerce in Scotland are almost solidly opposed to the plans.

For these and other reasons, the Conservative conference decided to oppose the Bill. And for the same reasons a multitude of MPs who feel obliged to support the assembly in Parliament for political reasons admit privately that they are worried about the consequences.

So, what should be done? Is it not necessary to make some move towards self-government?

Whatever the possibilities, the first step must surely be to reject the expensive and top-heavy albatross which the Government will be inviting the Scots to put round their necks in the referendum. Thereafter, we can plan the constitutional conference proposed by Francis Pym to consider improvements in the structure of Government – improvements which do not involve the threat to the unity of the United Kingdom inherent in the Government's plans.

For a start, it would be well worth while looking seriously at the possibility of establishing a Scottish select committee of MPs to sit in Edinburgh and to scrutinise the activities of the Scottish Office and its agencies. And there is a strong argument for having our standing committees of Scottish MPs doing their work north of the Border.

At the end of the day, the decision on the assembly is one for the Scottish people. But I have a feeling that, like members of Parliament and like my own party, the more they study the proposed assembly and the more they consider its implications, the more likely they are to give the plan a decisive and resounding 'No'.

The Conservative Party and Devolution

Francis Pym and Leon Brittan

From a pamphlet of this title published in 1978 by the Scottish Conservative and Unionist Party. Pym was Conservative MP for Cambridgeshire, and Brittan was Conservative MP for Cleveland and Whitby; both were official party spokesmen on devolution.

For over 18 months the Conservative Party has been calling for an all-party Conference to discuss devolution. During that time it has become quite clear that neither the Scotland Act nor any other individual scheme commands the degree of widespread acceptance that is desirable for such a major constitutional change.

. . .

The *precise* character of the Conservative submission to that conference would depend on the circumstances at the time. However, this paper indicates the form that submission would take and the proposals it would outline. We believe that unlike the Scotland Act all the options considered here *are* viable.

. . .

In casting their vote in the referendum, the people of Scotland should be aware that the Scotland Act is not the only possible form of devolution and that there are a number of serious implications for the rest of the UK in implementing that Act. Other viable schemes are available, and if the Scotland Act is rejected the Conservative Party will ensure that these are considered and that the changes made as a result will actually overcome existing defects in the government of Scotland without creating a whole new range of problems for its relationship with the rest of the UK.

– The Context of Devolution –

The call for devolution springs from many causes, only one of which is the dissatisfaction with the manner in which Scotland is governed today. The system that has gradually evolved over many years often does not seem to meet contemporary needs or to accord with what many people in Scotland want. Many of the problems have resulted from the increasing complexity of government and its extension into so many areas of people's lives. . . . In Scotland, this process has been accompanied by a growing awareness that Scotland's problems sometimes require different solutions from those elsewhere and an increasing desire to protect and emphasise Scotland's distinctive legal system, institutions and traditions. . . . In addition, the vast increase in the business of government and its associated agencies has placed a heavy burden on Parliament.

. . .

If any country is to preserve its unity, there are certain principles that should underlie both the distribution of authority and power within it and the relationship of its citizens to its institutions of government. In their application to the UK these principles are:

1. Each part of the State must belong to the Union on similar and compatible, though not necessarily identical, terms, so that all citizens are members of the state on the same basis, bearing the same relationship to those in power and authority at each level of government.
2. The lines of responsibility must be absolutely clear so that the citizen is certain where power, authority and responsibility for any decisions lie and from whom he should seek redress for any grievance.
3. All citizens should share the same basic civil rights in their relationship to the members of, and officials of, Parliament, government and the State.

. . .

– Option One: Reformed House of Commons – Procedures for Scotland

While a separate executive responsible to a separate legislature in Scotland could meet the desire to adopt specifically Scottish solutions to certain problems without any fear of creating unwelcome precedents for the rest of the UK, the establishment of such bodies is not a *necessary* pre-requisite for that. Given the right attitude on the part of the Government and the rest of the UK, and an understanding and recognition of Scotland's needs, it would be possible to extend existing distinctively Scottish policies to more spheres of policy, including the industrial sphere.

. . .

[I]t would be quite possible to establish a Select Committee on Scottish Affairs to cover the work of the Scottish Office. Such a committee could have a number of important powers. It could investigate the policies, expenditure priorities, programmes and activities of all the departments under the Secretary of State for Scotland with the power to propose new methods or better means of achieving agreed objectives. It would be able to call to account the work of the nationalised industries and public bodies which at present seem to be beyond investigation, and often give the impression of being unconcerned about those whom they exist to serve. In performing this task a Scottish Select Committee would be able to call before it Ministers, independent experts and the heads of public bodies, and could be assisted by its own independent staff.

. . .

[I]t might be appropriate for the select committee to act as a pre-legislative committee; it could investigate proposed Bills and scrutinise subordinate legislation. That would ensure that Scottish MPs had considerable influence before final decisions were made. Given the fact that the administrative and public bodies are in Scotland, the Select Committee should be able to meet in Scotland.

In addition, a reform of the Scottish Grand Committee could provide more time for the more general debates and questioning of ministers. Instead of meeting for debates on only about eight occasions a year, it could meet on a regular basis throughout the year, both to hold its own question time and to debate issues of concern to Scotland. It would be possible to draft in Ministers from other UK departments to answer such debates.

The advantage of such a proposal is that there would be a greater opportunity for a discussion on Scottish affairs as well as the possibility of a more detailed examination of important policies. At the same time, there would be no derogation of Parliament's responsibility for Scotland and no breach of the principles outlined above.

. . .

However, there would be even greater pressure than today on the time of Scottish MPs. They would also be expected not only to participate in wider UK debates and committees but also to play a full part in these Scottish procedures. It may also be felt that a specifically Scottish institution is necessary to preserve Scotland's distinctive institutions and traditions and that even a new structure of Scottish Committees in the UK Parliament would not be sufficiently independent to achieve this.

. . .

– OPTION TWO: AN INQUISITORIAL ASSEMBLY –

It is not a *necessary* pre-condition for the establishment of an independent voice for Scotland that it should have its own legislative and executive powers. It would be quite possible for there to be a Scottish Assembly carrying out the important inquisitorial function and role outlined above for the suggested Select and Grand Committees. Such an Assembly would be peculiarly appropriate for those matters in which there is a distinctive Scottish dimension.

. . .

The powers of such an Assembly would be very similar to those of the Select Committee and Grand Committee in Option one. It could:

1. Press Scottish opinions, views and needs on the UK government when taking decisions affecting Scotland.
2. Give powerful backing to the Scottish Secretary of State when he puts Scotland's case to the Cabinet or EEC.
3. Call to account the powerful Scottish Executive which Scotland already has.
4. Investigate and monitor the administrative decisions of the Scottish Civil Service in areas like education, housing, rates, local government, regional aid, planning and health.
5. Question the policies and decisions of public bodies and agencies like the Scottish Development Agency, the Highlands and Islands Development Board, the Scottish Tourist Board, the Forestry Commission, the Arts Council and Sports Council, most of which go unconsidered, and also of the health service and nationalised industries including electricity, gas and railways.
6. Form expert committees to examine, with the assistance of independent advisers, specific Scottish issues like regional aid, training of the unemployed, and attraction of new industries: and to suggest new policies or improvements to existing ones.

7. Debate expenditure priorities in Scotland and advise the Secretary of State on the allocation of Scotland's budget.

It might also be possible for the Assembly to be involved in Scottish legislation. The most convenient method would probably be for it to comment on proposals at the pre-Bill stage, though it might be possible also to devise a system whereby the Assembly could communicate proposed amendments which the appropriate Committee in Parliament would discuss.

It is true that such an Assembly would rely on exercising influence, through informed scrutiny, rather than power. However, the influence of informed scrutiny should not be underestimated. Governments do not like to be criticised, especially when the criticism is informed and realistic. Select Committees in Parliament have often been very influential in rooting out maladministration and in redirecting policies.

Indeed, the importance of Parliament as a 'talking shop' should never be underestimated. Constant criticism and scrutiny is our best guarantee of freedom. It is also the best guarantee both that executive decisions are justifiable and in the spirit of the strategy and policies Parliament has approved, and that legislation will be workable. Decisions that might otherwise go unnoticed or unchallenged have to be defensible and defended. It is in Parliament that vigilance is maintained in guarding against an abuse of power or disregard for the rights of an individual or a particular group.

. . .

However, it must be accepted that, in spite of all this, some people, will believe that [Option two] suffers from the disadvantage that decisions in those matters uniquely Scottish will still not actually be taken by an independent body in Scotland. They will claim that it is not sufficient that Scotland should have only an improved voice in the United Kingdom on these matters, and that it is necessary to ensure that there is executive and legislative power in Scotland in these areas. Only then will decisions be taken for Scotland, without fear that they will create precedents for other areas and without having to await the approval of the other partners, and the chain of command be shortened. Nevertheless, in the context of preserving the unity of the UK, and in the British tradition of developing our Parliamentary democracy by evolutionary means, there is a very strong case indeed for establishing an Assembly of this type in the first instance.

– Option Three: A Scottish Assembly with – Executive and Legislative Powers

. . .

An Assembly solely for Scotland could not be granted such a wide range of powers (e.g. over regional aid) as in a system of assemblies covering the whole UK because certain powers should either be devolved throughout the UK or not at all. In addition, the financial arrangement would be more complicated.

However, even for Scotland alone such an Assembly should be based on the clear division of powers, the clear lines of responsibility, the satisfactory procedures for resolving disputes in a judicial framework, and the contiguous exercise of legislative and executive power found in most federal systems.

. . .

The consequence of adopting an Assembly with legislative and executive powers for Scotland alone would be to bring to the fore the issue of the role of Scots MPs who would then be able to vote on matters for England, Wales and Northern Ireland, on which they could not vote for Scotland. . . . Even if there were an explicit acceptance of the anomaly in the short term, . . . it would be unlikely to survive a Parliament in which the voting patterns of Scottish MPs continuously determined the outcome of non-Scottish legislation. The only logical way in which to overcome the anomaly is to deprive Scots MPs of the right to vote on non-Scottish matters. It is unlikely that would commend itself for long. It would prove fatal to the concept of ministerial and cabinet responsibility because no minister could be expected reasonably to accept responsibility for a measure over which he has no control. Effectively, the Government would lose control over a wide range of non-Scottish affairs.

In those circumstances, the conclusion must be that if an Assembly of this kind were established in Scotland alone, sooner or later the system would break down. It is impossible to predict how the partners of the UK would handle that breakdown, but it is at least possible that it would evolve into a quasi-federal system under the weight of its own logic, whether or not that was actively wanted. That would at least bring compliance with the principles that must underlie any stable constitutional system.

. . .

– OPTION FOUR: A QUASI-FEDERAL SYSTEM –

. . .

In practice, this would mean that there could be four assemblies, each with the same powers, for Scotland, Northern Ireland, England and Wales. To demonstrate that sovereignty lay with the UK Parliament, it would retain authority to legislate on any matter for the whole United Kingdom, though a convention might grow out of this that, normally, it could only act at the request, or with the consent, of the subordinate assembly.

As with concurrent powers in Australia, Canada and Northern Ireland, where there was any conflict in the laws, those of the UK Parliament would have precedence and automatically invalidate those of the assembly to the extent of the inconsistency between the two. In effect, all devolved powers would be exercised concurrently, with the UK Parliament alone having any assigned to it exclusively.

Inherent in this simple procedure is the federal practice of a clear guide to which body is supreme and which laws have precedence in the event of a difference of opinion or in areas of overlapping responsibility. Moreover, with assemblies in every part of the United Kingdom, when the UK Parliament decided to act in a devolved area such action would be less open to the accusation that it was an attempt to overrule one part of the Union, as could be the case with a Scottish Assembly on its own.

This procedure would also supply the UK Parliament with a power of disallowance over Assembly Acts. Rather than a simple veto as proposed in the Scotland Act, it would have to pass legislation to repeal the Assembly Act in question. This would rarely, if ever, be used but the procedures involved would be a sounder safeguard, and less likely to lead to intense conflict, than a veto after a short debate. There would be no procedure to over-ride the assemblies in intra vires executive acts except the passage of legislation. If ever used, this power in the Scotland Act will lead to deep conflict; if never used it will in time become redundant.

. . .

– OTHER CHANGES –

The establishment of new institutions would need to be the occasion for a reconsideration of the procedures appropriate for the powers to be devolved if these bodies were actually to improve the operation of government rather than merely add to it.

– Specialist committees –

There might need to be specialist committees, representative of the parties in the assemblies, in each of the subject areas devolved, along the lines of pre-legislative or select committees. These would scrutinise the administration of policies in their field, call to account public bodies, and examine possible legislation. They would involve all the parties in administration and help to overcome the defects of a possible permanent minority always being out of power.

– Bill of Rights –

Rights are fundamental to individual liberty. Today more than ever citizens need protection from government and its agencies, especially in the sort of spheres that would be devolved. So it might be worthwhile to accompany the establishment of assemblies with the introduction of a Bill of Rights to set the framework for government action. Many people believe this is now a desirable advance in any case. While such a Bill would be difficult to entrench for the UK, Parliament could bind subordinate assemblies, as the official Conservative amendment to entrench a Bill of Rights in the Scotland Bill intended to attempt.

– House of Lords –

It might be right to try to incorporate such a quasi-federal scheme into a wider UK framework. At least some of the members of the House of Lords could be chosen to represent the regions. A House of Lords at least partially constituted in this way could act as a revising chamber for legislation from the assemblies. It could make suggestions based on experience in other parts of the UK; ensure all parts of the UK retained an interest in all other parts; and give the UK Government an opportunity to comment formally on such legislation, if it so wished.

. . .

– Assessment –

In as much as [a quasi-federal system] would not create an imbalance in the UK Parliament, it would be logically and constitutionally more acceptable than an assembly with executive and legislative powers for Scotland alone. However, the other partners in the UK would need to be convinced that they, too, would benefit. They could hardly be expected to undertake such a major change for the advantage of only one part of the country. Nobody pretends that a desire for such a change exists at present.

. . .

It is conceivable that if the people of England, Wales and Northern Ireland were to discuss the possible introduction of such a system, in time they might come to the conclusion that it would be a change worth making. They might think that the advantages of a more direct access to government, a Bill of Rights, and being able to make their own decisions (for example, in the case of England, free from the constraints of needing to take into account the Scots and Welsh) would outweigh the disadvantages of possible over-government. Alternatively, they might decide that the adoption of such a system would be preferable to the imbalance created if Scotland alone were to have an assembly with executive and legislative powers. However, that necessary process of discussion and thought has hardly even begun.

. . .

Nevertheless, it is right that it should at least be thought about at this stage with a number of possible conclusions in mind. For example, it could be noted as a possibility in the longer term but agreed that only the first step should be taken immediately. That is to say, if the people of Scotland clearly wanted it and if the other partners in the UK were prepared to accept the consequent anomalies, Scotland could be granted an assembly with executive and legislative powers based on a structure compatible with the evolution of a system for the whole UK.

Alternatively, it could be noted as acceptable in principle and possibly even desirable in the long term; but in view of the anomalies that would be created by Scotland launching out on her own, Scotland could be asked to accept Option 1 or 2 in the immediate future, on the understanding that there would be reconsideration in the light of experience and further public debate.

. . .

If the other partners were prepared to accept the anomalies, the first of the assemblies within such a system could be established for Scotland, leaving the other partners to determine their own pace of change or, indeed, to determine upon no change at all and an acceptance of the anomalies permanently.

. . .

Alec Douglas Home

Douglas Home gave the speech from which this extract is taken on 13 February 1979 at Edinburgh University. No written record of the full speech is available (although the general arguments can be gleaned from newspapers, as summarised in the Introduction to this Part). The text here was transcribed from the BBC, which filmed part of the speech. The interview which follows was with James Cox on the BBC Scotland programme 'Current Account' almost one year after the speech (12 February 1980).

– SPEECH –

I had thought of voting for this Bill because as a Scotsman – and I thought this was true of others too – I thought there would be disappointment if practical devolution was deferred. I do not believe that that is now the public mood, and I think that more and more people – even though this means more time – are concerned to get the matter right before we proceed to the final act of devolution.

. . .

Now, I confess that it is unfortunate that the only way to be certain that these flaws can be revised is to vote No, but that is how the question has been put by the government. But a No vote does not and need not imply any disloyalty to the principle of devolution.

– INTERVIEW –

Cox: Lord Home, . . . you entered the devolution debate by arguing that people should vote No because the form of Assembly proposed was the wrong one, and that a No vote might achieve a stronger, more effective Assembly with taxation powers among other things. Do you still stand by that now?

Home: Yes, that was, I think, right. What I hadn't reckoned with quite was the fact that the Scottish Nationalist Party, of course, had irrevocably linked devolution to independence from England; . . . that, in effect, has killed any further devolution as far as I can see ahead, in the form of an Assembly.

Cox: Do you remain, yourself, in favour of some form of devolution?

Home: Yes, I'm a decentraliser, and the more you decentralise, to my mind, the better. And so I would like a form of devolution, but I'm also a practical politician after all these years in the game, and I'm quite certain that you won't, either at this next election in four years time or the one after, get any agreement in Parliament on a devolved Assembly. Therefore you will have to go for something like . . . a Select Committee of Parliament looking at Scottish affairs and going up to Edinburgh, or . . . a reorganisation of the Westminster timetable [to allow] Scottish members to sit in Scotland, let us say on Mondays.

Cox: But didn't the Conservative Party, before the referendum, say that, while it was opposed to the present form of devolution that was on offer, it was in favour of devolution of some sort? Is your party not now reneging on its promises if it's not going to try to find any form of constitutional change?

Home: Well, I think that the form that will be found, probably, is either one of the two that I've been talking about . . . . That is a form of devolved activity, but I don't think you're going to get a Bill. . . .

Cox: Do you still think that you were wise, in retrospect, to say what you did, to say vote No for a stronger Assembly, if, as a consequence of what you call practical politics, it looks as if there's going to be no Assembly at all?

Home: Well, you have to say what you think makes sense at the time. I did think that there would be a chance of getting an Assembly, possibly on the lines of what we'd proposed in 1968 [Edward Heath and the Scottish Constitutional Committee]. To that, I would add . . . that the election would have to be on proportional representation. But circumstances change, and the circumstance was changed by this factor . . . of the link to independence, which really did scare people. They don't want separation from England. The merit of our proposal of 1968 was that it . . . kept the Scottish Executive part of the Scottish Assembly. In other words, the Secretary of State and all his ministers were part of that, so that our proposal was an extension of Westminster government, rather than a separation from Westminster government.

THE DEFEAT OF DEVOLUTION

Vernon Bogdanor

From *The Spectator* (10 March 1979, pp. 13–14). Bogdanor was a senior tutor at Brasenose College, Oxford (and is now a professor there), and has written extensively on devolution (for example, Bogdanor 1979, 1994).

The voters in Scotland and Wales have given Mr Callaghan's tottering administration the most stinging rebuff suffered by any British government in living memory. In Wales, only 11.9 per cent could be found to endorse devolution; in Scotland, the result was a majority for devolution so small as to make it impossible to proceed with the Scotland Act. How many other of this government's policies, one wonders, would have been similarly treated by an irate electorate if only it had been given the chance? For the referendum is coming to establish itself, as it has in Switzerland and Australia, as a powerful force for conservatism and stability.

Yet the result of the referendums could by no means have been foreseen when the Wilson administration embarked on what has been called 'the devolution caper'. In Scotland, opinion polls over the past ten years have consistently shown large majorities in favour of devolution; and in Wales the overwhelming rejection of devolution must be contrasted with the 60 per cent of Welsh voters favouring a Welsh Parliament in a poll conducted for the *Western Mail* in November 1967. Indeed, many who were later to become bulwarks of Unionism were swept along with the tide. Mr Teddy Taylor offered as one of his 'pledges to the people' in October 1974, 'a Scottish Assembly to ensure that decision-making is removed from London', and Mr Neil Kinnock proposed an elected Welsh Council to the voters of Bedwellty. As recently as January of this year, the 'Yes' supporters in Scotland enjoyed a 20 per cent lead over the 'Noes' and seemed confident of success.

But it would be difficult to deny that the 'Noes' had by far the better argument, both in Parliament and in the campaign itself. For the Scotland and Wales Acts were born, not out of a principled belief in the dispersal of power from Whitehall, but from expediency. Few in the Labour Party, with the honourable exception of the late John Mackintosh, cared for devolution for its own sake. Indeed, one adviser to the government assured me that only one and a half members of the Wilson Cabinet had been in favour of devolution, the one being Mr William Ross, a late enthusiastic convert, the half being Sir Harold himself.

Nor did Labour ever seek to secure the wider degree of political support necessary for a constitutional scheme of such magnitude. The overtures of Conservative devolutionists such as Mr Heath were rejected with contempt, and the Liberals were ignored until the exigencies of the parliamentary situation made their support essential. The proposals bore all the marks of the adversary conception of politics held by their presenter, Mr Michael Foot.

The scheme itself was an impossible one to defend, and indeed few attempted to defend it. For who could defend, as a matter of principle, the continued over-representation of Scotland in the Commons, the continued retention of the Secretary of State for Scotland in the Cabinet or the supreme folly of establishing a legislature with the power to spend, but not to raise taxes? The Nationalists, therefore, defended the scheme only as a step to separation, the Liberals as a step to federalism, and Labour as an essential pre-requisite for the continued existence of the government.

Nor did the timing of the referendums help the proponents of devolution: for at the fag-end of a dying Parliament the issue was bound to become entwined with the survival of a government already discredited by its inept handling of industrial disputes. Indeed it would be only a slight exaggeration to claim that anything advocated so strongly by both the Cabinet and the TUC already bore the mark of death upon it; and grass-roots enthusiasm amongst Labour voters, especially in Wales, was conspicuous only by its absence.

Yet one must look further than the deficiencies of the actual legislation to explain the defeat of devolution. For the Scotland and Wales Acts found themselves in conflict with a powerful public mood of disenchantment with institutional reform. After the reorganisation of local government, of the health service, and of the water industry, voters felt a deep yearning for stability, for the retention of familiar landmarks and an end to administrative scene-shifting. When Mr Foot told Welsh voters that devolution offered them an opportunity to do away with the 'cursed' structure of local government inherited from the Tories, he unwittingly provided the 'No' campaign with one of its strongest arguments. There can be no doubt that Mrs Thatcher identified herself with this deep-rooted desire for stability, and that she read the feelings of the electorate correctly.

The Labour Party, on the other hand, entered the campaign unhappy and divided. The Scottish wing of the Party was still smarting from the humiliation of having, at the command of Transport House, called a special conference in [August] 1974 to reverse the decision of its executive opposing devolution, a conference at which, according to one commentator, 'the devolutionists got their way by arm twisting'. Labour was unwilling to work in harness with the SNP and an earlier campaign 'Devolution not Separation' fizzled out since Labour's commitment appeared, in [MP] Willie Hamilton's words, as 'an act of blatant political appeasement'.

The SNP, of course, lives to fight another day. Admittedly, its support in Scotland lies at only 18 per cent and is still slipping. It would, nevertheless, be unrealistic to expect that it will fall back to its pre-1966 position as fringe party. The SNP has been discounted before when temporary troughs have been misinterpreted as indications of its rapid demise: it is likely to remain a permanent element on the political scene and Westminster will have to learn to accommodate itself to the prospect. Indeed, the SNP must be secretly delighted with the result of the referendum which enables it, when the next wave of support arrives, to claim that it was robbed of an Assembly solely because of Westminster's refusal to recognise the wishes of a majority of voters in Scotland.

For it would be a mistake to believe that Scottish devolution has been permanently killed by the result of the referendum. Both Mrs Thatcher and Lord Home assured the Scots that they could vote 'No' while retaining the option of devolution, and many Conservative devolutionists must have voted to reject the Scotland Act with this qualification in mind. Mrs Thatcher has herself been quoted as saying that 'she expected an Assembly to be established eventually, but that there might have to be a quasi-federal solution to achieve this' (*The Scotsman*, 17 May 1977, p. 9). It would be natural for her to establish a Commission, chaired by a figure of public weight and authority, to consider, not just devolution, but the broader issues of constitutional reform. For we need to escape from the piecemeal uncoordinated proposals which have dogged discussion of constitutional matters for so long.

The results of the referendums will have been misinterpreted if taken to indicate satisfaction with the structure and workings of British government. We remain the most centralised and top-heavy democracy in the Western world, and badly need to reinvigorate political institutions designed for a different age. The danger of the verdicts given last week is that they will freeze into immobility a structure of administration too congested and unwieldy to provide effective government.

Interview: Portrait of a Devolutionist

John Smith

From the *Bulletin of Scottish Politics*, a journal which only ever published two issues, in 1980 and 1981. This interview comes from issue 2, Spring 1981, pp. 44–54. Smith was Labour MP for Lanark North, and had been in charge of overseeing the passage through the House of Commons of the government's devolution legislation. The interview was conducted by Neal Ascherson and Tom Nairn, from the journal's editorial board.

How do you see the present position of the Labour Party in Scotland on devolution – after the decisions of the recent Annual Conference in Perth, for example?

The Party's position remains broadly the same, I believe, in the sense of firm commitment to devolution. However, it is also true that the more it debates the issue, the firmer the commitment appears to become. This does not mean it will ever become unanimous: I resigned myself to that a long time ago. One is unlikely to get unanimity in favour of this or any other proposal for major constitutional change.

It is also striking how the younger generation in the Party is much more attached to the devolution concept than its elders. This was probably always true; but it has grown more pronounced. Nor is the tendency linked especially to the left, among the younger members. It seems to cross the board politically. As you know the older Labour left was the source of much opposition. But there has been opposition on the right too. Now both left and right among the younger generation (with some exceptions) support devolution.

In that case, how do you see the process next time round? For example, what kind of test of Scottish public opinion would be needed, to avoid another disaster like 1979?

As regards public opinion, I must say first of all I very much hope there will be a rallying of pro-devolution opinion in Scotland. Our public opinion tends to be both ambiguous and volatile on the subject. It sways back and forth, as we have seen to our cost. At the moment polls indicate more enthusiasm than two years ago – doubtless reflecting the sense that this is a very English-dominated government, and one with a degree of animus towards Scotland. There is (I may add) a good deal of evidence to support this judgement. But we know now it is unwise to count on such moods alone. This is why I believe we ought to place much more emphasis on campaigns directed at rallying, at forming and steadying the climate of public opinion.

Then secondly, as regards a new test of that opinion, I think another referendum is inevitable. Without one, there is no hope of getting any significant constitutional change through parliament in a reasonable time scale. Also, given that we had to concede it once – albeit for tactical reasons – it would be difficult or impossible to refuse it on another occasion. I would add that this principle seems to apply in the case of the Common Market too. We have now definitely made referenda part of the constitutional equipment, and have to stick by that.

But the timing of the test should be different next time. I would urge the government to 'front-end' the referendum: let me explain what that would mean. Any new Labour government would of course confront the question of priorities in its legislative programme; and we would have to argue priority for a new Scottish Assembly bill. Now, it will be very hard to counter the objection that another government might find itself spending a disproportionate amount of time and energy on such a bill, only to get it rejected once more. So by far the best way would be to prepare a White Paper with a sufficient outline of that scheme – not necessarily all the detail – and hold the referendum on *that*. This would be an advisory referendum, which would give the government solid grounds for pressing ahead.

. . .

Do you now think there were defects in the last Scotland Act? How could a measure be improved, when you start to re-design the legislation?

As far as the main subject areas of devolution are concerned, I feel we have little to reproach ourselves with. We took the existing structure of the Scottish Office, and built on that, and I still think this was correct. It is essential to establish a continuum between pre- and post-devolution, making use of these structures. The fifteen Departments administered in Scotland should remain the starting point of the exercise.

And the main point of the exercise remains, in my view. The fact is the Scottish Office as it exists is a failure, and a lamentable failure. It has always been a kind of 'Mission Impossible', because you simply cannot have one Minister for these fifteen Departments of government. We *must* get elected politicians to control the apparatus. This is a principle of government, which I know from experience must constantly be asserted by Ministers, if they are to be effective at all.

But in the Scottish Office this is not possible. One is down at Westminster from Monday to Thursday; the civil servants in Edinburgh have some diversion ready and waiting for you on the Friday; and the result is you have no real access to or grip upon the senior administration. To have one's legislative body four hundred miles away is the perfect recipe for mandarin government – a description that fits the Scottish Office only too well.

What happens is this: if you take, say, some education issue, then the Secretary of State for Education is at the relevant Cabinet Sub-committee, looking after English interests quite naturally. Whereas Scottish interests are represented only by a Parliamentary Under-Secretary of State, someone much lower down in the political pecking-order, with correspondingly less weight. Unless, that is, the Scottish Secretary himself takes charge of the issue, by coming to the relevant Sub-committee, or by raising it in Cabinet. But he cannot do this all the time – not in education, and in agriculture, and tourism, and employment, and all the other areas. One man is being made to tackle an impossible job, so what really happens is low political input all round, from a Scottish point of view. One would be lucky to get one day's debate on Scottish education in the whole parliamentary year. Unless it is kicked upstairs to the Scottish Grand Committee, that is; but then it becomes a kind of remote, eccentric affair in the eyes of Westminster.

What about the objections made to the last Bill, like the absence of tax-raising powers, and economic powers? Won't any new Bill have to be improved in those respects?

At Perth, the debate centred on the proposal to give taxation powers to a new Assembly. The new document approved there makes it clear there is certainly a will to tackle the problem. However, these new ideas do not appear to me to have solved the essential problem. I still feel the importance of the matter has been exaggerated. People have repeated too often that an Assembly without such powers would be no use. This is an extreme position, frankly – as extreme as the opposite view, that any tax powers would fatally undermine the economic unity of the UK.

Last time, as the battle proceeded I came to feel more and more that all that mattered was to get an Assembly of some kind going. This is far more important than establishing a precise definition of its powers in advance.

. . .

There remain great difficulties in the way of getting economic powers, the same as we experienced last time. Mr Callaghan's government was very reluctant to concede much on that front, they were too worried about offending opinion elsewhere in the UK. This was the dilemma. Could we make the package more popular in Scotland . . . by including important economic powers, without thereby sabotaging the entire project in the eyes of the parliamentary majority which had to vote it through? Of course things were complicated by the fact that we did not have the majority in the House of Commons anyway. But even if we had the problem would not go away.

. . .

This leads us to ask your view of the 1970s, in retrospect. Why did it all happen? Would anything like that – and your own involvement in devolution – have taken place without the SNP break-through?

Well, there had always been a Home Rule strand in Labour Party thinking in Scotland, and people have recently taken to re-emphasising this. However after the Second World War this got pretty thoroughly overlaid by the new concern with central economic planing, nationalisation and so on. During that period the dilemma between a more or less 'cranky' Scottish nationalism on one hand, and 'Socialist Internationalism' on the other, became fixed for many people in the movement.

Then, for a period, the SNP managed to get themselves at the head of the moving forces in Scottish politics. The arrival of North Sea oil on the scene certainly contributed to that; yet – like many others – I am still puzzled in retrospect about just why the SNP captured the mood so completely. And equally puzzled about why it disappeared so quickly. At the Hamilton by-election in 1978 [which Labour won] I was acutely aware of this. One could almost see it evaporating day by day.

For a time the SNP crossed political class barriers to some extent, winning both middle-class support in the North East and working class support in the West. There then followed an extremely bitter battle on the ground between Labour and the Nationalists for local support across the industrial belt. This was so bitter that even today relations remain bad, and there was no hope of getting cooperation between the parties at the time of the referendum. Labour won the battle, by and large. We got them back. Yet I am still not sure just why we did win – why the whole phenomenon rose and fell in the way it did.

There was a connection with economic conditions, of course. As the clouds gathered in the later 1970s, optimism disappeared, particularly in Scotland. I believe that to bring about serious constitutional change one needs to be on a rising current: one needs to be buoyed up, and to be capable of some self-confidence. This is just what evaporated from Scotland, and what there is so little sign of just now. Psychologically at least, the contrast with the early 1970s is clear.

You mentioned earlier 'the ambiguity and volatility' of the Scottish electorate on devolution. How do you now view the referendum experience and its upshot?

As I look back, this is the thing which worries me most about the whole exercise. How, why, did we lose public opinion so completely in the last two or three months before the referendum? I have often wondered about this. As I said just now, no all-party campaign was possible, like the one conducted by the pro-Europeans in 1975; this was one factor. David Steel did approach me in the closing stages to suggest something of that kind, but it was too late. Apart from that – incidentally – the Liberals were more or less sitting out the process, whatever they say now. They were not at all active or pushing. Steel himself had begun to run into resistance on the ground, in the Borders, and was affected by this (and we saw how the Border vote went, subsequently).

But there was more to it than these party difficulties. The fact is that middle-class opinion moved very, very sharply against us. This was the most visible thing to me. I am afraid there is something about the Scottish professional middle-class – something which makes them take to their heels and run, when a real test arrives. They deserted in droves, after having been – equally characteristically – only too happy to toy with the notion of self-government, after being agreeably intrigued with it for some time. It was not Douglas Home's famous speech which changed their minds: that was nothing but a peg to hang their hats on. When it came to standing up and taking some risk – for that is how many of them saw what was happening – it was all suddenly different.

. . .

Then, of course there were the rural fears about being ruled by these dreadful people in Strathclyde, there was the forty per cent rubbish and there were the confusions about local government, and too many people saw it as another chapter of the same process. There is enough confusion about the two-tier system of Regions and Districts, without adding to it.

Our opponents found it easy to exploit such fears. I now think that a new attempt at devolution ought to be associated with some reform of that system. The Assembly could perhaps relieve the Regions of some of their responsibilities. The police force, for example, could be run on a national Scottish basis, not a Regional one.

Part III: Reactions to Thatcherism, 1983–92

Introduction

The main political development of the 1980s was the convergence of almost all left-of-centre political currents behind the idea of Scottish self-government. Although some of this was acquiescence rather than enthusiasm, it was nevertheless a remarkable agreement considering the divisions which had existed a decade earlier. The key reason was Margaret Thatcher. The perception of her regime as alien and destined to last for ever is summed up in the short extract here from a 1983 interview with Robin Cook, an opponent of devolution in the referendum but, by then, a supporter. Of course, these were reasons of their time: as it turned out fourteen years later, Britain was not as permanently polarised politically as it had seemed (an observation which Cook himself made when giving his agreement for this extract to be reproduced). But the important point is how things looked at the time, as David McCrone analyses in his 1989 article here.

An initially defensive reaction then began to contribute positively to constructing an agreed scheme for a Scottish parliament. The Campaign for a Scottish Assembly – which had been founded in the aftermath of the 1979 referendum – proposed a Constitutional Convention: its views are summarised in the article here by Alan Lawson, who was a leading activist in the CSA. From 1985, Lawson was also editor of the magazine *Radical Scotland*, which was becoming highly influential in this debate, and a unifying forum for the Scottish left. Indeed, concentrating on the constitutional question helped to ensure that the left in Scotland would not be as deeply fragmented as the left in England, which was suffering the debilitating split between Labour and the Social Democrats.

The main political impetus towards a Convention came after the 1987 general election, which Thatcher won but in which the Conservatives' Scottish representation fell from 21 seats to 10 (and just 24 per cent of the vote). The CSA set up a committee which produced the *Claim of Right* in 1988, key passages of which are reproduced here; part of its argument was that there should be a Convention (Edwards, 1989). The document was drafted by Jim Ross, a retired civil servant, who had been closely involved in the 1970s in the Scottish Office's work on the devolution proposals. Writing in May 1997 (and thus before the referendum of that year), he has summed up the significance of the *Claim*: 'without it, the Constitutional Convention might not have come into being, and insofar as our new [Labour]

Government [of 1997] is committed to anything specific on devolution, those commitments have arisen largely out of the dealings of the Convention' (personal communication to the editor). A similar conclusion is reached here by James Kellas, writing somewhat earlier (1992) but foreseeing what would happen if a Labour government was elected.

The *Claim* immediately had an effect on the debate. Donald Dewar – who was then shadow Secretary of State for Scotland – welcomed it, and essentially committed Labour to joining a Convention. Extracts from the speech in which he did this are included here; he gave it well before the SNP won a parliamentary by-election in Govan, and so the accusation that Dewar was reacting to Labour's defeat there is simply untenable (but the SNP victory probably did help to concentrate Labour minds). Gradualists in the SNP would have liked their party to join the Convention too, as MacCormick argues here, but they failed as the SNP adopted an increasingly intransigent attitude towards Labour (which was reciprocated). This attitude to Labour is found in, for example, the piece here by Jim Sillars, who was the new MP for Govan. MacCormick's paper was not just a reaction to events, however: it is also a detailed and lucid statement of the case for gradualism, for allowing a Scottish parliament to evolve towards independence.

The Convention first met in March 1989, and it included most Labour and Liberal Democrat MPs, all the Labour members of the European parliament, representatives of most local authorities – whose experience of the Thatcher government had led them to support a Scottish parliament as a way of protecting their own autonomy (see McKenna in Part IV) – and representatives of various civil society bodies such as the STUC, women's organisations, the churches, the Federation of Small Businesses, and groupings of ethnic minorities. At this meeting, the participants signed a statement that sovereignty lay with the people of Scotland:

> We, gathered as the Scottish Constitutional Convention, do hereby acknowledge the sovereign right of the Scottish people to determine the form of government best suited to their needs, and do hereby declare and pledge that in all our actions and deliberations their interests shall be paramount.
> We further declare and pledge that our actions and deliberations shall be directed to the following ends. To agree a scheme for an Assembly or Parliament for Scotland; to mobilise Scottish opinion and ensure the approval of the Scottish people for that scheme; and to assert the right of the Scottish people to secure the implementation of that scheme.

The inclusion of the word 'parliament' here illustrates the return to that word even among home rulers after the 1970s preference for 'assembly' as a way of distinguishing home rule from independence. By the early 1990s, 'parliament' had become normal among supporters of both home rule and independence, while 'assembly' tended to be used by sceptics (as items later in this book illustrate).

The notion of a 'claim of right' had some theological origins, and, in fact, the churches had been active in redefining the relationship between the individual and the state. The presbyterian and the Catholic positions on this are summarised here by two statements in 1989. (See also Forrester, 1993; Mitchell, 1992; Shanks, 1996; and Storrar, 1990.) As well as the notion of a covenant (or its Catholic analogues), the other key theological idea which entered the debate was on the limited character of sovereignty. This, in turn, linked the debate to secular aspirations towards a type of politics that would be inclusive of all sections of the community (something which was anticipated by Isobel Lindsay in the text which was included in Part II). The most influential source of this thinking was from the women's movement, illustrated here by a paper from the women's committee of the STUC and by a summary (by Alice Brown and Yvonne Strachan) of a discussion in 1991 among representatives of diverse women's organisations. The same aim of inclusiveness pushed the Convention towards accepting that elections to a parliament should be by a proportional system, encouraged by the Liberal Democrats and the STUC, but acceptable to Labour as a way of keeping the broad coalition together.

The presence of feminism in this phase of the debate about a Scottish parliament was unprecedented. In the 1970s, people discussing Scottish self-government paid little attention to specifically feminist issues (although there were exceptions, such as Stephen Maxwell, 1977b). It was also still possible then for a Scottish cultural magazine to devote an entire issue to the international women's movement without mentioning the specifically Scottish aspects of it, far less the issue of Scottish self-government (*New Edinburgh Review*, 1972). But that changed partly because the policies of Margaret Thatcher were believed to have harmed women particularly (Breitenbach, 1989, 1990; Brown, McCrone and Paterson, 1998, chapter 8), and partly because the consensual character of the Convention process offered a new opportunity to influence public debate.

The other main source of new thinking on Scottish government at this time was the SNP, outside the Convention but forced to pay attention to what was going on. Jim Sillars had argued since 1976 that UK membership of what was then called the European Economic Community necessitated Scottish independence; that policy also conveniently dealt with the accusation that the SNP would isolate Scotland. Sillars's 1989 paper here has probably been his most important contribution to Scottish political debate: its legacy will continue to be felt long after the Scottish parliament is established, because independence in Europe will then be the only politically viable alternative to what will then be the constitutional status quo. Enthusiasm for the European Union (as it now is) can now be found across Scottish politics, as we will see in the next Part, but that was not always so. Up until the late 1970s, it was conventional to assume that a devolved Scotland would not be very pro-European, largely because, in the 1975 referendum, Scotland had voted less clearly in favour of continuing membership of the EEC than had England (see Massie, 1978; Fry and Cooney, 1979). Nevertheless, several commentators had predicted that the EEC would provide a convenient defence against charges of separatism (Maxwell, 1973; Massie, 1978).

The Conservative party refused to join the Convention, a decision later regretted by one of its leading members because it precluded any Conservative influence on the scheme that eventually was endorsed in the 1997 referendum (Brian Meek in *The Herald*, 24 July 1997, p. 17). Conservatives paid little attention to the issue of a Scottish parliament in the early and middle 1980s, and, when they did, they rejected it uncompromisingly (as the pamphlet by Allan Stewart from 1987 shows). In that, they were reflecting the attitude of most business people (see, for example, interview with John Davidson, director of the Scottish Confederation of British Industry, *Scottish Business Insider*, June 1988, pp. 20–2): business largely left Conservative politicians to deal with the issue in public. Insofar as the right had a position on Scottish government, it was the radical opinion that the only true devolution is that which transfers power to individuals in opposition the state (a view which Isobel Lindsay notes in her 1976 paper in Part II). This approach is summarised here in the article by Allan Massie (1984). In this New Right view, the problem with Scotland was too much dependency on government: as Massie put it later (1991), Scotland suffered from 'the mentality that sees salvation as coming only from the public sector' (p. 9), and so 'devolution . . . would probably reinforce the dependency culture' (p. 10). Similar views can be found in a pamphlet by Beat et al. (1991).

In the approach to the 1992 general election, the Conservatives did start to respond to the apparent popularity of the Convention's scheme and to the risk that they might lose seats. In the event, they recovered slightly from the 1987 disaster, and so they were – to their own surprise – actually in a position to do something about the ideas they had put forward. These are dealt with in the next Part.

INTERVIEW: DEVOLUTION

Robin Cook

From *Radical Scotland*, a magazine which was published every two months between summer 1982 and July 1991. The interview was in issue 4, August/September 1983, pp. 9–11. Cook was MP for Livingston.

Radical Scotland: Your position on devolution of power to Scotland has changed recently – what brought this about? What has made you advocate, as you did recently at the 'What now for the Scottish Left?' conference [July 1983] a form of federalism?

Cook: The key ground is that the election does show the change in the pattern of British politics which has created quite a distinctive and different political outcome in Scotland from that in England. It was credible previously to regard British politics as essentially a swing between Conservative and Labour, albeit that was an over-simplification of what was actually happening in the electorate. On that basis there were grounds for maintaining a central decision-making Parliament because only on that basis could you deliver Labour policies on domestic issues to areas of England which were voting Labour. The time has now come when one has got to recognise the reality of the divergence of the political pattern of the south of England from Scotland and therefore I think that should be recognised by some different form of constitutional settlement which allows the Scots to take their own decisions concerning domestic issues which can be settled by a state within a federal system. It remains my own view, my overwhelming view, that there is no way in which you can establish separate decision-making in Scotland over the major economic and industrial issues. The extent of economic and industrial integration with the rest of Britain has advanced to such a degree that it is impossible that meaningful decisions can be taken in a purely Scottish context on these issues.

. . .

However, I think that it would be a mistake if we were to think that the mass of the Scottish electorate are going to be mobilised into a popular campaign on the constitutional question. Where we will undoubtedly get a mass campaign with popular backing is where we are resisting the consequences of the economic, industrial and social policies pursued by Thatcher. Through that resistance, and the mass support for that resistance, will then come the lesson to those taking part that these policies demand a constitutional solution as well as a political solution to the particular set of policies being pursued by central government. Now that is why I think that, in terms of maximising support for a separate constitutional settlement, it would be a mistake to concentrate immediately on the constitutional issue and not on the question of jobs, of industry, of the welfare state which will have a more immediate resonance amongst the mass of the Scottish electorate.

SCOTLAND – OMEGA ONE

Allan Massie

From *The Spectator* (14 January 1984, pp. 9–10). Massie is primarily known as a novelist, but he has always also engaged in debate about public affairs. He is relatively unusual in late twentieth-century Scotland in being a novelist who is on the right politically.

The 1970s were a period of unusual intellectual excitement in Scotland. It's hard to say quite why, but three elements may be identified. There was first the coming of age of the wartime and post-war generation, many less committed a priori to the idea of the British state. Secondly, there was the stimulation of the state's manifest troubles, which reached their limit (though that wasn't realised) in the Scottish National Party's annus mirabilis of 1974, that grotesque year when *Time* and *Newsweek* were speculating about a British Revolution, and ex-army clowns were mustering private armies. It was all a fantasy of course, but, my word, it did stimulate. Then thirdly, there was the prospect of North Sea oil, itself fruitful of fantasy. I can remember having it patiently explained to me that if Scotland made a democratic decision to secede, England would naturally have no choice but to surrender the oil field to the new Scottish state; and I doubt if you could ever get more fantastic than that, north of the Mason-Dixon line anyway. Well, that house of cards tumbled down after the botched referendum.

But before that happened there was a lot of thinking done about the future of Scotland. And naturally enough, in the circumstances, most of this was concerned with political structures. It was assumed by many intellectual enthusiasts that North Sea oil would enable Scotland to free herself with one leap, like the hero of a pulp serial, from the constricting bonds of history. A bit of a damper was cast by the odd economist who unkindly suggested that an oil-backed Scottish pound would soar through the roof, killing off export industries and inviting a torrent of imports. But such judgements were too like the real world for the fantasists.

Of course, most people were a bit more modest. They didn't look for independence, but were content with the timid and muddled scheme of devolution on offer. And, since this was conceived in political language and involved the setting up of an Assembly in Edinburgh, it was assumed that such economic powers as were devolved would result in a still higher level of state activity in the economy; after all, you had to give the damn thing something to do, and the obvious course was state-inspired 'industrial regeneration'.

. . .

This wasn't surprising, for most of the thinking came from the Left. It might, though it is doubtful, have been different if the Tories, still committed by Heath's Declaration of Perth to the principle of devolution, had won one of the 1974 elections. But they didn't. The clumsy Scotland Act was then pushed through by Labour, however reluctantly. Most enthusiasts were left-inclining. The prospectus offered a managed economy in a more-or-less socialist Scotland. Of course, many who supported devolution hadn't thought much about economic affairs. They just assumed (with an optimism that wasn't unreasonable) that we might make a better shot at managing our own business than London did.

The corollary of all this was that the Tories were pushed on the defensive. They either had to pose as defenders of the Union, or, if they were Home Rulers, couldn't conceal from themselves that what was on offer was less than promising. They saw the Assembly as yet another layer of government, which could not fail to meddle in the economy, imposing still more state direction and artificial, theory-inspired 'stimulus'. The prospect seemed to numb their minds. Consequently the Scottish Right said nothing that was intellectually challenging. It just dug itself into a trench.

It would be too much to say that all this has changed. (You've only to look at the Scottish Conservative Party to see what a fantasy that would be.) But something is stirring. Last week for instance the Adam Smith Institute (London-based, admittedly) published its *Omega Report on Scottish Policy*. And it does suggest a new energy and some sense of there being 'une idée en marche'.

Its authors are minimal-state men. Consequently, they have no present interest in any sort of government in Edinburgh. On the contrary their working assumption is that a distant government can make less of a nuisance of itself than one on the spot. Since they see that any Edinburgh government would be interventionist, they are happy without it. 'Government intervention in the 1960s and 1970s', they say, 'stimulated only a series of disastrous schemes . . . Governments almost invariably opt for ambitious prestige projects which may enhance their own political reputation but which do nothing to mobilise the creative power of the population . . . The Scottish Office cannot know what technologies will flourish in the future and has usually backed the wrong ones . . .'. Such phrases, perhaps little more than the commonplaces of Thatcherism and Tebbitry, stud the report; in the Scottish context however they challenge dominant opinion. Though they don't make the historical comparison, the authors of the report are in fact asking for a return to the political conditions of the eighteenth century when Scotland experienced minimal government, the Enlightenment and the Industrial Revolution simultaneously.

So they would scrap all regional aid ('distorting'), scrap the Scottish Development Agency ('the embodiment of corporatist thinking that has typified Scottish policy for the last forty years') and transfer the functions of the Highlands and Islands Development Board to the Highlands Regional Council. They say, 'any part of Scotland which can support the status of enterprise zone or freeport should get it', insisting also that these zones should be what they are not in fact now, that is, free. They would change the taxation system in the North Sea, expose North Sea gas to market forces, privatise the two electricity boards, and, most interestingly of all, reform Scottish banking by freeing Scottish banks from the control of central monetary policy; 'they should be able to issue as much of their own currency as they judged to be right for the conditions of the Scottish economy'.

. . .

[T]he first importance of this report is the evidence that the Scottish Right is stirring, that it has got itself out of its dull statist and unionist trench, and is thinking again. 'In the 1970s', it states, 'it was thought that the way to open up and democratise Scottish government was through a directly elected assembly. Our alternative is to set about the systematic removal of powers, especially economic powers, from central government . . .'.

It is an alternative that will meet resistance from the vested interests of bureaucracies and quangos, which were not threatened at all by the schemes of political devolution, but battle has been joined; and it is one worth joining.

Towards a Constitutional Convention

Alan Lawson

From *Radical Scotland* (no. 17, October/November 1985, p. 6). Lawson was editor of the magazine.

In recent years, support amongst the Scottish electorate for the setting up of some form of separate Scottish government has been consistently in the region of 70 per cent, with further opinion polls showing that considerable economic powers were desired by most of our people. However, although all the political parties (except the Tories) now have policies in favour of a Scottish Assembly, there is still considerable concern as to how that goal is actually to be achieved. It is this essentially practical concern about how we get from A to B which has motivated the C[ampaign for a] S[cottish] A[ssembly] to produce their current consultative paper.

The original impetus came from the despair of the 1983 election result and its aftermath, in which there appeared to be growing permanency about the heavy Tory voting of south Britain and the heavy anti-Tory voting of Scotland. There was a feeling that such a scenario could not be allowed to continue virtually unchallenged indefinitely, and that a representative body of Scottish political opinion would somehow have to be gathered together immediately after any further similar election result, with a view to creating a national forum; that forum would articulate Scotland's demands for some form of self-government and oppose the alien policies of the southern establishment. Such unilateral action would probably be declared 'illegal' by a hostile Westminster government, but (the argument goes) wide-spread support would give it de facto legitimacy, given that people's grievances were not being satisfactorily met otherwise.

The second impetus behind the CSA initiative came from the realisation that even a 'friendly' government at Westminster (Labour or Alliance, or some conjunction of the two) would have the greatest difficulty in implementing any Scottish Assembly proposal. After all (it is argued), the situation in Britain when the next government takes office will be far worse than it was in 1976 and the pressure on parliamentary time is likely to be enormous, possibly throughout the entire term. CSA Convener Jim Boyack believes that this concern 'is already being understood by leading Scottish political figures' (thought to include Donald Dewar), following private meetings in London and Scotland.

One of the prime movers behind the new CSA movement is Jim Ross, who was Under-Secretary responsible for Devolution at the Scottish Office 1974–9. Citing the bumbling way in which British government fell into referendums in 1979 and in 1975 (EEC), he states quite firmly that 'Britain has no democratically respectable means of achieving constitutional change', and he cites the current process of altering the nature of local government as an oblique illustration of the same truth. Having been so closely involved in the process last time round, his views on the prospects for success next time are particularly relevant: 'The prospects of getting priority for a complex Bill to be taken entirely on the floor of the House are not good. The prospects of agreement to a short Bill, with most of the substance left to statutory instruments is not good either, unless the Government have a very decisive majority. But even if there were such an agreement, it would not be democratically responsible and could lead to the kind of haphazard wrecking votes which were a feature of the last venture.'

From these concerns, the CSA produced their proposals, although they accept that, as it is uncharted territory, considerable changes to those proposals may be made over the next two years. The scheme envisages a Convention being formed within a short period after the next General Election, with the following remit:

1. to articulate and represent the demand for a Scottish Assembly;
2. to draft the provisions of an Assembly scheme, setting out the powers of the Assembly, its source of finance, and its relationships with the British government;
3. to negotiate with British government the time-table and implementation of that scheme;
4. to arrange any necessary test of Scottish support for the Assembly scheme – e.g., by referendum.

The details of who would form the Convention and how it would come into operation are dealt with in the CSA Paper as a set of 'options', depending on the attitude of the incoming British Government. The main option discussed involves the newly-elected Scottish MPs forming the 'core' of the Convention, which could then be 'topped up' with representatives of the many political and other organisations in Scotland who could legitimately provide some input to the deliberations. Alternatively, the membership of the Convention could be elected at a set of elections held specially for that purpose, either officially (if the Westminster regime was favourable) or possibly unofficially (if the London regime was hostile). However, leading members of the CSA stress that the precise machinery may be of less importance than 'campaigning to impress on all concerned both the priority of a Scottish Assembly, and what is involved in bringing it about'.

During early consultations on the Paper, some members pressed for the Convention to be set up now, such that its work would be in place in time for the next election; others were of the view that such a move would lack credibility at this stage, and that time was needed to build up interest, knowledge and support behind the Convention scheme. The Paper has now been sent out to all the Scottish MPs, political parties, Trade Unions, Local Authorities, university principals, Chambers of Commerce, and cultural and religious organisations, as well as to the CSA's own members and affiliated organisations; considered responses are now being sought, prior to the next round of discussions and refinements to the proposals.

It is not easy to see at this stage exactly where this initiative will lead, but as Jim Ross says 'there is everything to be said for acclimatising the Scottish people to the idea of the Scots – through some form of clearly representative body – laying firmly before Parliament exactly what they want'.

THE DEVOLUTION MAZE

Allan Stewart

From *Apostles Not Apologists*, a pamphlet published by Eastwood Conservative Association in October 1987. Stewart was Conservative MP for Eastwood.

Slogans are easy and useful. Appeals for 'decisions in Scotland by Scots' have an immediate appeal. For opponents of the Government, the idea of a Scottish Assembly has considerable uses. Support for it can be portrayed as being 'pro-Scottish'. Unsullied by experience, it is the convenient answer to every grievance, real or imagined. There can be few social or economic problems for which devolution has not been put forward as the solution.

The case for a Scottish Assembly now is not seriously argued on its merits. Down the years the motives of the proponents of devolution have been partisan. Who can now seriously doubt that the interest in devolution of the last Labour Government was directly related to the rise of the SNP?

. . .

Now the proposals are for an Assembly with tax-raising powers and a 'greatly strengthened' role in the economic field. A body with those powers is seen as a secure Socialist power base from which to challenge Westminster.

The strongest supporters of an Assembly are to be found among those who have mismanaged many councils, driven rates up and business out, disastrously mishandled housing policy. We are asked to believe that extending their power and policies to the whole of Scotland will magically replace failure with success. We have seen what Labour have tried to do in London, Liverpool and Lothian. But local councils cannot pass laws or raise taxes irrespective of Parliament's views. Labour's Scottish Assembly would do both.

Conservative supporters and sympathisers who have advocated a Scottish Assembly since the election have done so purely on grounds of supposed party political gain. 'People want some devolution – this particular scheme would dish the Labour party' come the cries. Even on its own extremely limited merits that argument does not stand up. Neither opinion polls, public meetings or canvass returns suggest support for an Assembly was a significant issue at the last election.

The idea that voters will swing to the Conservatives because we are in favour of an Assembly but less enthusiastically than our opponents is to put it mildly implausible. To put forward some half-baked scheme would be to get the worst of all possible worlds. It would be derided by our opponents. Such a course would appal many supporters, especially in the business community, who have thought very seriously about the implications.

It is no answer either to suggest some watered down scheme without the dangerous new powers proposed by Labour. An Assembly without them would lobby continuously for them and under pressure Westminster would be bound to concede, especially as the subsequent damage would be largely confined to Scotland.

What then are the realities? They are that an Assembly would: impose real costs on Scotland and resolve no problems; reduce Scottish influence where it matters – at the House of Commons and in Cabinet; receive and spend less Treasury funding than it wished and make up the difference with extra Scottish taxation; lead inevitably to continuing conflict which would break up the United Kingdom.

The obvious cost of an Assembly is setting it up and running it. That is estimated at £50 million a year – £50 million which could otherwise be productively used. Local government would need to be reorganised – more expenditure. For a period of several years there would be considerable confusion about who was going to be doing what in Scotland. The costs of uncertainty and delay for business and individuals would not show up in the public sector's accounts. But they would be very real and very damaging to those affected. For companies making decisions on whether to invest in Scotland or elsewhere, the wise course of action would be clear.

Given the claims made for it, an Assembly would be set up with high expectations. But the hard reality is that it could not change the economic facts of life. How could constitutional change alter the world markets for steel, ships or anything else? An Assembly does not magically produce better houses, faster roads, or more wealth creation. Socialists believe that the answer to most problems is to throw public money at them. But where would the money come from? There are only two possible sources – the Treasury or extra Scottish taxation.

So an assembly would be financed in part from a Treasury block grant. Funds for an Assembly block grant are funds which could be allocated elsewhere. Public spending per head in Scotland has been consistently higher than in England or in English regions with arguably similar needs. Under successive Governments, Scotland has had high public spending levels as a result of political pressure from a Secretary of State backed by the Scottish Office and (at least when it comes to extracting money) Scottish

MPs. . . . That system may well have damaged Scotland in a number of ways. It would certainly go into sharp reverse when a Scottish executive had to negotiate annually specific sums with a Treasury answerable to a Cabinet in which the Secretary of State was at best a marginal member without his own Department, if the office existed at all. In the House of Commons the allocation of funds would come under rigorous scrutiny from Members from all parts of the United Kingdom.

As the President of the CBI has pointed out 'the pressure on others to look again at Scotland's share of national expenditure in the changed circumstances of a tax-raising assembly could be considerable'. The ambition of Assemblymen to spend more of other people's money than the Treasury would allow would have one inevitable result. The inability to fund every pet project would be blamed on the Treasury and the House of Commons. These frustrations would lead to disenchantment as the imperfections of an imperfect system became clear. It would be a perfect scene for the SNP, an ideal vehicle for protest, to succeed with their argument that what an assembly needed was real economic and fiscal powers – in other words independence.

An Assembly with tax-raising powers means one thing – higher taxes. Which ones? you may well ask. Over the years all possible sources of extra revenue have been exhaustively examined. Some are clearly ruled out – regional differentiation of VAT is not permitted under EEC rules. Some are difficult but possible. Higher Scottish income tax and excise duties would do wonders for the housing market and retail sales in Carlisle and Berwick upon Tweed! A surcharge on the new community charge would also be possible. But it would be likely to be unpopular and would certainly lead the whole electorate to question what good an Assembly was doing them. Bad politics!

That leaves taxes on businesses as by far and away the most attractive option for an Assembly. Corporation tax and a new tax per employee are possible targets but the easiest one is business rates – an area where the Assembly would clearly have legislative authority. During the debates on the replacement of domestic rates with the community charge and the pegging of business rates, Opposition spokesmen consistently argued that high rates on businesses had either no effect or very little. An Assembly could also decide to reintroduce domestic rates, perhaps only for property above a certain value. Both measures would be possible technically and would not immediately affect many voters.

The long-term effects would be quite a different matter. Additional rates are an unavoidable overhead. They could undermine the competitive position of Scottish companies in Scottish, English and international markets. They would undoubtedly bias investment decisions against Scotland.

How would the House of Commons work and how would Scotland's interests be served? Currently the Secretary of State for Scotland sits not only in Cabinet but also on all Cabinet Committees and groups whose deliberations do or could have an effect on Scotland. If he and his Ministerial team existed at all with an Assembly, deprived of a department and real authority their influence would become increasingly negligible.

Pro-Assembly spokesmen have generally tried to pretend that problems about the role of Scottish MPs with an Assembly would be 'technical' or 'could be solved with goodwill'. They are not and could not be. The problems about the role of Scottish MPs are the most obvious example of the impracticality of inserting a Scottish Assembly into the Parliament of the United Kingdom. Scotland is relatively over-represented in the House of Commons. The reasons are currently defensible – notably, separate Scottish legislation. That over-representation could hardly survive a Boundary Commission Report when there was virtually no Scottish legislation in the House of Commons. That would mean less influence. But a mere cut in numbers does not solve the problem. Why should English MPs allow Scots MPs to vote – possibly decisively – on legislation affecting English housing, education, local government and so on when none of them could vote on comparable Scottish matters?

Some Labour MPs argue that the answer is that Scottish MPs would not vote on purely English matters. Quite apart from the immense difficulties of definition this raises, that is workable only where the Government has a working majority irrespective of Scottish votes. What happens if a Government rules on Scottish votes (or Scottish and Welsh as the case may be) – like the recent Labour Governments of 1964 and 1974? Not only could that Government not get its English legislation through. It could be easily forced out of office not by a combination of parties as in a hung Parliament but by its leading opponents. They would simply vote down purely English measures they disagreed with and those essential to continued Government – like the English Rate Support Grant Order. Then what?

So an Assembly would lead to constitutional instability both because of pressures from the Assembly and within the House of Commons. This would be bound to lead to continuing uncertainty with all the obvious consequences for the environment, for business and for the quality of decision-making. In both the Assembly and the House of Commons pressures for complete separation would rise inexorably.

These fundamental difficulties apply to all proposals for a legislative

Scottish Assembly whatever detailed powers it might start with. A Scottish Assembly would resolve no problems. It would . . . mean extra taxes for Scottish business. Constitutional conflict and uncertainty would be inevitable with the SNP the political beneficiary and the climate of business confidence the obvious loser.

A Claim of Right for Scotland

From the report of this title issued on 13 July 1988 by the Constitutional Steering Group set up by the Campaign for a Scottish Assembly. The Group was chaired by Sir Robert Grieve, a planner and academic who had been the first chair of the Highlands and Islands Development Board when it was established in 1965. The secretary was Jim Ross.

– Introduction –

We were appointed because, in the opinion of the Campaign for a Scottish Assembly, Parliamentary government under the present British constitution had failed Scotland and more than Parliamentary action was needed to redeem the failure. We share that view and in this report set out what we consider must be done if the health of Scottish government is to be restored.

Our direct concern is with Scotland only, but the failure to provide good government for Scotland is a product not merely of faulty British policy in relation to Scotland, but of fundamental flaws in the British constitution. We have identified these and pointed out their relevance to the problems of Scotland. They do not, however, afflict Scotland only. So far from giving Scotland an advantage over others, rectifying these defects would improve the government of the whole of the United Kingdom, more particularly those parts of it outside the London metropolitan belt.

In this report we frequently use the word 'English' where the word 'British' is conventionally used. We believe this clarifies many issues which the customary language of the British government obscures. Although the government of the United Kingdom rests nominally with a 'British' Parliament, it is impossible to trace in the history or procedures of that Parliament any constitutional influence other than an English one. Scots are apt to bridle when 'Britain' is referred to as 'England'. But there is a fundamental truth in this nomenclature which Scots ought to recognise – and from which they ought to draw appropriate conclusions.

. . .

– The Past: Essential Facts of Scottish History –

Much ink is wasted on the question whether the Scots are a nation. Of course they are. They were both a nation and a state until 1707. The state was wound up by a Treaty which clearly recognised the nation and its right to distinctive government in a fundamental range of home affairs. The fact that institutional forms, however empty, reflecting these distinctions have been preserved to the present day demonstrates that no-one in British government has dared to suggest openly that the nation no longer exists or that the case for distinctiveness has now disappeared.

Scottish nationhood does not rest on constitutional history alone. It is supported by a culture reaching back over centuries and bearing European comparison in depth and quality, nourished from a relatively early stage by an education system once remarkable by European standards. Since the Union, the strength of that culture has fluctuated but there is no ground for any claim that, overall or even at any particular time, it has benefited from the Union. On the contrary the Union has always been, and remains, a threat to the survival of a distinctive culture in Scotland.

The international zenith reached by that culture in the late eighteenth century is sometimes facilely attributed to the Union, but that leaves for explanation the subsequent decline of the culture as the Union became more established. No doubt some benefit was derived from the relatively settled state of Scotland at the time. More, probably, stemmed from the minimal interference of London in Scottish affairs in those days. But the roots of that philosophical, literary and scientific flowering lay in the social soil of Scotland itself and its long-established cross-fertilisation with mainland Europe.

That cross-fertilisation diminished as the pull of London increased and the effects of the removal of important stimuli to Scottish confidence and self respect were felt. In mid-nineteenth century, Scottish culture eroded and became inward-looking in consequence. It has struggled with mixed success to revive as Scots realised what they were in danger in losing. The twentieth century, up to and including the present day, has been a period of extraordinary fertility in all fields of the Scottish arts: literature, visual and dramatic arts, music, traditional crafts, philosophic and historical studies. In particular the indigenous languages of Scotland, Gaelic and Scots, are being revived in education, the arts and social life. We think it no accident that this trend has accompanied an increasingly vigorous demand for a Scottish say in Scotland's government.

The nation was not conquered but it did not freely agree to the Union of Parliaments in 1707. We need not go into the details of the negotiations about the Union. What is beyond dispute is that the main impetus for Union came from the English and it was brought about for English reasons of state. Likewise, the form of Union was not what the Scots would have chosen but what the English were prepared to concede. However, the considerable guarantees which Scots won in the Treaty of Union reflected the fact that, until the Treaty was implemented, they had a Parliament of their own to speak for them.

The matters on which the Treaty guaranteed the Scots their own institutions and policies represented the bulk of civil life and government at the time: the Church, the Law and Education. However, there was never any mechanism for enforcing respect for the terms of the Treaty of Union. Many of its major provisions have been violated, and its spirit has never affected the huge areas of government which have evolved since. The say of Scotland in its own government has diminished, is diminishing and ought to be increased.

The forms of Scottish autonomy which, until recently, had multiplied for almost a century are misleading. The Scottish Office can be distinguished from a Whitehall Department only in the sense that it is not physically located in Whitehall (and much of its most important work is done in Whitehall). The Secretary of State may be either Scotland's man in the Cabinet or the Cabinet's man in Scotland, but in the last resort he is invariably the latter. Today, he can be little else, since he must impose on Scotland policies against which an overwhelming majority of Scots have voted.

The apparent strengthening of Scottish institutions of government since 1885 – the creation of a Secretary of State, the enlargement of the functions of the Scottish Office, the extension of Scottish Parliamentary Committees – has been accompanied by an increasing centralisation and standardisation of British government practice which has more than offset any decentralisation of administrative units.

– THE PRESENT, AND THE FUTURE BEING FORCED UPON US –

Scotland has a team of Ministers and an administration who are supposed to exist in order to provide Scotland with distinctive government according to Scottish wishes in those fields of British government which affect Scotland only. They cannot possibly do so.

The creation of these offices and procedures was a sop to Scottish discontent, not a response to Scottish needs. The team of Ministers is chosen from whichever political party has won a British general election. That election must be fought on British, not Scottish, issues. The Scots cannot concentrate on Scottish issues when casting their votes, but must simultaneously reflect their opinions on such matters as foreign policy, defence, the EEC, and Northern Ireland. So far as the Scots vote for United Kingdom parties, these parties will themselves regard Scottish issues as subsidiary to the winning of British votes. At present, the Scots cannot vote for other than a UK party without implying a vote for independence. And the political arithmetic of the United Kingdom means that the Scots are constantly exposed to the risk of having matters of concern only to them prescribed by a government against which they have voted not narrowly but overwhelmingly. Yet Scottish Ministers and the Scottish administration must implement these policies, even where their implementation only affects Scotland.

Scottish Ministers and the Scottish Office are not the only parts of the special machinery of current Scottish government. But the other parts are no more effective. There is a Scottish Grand Committee for general debate of Scottish issues in Parliament; there are Scottish Standing Committees for detailed consideration of Scottish legislation; and there used to be a Select Committee on Scottish Affairs to scrutinise the working of Government policy in Scotland.

The Scottish Grand Committee rarely votes. Its debates have no effect except so far as the Government chooses to pay attention to them and its agenda is subject to Government manipulation. The Scottish Standing Committees operate only when the Government chooses to handle Scottish legislation separately. If it prefers to combine Scottish legislation with English, it can usually find an excuse for doing so. And if need be, Scottish Standing Committees can be filled out with English members. The Select Committee on Scottish Affairs must have a Government majority, no matter how slight a minority the Government may be in Scotland.

Even this unsuitable and inadequate 'government' of Scotland is no longer working. There is a constitutional flaw in the present machinery of Scottish government; it can work only within a limited range of election results. Providing a Scottish Ministerial team, Scottish Whips and Government representation on Standing and Select Committees, requires a certain minimum number of Government party MPs from Scottish constituencies. There is no guarantee of such a number being elected.

At present the governing party is below the minimum and there is no certainty that this situation will be short-lived. As a result, we have no Select Committee on Scottish Affairs, so Government policy in Scotland is not subject to the scrutiny thought necessary elsewhere. And the use of the other elements of Scottish Parliamentary procedures is being minimised.

We are not aware of any other instance, at least in what is regarded as the democratic world, of a territory which has a distinctive corpus of law and an acknowledged right to distinctive policies but yet has no body expressly elected to safeguard and supervise these. The existing machinery of Scottish government is an attempt either to create an illusion or to achieve the impossible.

In that attempt it was bound to fail eventually and the failure can no longer be hidden. The choice of adhering to present Scottish government is not available. Either we advance to an Assembly, or we retreat to the point at which Scottish institutions are an empty shell and Scottish government is, in practice, indistinguishable from that of any English region. The latter process has already begun.

So far as Scottish Ministers and the Scottish Office have a real, as distinct from an illusory, purpose it is merely to solicit for Scotland a larger share of what the British Government of the day thinks Scotland ought to want. Even when this soliciting succeeds, it regularly fails to produce what Scotland wants and there can be little confidence that it produces what Scotland needs. It is also invidious within the United Kingdom. It arouses the jealously of English regions and it concentrates Scottish attention on lobbying in London rather than initiating in Scotland. It creates the very dependency culture of which the present Government professes to disapprove.

Because of the constitutional flaws long latent in Scottish government, also because it is now imagined elsewhere that Scotland has an unfair advantage, Scottish government as developed over the last century is being rapidly eroded. It cannot be preserved. It must be rejuvenated or it will fade away.

– The English Constitution –
an Illusion of Democracy

The English constitution provides for only one source of power, the Crown-in-Parliament. That one source is now mainly embodied in the Prime Minister, who has appropriated almost all the royal prerogatives. She/he appoints Ministers who, with rare exceptions, can be dismissed at will, and has further formidable powers of patronage. Because of Party discipline and the personal ambition of members the consequence is that, so far from Parliament controlling the Executive (which is the constitutional theory), it is the Prime Minister as head of the Executive who controls Parliament.

. . .

However convinced Scots may be of the defects of their present system of government, some may be daunted by the apparent complexities and uncertainties of change. It is not our function to draw up a scheme for a Scottish Assembly. But it is part of our terms of reference to convince doubters not only that present Scottish government is bad but that an Assembly would make it better. . . .

– AN ASSEMBLY AND INDEPENDENCE –

It is sometimes argued against an Assembly that it will inevitably lead to 'separatism', by which those concerned presumably mean Scottish independence. As those who profess to think this usually also profess the opinion that, if Scots want independence they ought to have it, we must conclude that they believe that an Assembly will somehow lead the Scots into independence without wanting it.

The planning of a Scottish Assembly within the framework of United Kingdom government is a complex task, made considerably easier, however, by the fact that a great deal of it has already been done. The negotiation of Scottish independence would be a vastly more complex task. It would take considerable time, it could not be kept secret and its details would be the subject of active public debate. The Scots could not be faced with independence either suddenly or in ignorance of its implications. Hence, the argument that an Assembly will inevitably lead to independence can imply only one of two things.

On the one hand, it may imply a belief that independence offers the best long-term prospects for Scots and that an Assembly will help them to perceive this. That is a legitimate and honest belief but there is no guarantee that it will prove well-founded. It is at least equally possible that refusal of an Assembly will convince the Scots that only independence offers them any prospect of acceptable government, whereas achievement of an Assembly will satisfy them.

Alternatively, the argument implies an insult to the Scots by suggesting that, once an Assembly is in place, they will lose all power of political judgement and will be manipulated by a particular faction despite their own interests. The Scots will indeed have lost their political judgement if they succumb to such an argument. They are entitled to point out that they already suffer from an English constitution which allows manipulation by a particular political faction and that the quest for an Assembly shows a determination to put an end to such manipulation and a resolve to decide for themselves.

. . .

– The Way to Resurgence –

In [the situation we have described] one would expect to see signs of a breakdown of respect for law. They are beginning to appear.

It is not part of the Committee's remit to pronounce on the legislation for what is generally know as the poll tax. But the existence of, and the reaction to, that legislation illustrate our point. Whatever the arguments for and against the legislation, its unpopularity is beyond dispute. Equally beyond dispute is the fact that it is attracting greater resistance and creating a more serious risk of disobedience to the law than any other issue in living memory. Now that the legislation is being enacted for England and Wales, its defects are being highlighted by the Government's own back benchers, though nothing was heard from them when it was forced through for Scotland against the opposition of six sevenths of the Scottish MPs. Probably no legislation at once so fundamental and so lacking in popular support would have been initiated other than in a territory within which the Government was unrepresentative of and out of touch with the electorate.

We fully understand the pressure for refusal to comply with the requirements of the poll tax legislation. In all the circumstances the Government cannot reasonably expect anything else. But we do not believe that random rejection of the law on particular issues is the answer to the problem facing Scotland.

Misconceived and undemocratic legislation for Scotland is not the product of occasional aberration by a particular British Government. It is a consequence of the flaws in the machinery of government which we have already pointed out. Resistance to one mischief will not prevent other mischiefs and may well fail because it does not address the real weaknesses of the Government's case.

Scots must create for themselves a focus of resistance and political negotiation, which rejects comprehensively the authority of existing government on matters peculiar to Scotland, which describes and demands the appropriate cure of present ills, namely a new form of Scottish government, and which encourages civil disobedience of any kind only so far as this forms part of an orderly programme to achieve it. The appropriate form of that focus of resistance is a Constitutional Convention.

A Constitutional Convention is a representative body convened to fill the democratic gap when the government of an existing state has partly or wholly failed, or when a government needs to be created for a new, or re-created for an old, country. It may perform several tasks, but one invariable task is to draw up a new constitution.

A definition applicable to Scotland was given in a Consultative Paper issued in 1985 by the Campaign for a Scottish Assembly. This stated that a Scottish Constitutional Convention would:

1. articulate and represent the Scottish demand for an Assembly;
2. draft the provisions of an Assembly scheme, setting out the powers of the Assembly, its sources of finance and its relationship with British Government;
3. negotiate with British Government the timetable and implementation of that scheme;
4. arrange any necessary test of Scottish support for the scheme, e.g., by referendum.

. . .

The originating mechanic of Conventions have ranged along a spectrum from, at one extreme, formal de jure legitimacy with direct elections and a remit prescribed by Government to, at the other extreme, semi-clandestine gatherings, mainly appointed or delegated and with only a de facto claim to be representative. The 1975 Northern Ireland Convention is an example of the first. The German Vorparlament of 1848 and the French Assemblé Consultative, which began work in Algeria in 1944 and was later transferred to France and enlarged after the recovery of Paris, are examples of the second.

Two other possible aspects of Constitutional Conventions are worth noting. They need not spring up full grown in the first instance; and groups or bodies initially formed for another purpose may turn themselves into Constitutional Conventions. The French case mentioned is an example of gradual growth. Examples of transformation can be found in France, where the Estates General of 1789 turned themselves into a National Assembly with the remit of drafting a constitution, and Ireland at the end of the First World War, where MPs elected in British elections withdrew from Westminster and set themselves up as a Dáil in Ireland.

The essential is that a Convention, whether its origins are de jure or de facto, whether it is created complete as a single act or grows gradually, must achieve acceptance by those on whose behalf it presumes to speak and act. The more difficult the circumstances in which the Convention is created – in other words the less help it gets from established government – the more difficult it will be to make it wholly representative. By strict criteria, most Constitutional Conventions to date have been representative only to a limited degree. However, a wise and mature community should be tolerant about the criteria of representativeness when the body representing it has been convened in circumstances of difficulty and obstruction.

LECTURE

Donald Dewar

From a lecture at Stirling University (21 October 1988). Dewar was Labour MP for Garscadden and shadow Secretary of State for Scotland. He later became Secretary of State in the Labour government of 1997.

. . .

I start from the premise that Britain is an over-centralised state. This is not always obvious. We have a Government which believes in the market, in the break-up of the bureaucracy and is apparently committed to contracting out what many would see as the essential role of the Civil Service. For all that, there clearly is an undesirable concentration of power in Whitehall and, at times, an unhealthy suspicion of any competing centre of influence of the kind provided by Local Government. There is no essential virtue in the concentration of power in and around the capital and there is no reason for thinking that a different approach leads to inefficiency or a substandard economic performance. Even the most superficial examination of what has happened in Federal West Germany makes that point.

The argument about local democracy is important. Local Government is not always popular, but the community does depend on the basic network of services it provides. There is nothing romantic about sewage and street lighting, but there is no argument about its importance. Councils are democratically elected and respond to public opinions. It is a process often surrounded by controversy, but it matters. I believe it would be a disaster if local authorities were to be reduced to occasional meetings to rubber stamp formally decisions taken elsewhere. It may seem an alarmist picture, but the thrust of current policy is unmistakable and the damage is already very real. . . .

There is, too, the looming presence of Europe and the Common Market. It is something that can not be ignored. I voted 'yes' in the European Referendum. I believe the EEC is part of our lives and increasingly important in economic terms. I am conscious of the danger, however, that Scotland, despite our best efforts, will be a country on the outer edge of Europe and the wrong end of Britain.

. . .

The key question is the place of Scotland in the United Kingdom. Here, in recent times, there is evidence of a determined attempt to polarise the argument. This results from an alliance of unlikely forces cemented by little but partisan self-interest. The pitch is that Scotland must pick between a full incorporating union or total independence. The suggestion is that there can be no workable middle way and that those who advocate some form of devolution are in effect impossiblists. I do not believe that this is necessarily so. It is a strange argument to come from those, like Lord Home and indeed the Prime Minister herself, who claimed that the repeal of the Scotland Act [1978] was not the end of the devolution debate.

It is important to stress the fundamental distinction between devolution and independence. They involve the pursuit of very different objectives and the one is not inevitably a way of achieving the other. I do not to subscribe to the theory of the slippery slope. This distinction may be thought to be self-evident, but many try to blur the position and it is a difference that must be hammered home again and again. Of course, Scotland has a right to self-determination, but it has an equal right not to exercise that option.

I am an unashamed supporter of John P. Mackintosh's theory of dual-nationality. We are both British and Scottish, and the two are not exclusive but essentially compatible. Political statehood is not essential to 'the status of genuine nationalism'. What is needed is a political solution which recognises and buttresses the Scottish identity within the framework of the United Kingdom.

What then is to be done? There are undeniable attractions to federal models that have been put forward. Sadly, this is an academically interesting but sterile debate. Federalism is not on the agenda for the simple reason that there is very little support for it outside Scotland. I welcome the growth of interest in forms of provincial government as an innovation which may do something to bridge the gap between Scotland with an Assembly and the rest of the country. We should not, however, imagine that the two phenomena are comparable. Those who argue the federal case draw their complicated constitutional blueprints in the sand. They are not likely to be called to account. They have no expectation of being asked to implement their ideas.

If we accept that federalism is not an immediate option, then the task is to evolve a distinctive Scottish solution within the United Kingdom which is workable and acceptable to both sides of the Border. The Labour Party's proposals are well known. They are also frequently attacked and vilified. There is no more familiar but tiresome tale than the 'I would have voted "yes" in 1979 if it had been a better Bill'. The more you look at the devolution possibilities, the more you settle on the broad shape which John Smith and his colleagues piloted through ten years ago.

The problem is not geographic isolation but the way in which the system fails to respond to the perceived needs of the people of Scotland. Administrative devolution has grown over the years, but there is a great need for parallel democratic control. It really is a nonsense that one Junior Minister should be in charge of areas of policy split between four or five of his colleagues South of the Border.

It is said that a directly elected Assembly with wide and impressive legislative powers will be no more than a talking shop. I would have thought that anybody responsible for health, education, housing and local government could hardly be described in that way.

It is argued very strongly that the power to raise revenue is a fatal flaw. The attack is less than impressive because it usually comes from groups who in 1979 were urging the exact opposite. Then we were told that any elected tier of government without the right to raise its own revenue was constitutionally irresponsible. There is the smack of parish pump politics about the stories of an over-governed Scotland. There is an overwhelming case for single tier, all-purpose authorities working with the Assembly. It is a matter of scale and common sense. The Assembly itself draws its power from Westminster and the much trumpeted new bureaucracy is already in place in the Scottish Office.

The important thing is that there should be no false prospectus. No one suggests that a change in the structure of government will suddenly wish away our economic problems. Obviously an Assembly with the power to decide on public spending priorities, which controls the Scottish Development Agency and is responsible both for Section 7 Grants to Industry and Employment Training, will have great influence. That is not to suggest, however, that with one bound Scotland will be free. The aim is a balanced approach with devolution giving a measure of control over Scottish legislation to Scots but with the United Kingdom maintaining its economic integrity and, hopefully, using its muscle to ensure an effective use of the opportunities presented by Europe.

If there is broad agreement about the right approach, how can Government be persuaded to act? Present problems – an obstinate Government unwilling to respond – could be anticipated but solutions are more difficult to find. One of the questions that arises is whether the Constitutional Convention now proposed offers some way forward.

. . .

I hope that the Campaign for a Scottish Assembly's *Claim of Right* will be the basis for a real attempt to agree common policy on Scotland's place in the United Kingdom. I do not underestimate the difficulties of maintaining progress or resisting the calls for unrepresentative action from unrepresentative groups who are simply interested in outflanking and discrediting those with whom they disagree. Any talks should be a genuine attempt to find that common ground and to evolve an agreed package – that means that the process must be seen as a way of finding the right reform within the United Kingdom and not breaking away from it. It means, too, the Labour Party must be prepared to negotiate and not simply seek to enforce the devolution package that we already have before the public. Any convention will be based on Scottish MPs, but there may be a case for broadening its membership to include representatives from other bodies. Any formula, however, must represent the realities of Scottish politics, and the price of adding to the Parliamentary core must not be to expose the Assembly to a constant harangue mounted by people who would be a bad joke if they risked the judgement of the electorate.

The significance of the Constitutional Convention should not be shrugged off by Government. It is based on the assumption that it is possible to mount pressure even on a hostile administration and that there are tactics other than simply working for national victory at the next election. It is essential, however, that we look long and hard at what happens if the Government does say no to any formula that might emerge. The devolution campaign would, of course, continue in any case, strengthened and reinforced by the broad based support for the new proposals. Government obstruction does not mean an inevitable drift into policies of civil disobedience, to the boycotting of Westminster or some other tactic designed to make Scotland ungovernable, or to create a constitutional crisis with the intention of stampeding the country into a quasi nationalist stance. The most important virtue will be realism and an ability to reflect what Scotland wants.

There are Scots politicians who will happily dance on the head of a pin or, at least, argue with Presbyterian zeal about the theology of devolution. The real question is whether Scotland is ready for it. Muriel Spark, talking about the Edinburgh of Miss Jean Brodie, described what she was pleased to call the 'nevertheless' syndrome. The story was of 'tough, elderly women in musquash coats taking tea in McVitie's' who would ceremoniously accumulate vast evidence pointing to one conclusion and then confound the logic with the triumphant use of the one word 'nevertheless' followed by a stark denial of all the facts.

In the past the devolution argument has proceeded on the 'nevertheless' principle. What we have got to do is to persuade Scotland that fear must be conquered and that canny caution be put on one side. The people must decide if they are prepared to live a little dangerously in order to achieve what they want. Poll after poll has shown support for devolution and a rejection of the independence option. If they stand by that, the second challenge will be whether our system is flexible enough and our politicians sensible enough to respond. There is a tough, disciplined debate ahead if we are to make progress.

UNREPENTANT GRADUALISM

Neil MacCormick

From a collection of essays discussing the *Claim of Right* (Edwards, 1989, pp. 99–109). MacCormick was a prominent member of the SNP and had stood for parliament for the party on several occasions. He was (and is) professor of public law at Edinburgh University.

. . .

This is written by a signatory of the *Claim of Right* who is also a member of the Scottish National Party, but one who at the time of writing finds himself in sharp and public disagreement with the party leadership's posture of opposition to the convening of a convention on the terms proposed in the *Claim*. Rather than pretend to academic objectivity, I shall therefore here present an amalgam of blatant advocacy and apology for a view not much in fashion among my political friends. I hope the argument will succeed as apologia, rather than be dismissed as a mere apology for an argument. However that may be, the argument is not a new one, not even new in the context of the particular present debate in Scotland. At the Scottish National Party conference in Inverness in September 1988, I had the honour of being invited to present the annual 'Chairman's Lecture', taking as my subject 'Constitution and Democracy'. The case I put then will be substantially restated here. If I now have the misfortune to disagree with the leadership of the party to which I (perhaps all too loosely) adhere, I shall at all events be stating the very same view as I stated to the party conference well before the outbreak of controversy.

The argument here has two main sections. In the first, I state some elements of a general political creed under the rubric of 'Constitutionalism, Democracy, Gradualism', showing the connections of this with some of the themes of the *Claim of Right*. In the second ('On Present Discontents'), I try to justify a view about the way the SNP should respond to the challenge of a Convention, and concede some points of fault in my own view.

– CONSTITUTIONALISM, DEMOCRACY, GRADUALISM –

'Constitutionalism' and 'Democracy' are in my view concepts or ideals essential to the ever elusive goal of human freedom in political society. To make this bold statement is, however, to assert a relatively uncontroversial, not to say vapid, thesis. The real question is not whether these concepts are involved in the issue of political freedom, but what conceptions of them we should propose as defining a favoured ideal of liberty in community. The ones which I propose are certainly congenial to the long standing style and spirit exhibited by the Scottish national movement in almost all its manifestations and most particularly to the political approach of the SNP. The SNP has been devoutly and unshakeably constitutionalist and democratic throughout its history, and is so now. Even if there were shortcuts to its cherished goal of a free Scotland, the party has never shown any inclination towards them, and rightly, since attempts to dodge round either would put at profound risk the integrity of the objective sought. The general temper of Scottish politics in modern times provides its own guarantee against any successful adventures down such shortcuts.

The point about integrity is fundamental. For the goal of a 'free Scotland' in the favoured sense must be taken as prescribing the freedom and equality of all citizens regardless of creed, class or ethnic origins, and the free participation of them all as equals in the processes of self-government. In a word, democracy. It must also, however be understood as requiring what our forebears such as George Buchanan and David Hume used to call a 'free government', that is a government which is not only freely chosen by the people but which conducts the business of government with respect to the freedom under law of each citizen and of all of them in such associations as they pursue. In a word, constitutionalism. If the goal of a free Scotland is understood in this way, pursuit of it entails both practical and logical limits on the means that could be adopted for attaining it; if it is not so understood, it is not a goal fit to be pursued.

Sometimes one almost thinks of democracy and constitutionalism as though they were run together and hyphenated, constitutionalism-and-democracy, just one great big compendious concept. This is unhelpful, since it obscures the need for a balancing of values by presenting the balance as already struck pre-analytically. Constitutionalism and democracy represent two internally complex values, two poles to each of which our political life and thought has to be oriented, albeit in tension between the partly opposing pulls from them.

Democracy as a value stresses the equality of citizens (the equal worth, dignity and civil and political rights of citizens), and the sovereignty of the will of the totality of the citizens acting as equals. Constitutionalism is about the need for all sovereignties, not least popular sovereignty, to be constrained and restricted within political structures and legal or quasi-legal limits. It points to the dangers of every sort of absolute and arbitrary power, and stresses the need to divide into parts the powers of a commonwealth, distributing them among several agencies and estates, each jealous of any overweening pretensions of any other, all supplying 'checks and control' (as Hume would say) upon all the others. As well as limits of form and structure, in the modern world constitutionalism is increasingly and rightly seen as stipulating limits of substance upon governmental power, spelt out through charters or bills of right – or 'Claims of Right' such as those stipulated by the Scots Estates in convention in 1689.

Democracy says the people should be sovereign; constitutionalism denies that any sovereignty should be absolute and free of restraints or limits. Rather than plainly asserting the power of the people, it says that even the people will not exercise power wisely or justly save under acknowledged limits. Constitutionalist governments are carefully respectful of the limits on state power. Constitutionalist citizens make it their pride to pursue just reforms through the forms of legality and constitutional propriety – but they must also have the most watchful jealousy against governmental encroachments of constitutional power practised through any of the branches of government.

The long-standing constitutional policy of the Scottish National Party is in my view one which postulates a well-balanced equilibrium between the two poles of democracy and constitutionalism. It insists on equality of citizenship for all residing here. It proposes to entrench equality of voting power for everyone through a fair system of proportional representation in elections. It guards against abuses of majority power by proposing to give substantial minorities in parliament a power of veto subject to control by referendum or fresh general election. It sets out an elaborate scheme to depoliticise judicial appointments and to make the independence of the Courts as nearly as possible absolute. Faithful to understood traditions and usages, it provides for a Parliamentary Executive under limited monarchy. Lastly, but of fundamental significance, it proposes a restriction on all governmental powers under a justiciable Bill of Rights based on the European Convention, but somewhat strengthened.

It is not necessarily a paradox that the party proposing the most radical constitutional change, through dissolution of the present incorporating union of Scotland with England and its replacement with a partnership of equals within the European Community, nevertheless proposes a draft constitution for this independent Scotland in Europe which would guarantee strong elements of constitutional continuity from the present. On these proposals, the form of self-government in Scotland would, as it should, be instantly recognisable as government within the traditions of governance tested by experience in these islands over four centuries and perhaps more. Such a respect for tradition is, I believe, another practical necessity of constitutionalism. The structure established by and the limits prescribed in the constitution have to be meaningful to the people whose constitution it is. At least, they have to be so if democracy is to have any chance. For democracy requires that the popular exercise of power is an intelligent one made by persons who understand the constitution within which they are working. And that entails in effect that the wisdom of many generations tested out in constitutional experience has to be gladly accepted as a limit on the ingenuity and inventiveness of any particular moment.

The important truth that all constitutions presuppose and depend on tradition and custom rather than on acts of momentary will is another of the discoveries of the Scottish Enlightenment, particularly well articulated by David Hume. It used to be regarded, not unjustly, as a special gift of political conservatism to common political wisdom. This makes it all the stranger that the Conservative Party under Mrs Thatcher appears to have abandoned it in face of an overwhelming commitment to a political ideology, that of the so-called 'enterprise culture'. Mrs Thatcher has even on occasion brought to Scotland a homily for the fathers and brethren of the Kirk in assembly, not to speak of her sundry lectures to obsequious gatherings of her party's faithful. In these interventions she has risked startling the public intelligence with a reading of the Scottish Enlightenment which almost parallels in strangeness and audacity her interpretation of St Francis as a patron saint of Thatcherism or the Good Samaritan as an advertisement for the unique humaneness of unqualified capitalism.

In fact, the present government more than any other in living memory has perfected the skills of what Lord Hailsham used to call an elective dictatorship (his lordship's anguish against such monstrosities having evidently been mightily soothed by regular application of a woolsack to his nether parts). The elective dictatorship is a perversion of democracy and a corruption of constitutionalism. As to democracy, our present electoral system regularly awards a clear and often an overwhelming majority in Parliament to what is no more in the country than – again let me use Lord Hailsham's words – merely the 'largest organised minority'. Disproportional representation denies equality and clothes substantial minorities with powers so unrestricted that they would be dangerous if exercised by bona fide popular majorities. This is true, mark you, at the UK level or that of England alone – recall Mrs Thatcher's remarkably low winning percentage of the vote in 1987. In Scotland it simply parodies itself when a party has to crowd all its unalienated members into the Scottish Office just to make up an administration. And there is something a bit too self-serving about the thesis that it is only fair for Scotland to put up with a minority administration from time to time since England gets her share too when the left is ascendant in Scotland and Wales. You only have to reflect on the impossibility for a party holding a seventh of the English seats to form a British government in order to see the very restricted conception of equity here involved.

All very well, you may say, to criticise the undemocratic quality of the elective dictatorship. But have I not to admit that it is the traditional British way, hallowed by the constitutional usages and hence as constitutionalist as you like; tried and tested by practice even if criticisable from the view point of fancy theories about proportional representation? The fact is anyway contrary to the objection. The British system as it has evolved presupposes that those who exercise power accept and observe largely conventional constraints on the way power is to be exercised. This has functioned as a necessary counterweight to the massive and potentially arbitrary power held by a proclaimedly sovereign Parliament in fact controlled by an executive with a secure majority from a well-whipped party most of whose members depend on the government for their own secure continuation in Parliamentary if not also governmental office. A Prime Minister as dedicated to a single ideological line (and as intolerant of alternative opinions) as the present one can further, during a long period in power, establish a scarcely challengeable personal ascendancy over the whole apparatus of state.

This is not just an abstract or theoretical danger. It is the way we live now. Local Government when found inconvenient has been swept away without inquiry or commission or any attempt to find or establish a consensus. Local taxation in a new form has been thrust upon us, and in Scotland this was initially done without thought that such a thing, done without local popular mandate and otherwise than as part of a uniform UK scheme, was contrary probably to the letter and certainly to the spirit of the Articles of Union increasingly recognised in modern scholarship as the true fundamental constitution of the United Kingdom as a constitutional union. That particular and strong constitutional objection was no doubt mitigated by the carrying of the parallel measure for England and Wales. Yet what very many see as the profoundest injustice still faces us in the garb of legislation, but legislation thrust through Parliament on the say-so of a ministry without any of the normal, traditional and wise prior airing of ideas and problems in the light of suggestions, objections and considerations from all quarters. A whole system of taxation has been substituted for an ancient and admittedly unsatisfactory one by a process which might have been reasonable for some kind of civil emergency, not by the kind of reflective, well deliberated and consensus-seeking measure appropriate to changes of this kind. (I am not naively supposing that oppositions do not or should not oppose; but the really alarming thing was the way in which the government simply defied the idea that it ought to seek a real consensus among its own supporters.)

Most serious of all has been the steady attrition on freedom of speech and of information, and the withering attack on public institutions of free inquiry. . . .

The recently published *Index on Censorship* has driven home all of such a critique of this government's small respect for constitutionalism in the sphere of freedom of information and of opinion-formation. Perhaps even more telling, because yet wider-ranging, is the critique of present British constitutional doctrine and practice which makes up a substantial part of the argument in the *Claim of Right* report itself. The erosion of constitutionalism in the UK exposes the distortions of democracy in a cruel light. Liberties long taken for granted are under threat. The old semi-autonomy of Scottish government within the UK compromise is a thing of the past. There is just one say in the state, and that say goes regardless of the measure of popular support, regardless of restraints traditionally observed in constitutional practice. Whatever be thought of the *Claim*'s proposals and prescriptions, its diagnosis of present ills in Scotland and indeed the UK at large deserve attention in their own right.

What is to be done, then? One possibility from the SNP's point of view is certainly to stand clear of any proposals other than that for independence, or for independence in Europe, and to press these forward in every forum and election available, starting with the elections to the European Parliament in June 1989. From this point of view, there would be serious objections of principle to any proposal for any sort of all-party convention or conversations which did not include the possibility of a resolution in favour of such a constitutional settlement. Notoriously, however, the *Claim of Right* proposed an attempt to establish a more restricted and perhaps more tactical than strategic short-term consensus towards constitutional change in and for Scotland. The proposal was that in favour of convening, with or without the endorsement of Westminster, a Scottish Constitutional Convention consisting of all the Scottish MPs willing to participate, together with appropriate representative others. That Convention was envisaged as settling after careful debate a proposal for the future constitution and governance of Scotland, whether inside the UK or outside it. Given the effects of the present electoral system's principle of disproportional representation, the proposal necessarily had undesirable effects in relation to the relative representation of parties in the Convention, and proposals for additional counterweighing members from under-represented parties fell well short of fair proportionality. Further, the electoral opinion represented was that of a quite long past election (that of 1987), not of the present, nor yet of whatever the European elections will reveal.

These are serious deficiencies. They are, moreover, deficiencies of principle if we judge by reference to the ideal of democracy sketched above. What for me justifies the Convention proposal despite the deficiencies and despite their serious character is that it seems to me to offer the best first opportunity to achieve an agreed first step in the way of Scottish constitutional reform. Either before or after the next general election, a plan agreed by a massive Scottish majority and backed by their representatives elected to Parliament will have been determined. If in these circumstances no reform were forthcoming from Westminster, there would be a serious crisis for democracy and the conditions for a deeper recourse to popular sovereignty would have been summoned into being. The Westminster reply, if it were made, that Scotland must either secede or remain in an unreformed incorporating union would certainly polarise the issue in a manner eminently fit for recourse to a referendum in Scotland at a point at which it had been made clear beyond doubt and across party lines that no serious middle way was available for consideration within the time scale of the crisis.

For myself, I seriously doubt if it would come to that. Just conceivably Mrs Thatcher might choose to remain as implacably opposed to any devolutionary reforms as she is now. But it is open to question whether she could then still command support in party, parliament or perhaps even palace. I strongly believe in the importance of an initial establishment of a Scottish Parliament upon terms of the broadest consensus available, even if such must necessarily fall short of that which the SNP will at the same time propose in the elections it contests.

This view is fairly open to attack as nothing more than advocacy of 'back to gradualism', back to a policy which many hold to have been discredited by the experience of the Scotland Act and the 1979 referendum. Such an attack I regard as wholly to the point but also wholly wrong. For myself, I am an unrepentant gradualist. Gradualism is an all but inevitable corollary of constitutionalism, but also of a commitment to democracy, for we should seek to go at the speed of the greatest majority in promoting constitutional change. On reflection after ten years, I think that what was discredited in 1979 was an insufficient gradualism, a half-hearted gradualism. I remember Jo Grimond challenging members of the SNP during the debates about devolution to promise that we would work for ten years within the framework of a Scottish Assembly, before again raising the issue of full independence as a concrete policy proposal (as distinct from an ultimate aim). The idea got short shrift then. Ten years on, we in the SNP can say that we did not sully ourselves with compromise. We also did not have an assembly of any, however inadequate, sort all these ten years. It is not certain that we would, had we been more openly accommodating to ideas of that sort. It is certain that we have had nothing as things have been. One's deepest doubt has to be that Scotland will go on having no democratic forum of legislation and government if those who most wish most in the way of self-government find themselves unable to strike compromises with those who will go some way, but not the whole way yet.

– ON PRESENT DISCONTENTS –

It is not hard to see why the view I just stated may be challenged. The trouble is the gap which is left between the principles stated as premises and the practical conclusion argued for, namely the setting up of a constitutional convention as proposed in the *Claim of Right* and subsequently set in motion by the Campaign for a Scottish Assembly. After all, if the arguments of principle start out by being grounded in democratic equality, it has to be said that the departure from proportionality is considerable. Those in the SNP who have lately argued that the convention ought to be directly elected for the purpose can rightly appeal both to precedent and to the principle of the thing, as well as to the SNP's own historical commitment to the idea of setting up a convention. Further, it can fairly be said that a constitutional convention in the full sense ought to be preparing proposals which may ultimately be put to the sovereign people in a referendum as the most appropriate test of popular approval. Finally, it has to be acknowledged that so long as what is proposed is revision or alteration of the constitution of a United Kingdom of which Scotland is to remain a part, one cannot either upon democratic or upon constitutionalist grounds, to say nothing of elementary fairness, assert a right to impose change without the consent of the whole body politic in some form or another.

These thoughts at the very least require some admission of fault on the part of at least one member of the team who drafted the *Claim*. To put the point plainly, while I for my part do believe we were correct in supposing that the greatest care was called for in the framing of convention proposals if these were to be capable of winning the participation of the Labour Party, yet I now have to say also that I at least ought to have contemplated yet more carefully the question what would be sticking points for other parties, particularly the SNP, particularly in the light of its established approach to issues of democracy and of constitutionalism. Whether Labour could ever have settled for anything less than the terms of the *Claim* is far from clear; that more has been asked of the SNP than its officers and tacticians are willing to give is now clear also.

Let me not seek to disguise or to excuse this fault. Still I shall argue on the other hand that the goal we set is a good one. Somehow, some day, we have to find a way of bringing together all those who desire home rule in Scotland, under circumstances which fundamentally challenge the right of governments to continue to override the popular will here. Nothing but a massively majoritarian endorsement of some concrete proposal for workable change can un-jam the present constitutional log-jam. Certainly, this might give rise to charges of double-thinking, even duplicity, on the part of the SNP if it appears to be pretending to endorse a devolutionary or quasi-federal proposal while it is at the same time known to be favouring independence in Europe.

To that, and to the horror of so many in the party over any blurring of the ultimate end, there is I believe a simple reply. There is surely no reason for the SNP ever to campaign electorally on anything other than the plain theme of its well-known policy as that which will be mandated by a sufficient majority vote for the party's candidates. But there is another question to which it is not defeatist to seek a ready answer. That is the question what the SNP would demand and would support politically in the not unlikely event of a repeat of some variant on the 1987 election result, that is, a massive defeat for the Conservatives in Scotland, an increase in SNP support falling short of a majority even of Westminster seats, far less of votes, and the balance of the votes and seats split between Democrats and Labour with a probable large predominance for Labour. Whether the UK Government formed after such an election were Conservative, Labour or some sort of coalition, we should require clarity as to interpretation of the Scottish result. A highest common factor of a home rule scheme worked out well ahead of time by the proposed convention would answer that question.

Some will say that the very act of working out such a scheme would so dilute the SNP's commitment and demoralise its workers that it would be counter-productive. I doubt it. Further, when one takes it the other way and speculates on the morale and drawing power of a party which appears to have walked away from the attempt to articulate an all Scotland consensus as to one workable scheme, one is left doubting whether the course of non-participation in the convention is not the course which incurs by far the greater damage. I am sure it is. I admit some measure of fault in the *Claim*'s proposals, given the severe strain they cause for the SNP. But I have to conclude still that, in terms of Scotland's good, the greater fault is in non-participation. I hope it will not prove permanent.

Church of Scotland

From a report issued in 1989 by the Church and Nation Committee of the Church of Scotland, reproduced in a booklet edited by Jock Stein (1989, pp. 14–23).

. . .

The Church of Scotland can only make a distinctive and effective contribution to the current debate about the government of Scotland if it grounds its position in its own historic theological and constitutional convictions as a national Kirk within the Reformed tradition. . . . The heroism of a Reformed Church derives from its unflinching commitment to fundamental principle. Underlying the proper party political debate and electoral contexts on the question of the government of Scotland, there is a basic constitutional question which it is proper for the Church to address.

– THE CLAIM OF PRINCIPLE –

It is the Committee's contention that the present crisis in the democratic control of Scottish affairs cannot be understood or dealt with apart from a study of how this crisis has arisen, constitutionally and historically. Only in this way can the issues of truth be perceived that are the heart of the crisis and a way forward be found to the creation of a Scottish democracy. It is a crisis that is more apparent than real, according to some protagonists who oppose any form of devolution. It would be truer to say that it is a crisis which is more real than apparent. It is a crisis within the constitutional foundations of Scotland and the United Kingdom. For those with eyes to see, it is apparent within the present public concern over the direction of Scottish education, the leadership of Scottish cultural institutions, the financing and autonomy of local government, the lack of local control of key parts of the Scottish economy and the failure of the British constitution and government within Scotland to reflect the electoral preferences of the Scottish people. The crisis is real in that it involves a clear conflict between totally opposing notions of sovereignty in the Scottish and English constitutional traditions; a conflict made apparent by the polarising tendencies in British society in the 1980s but always present and underlying the relationship between the two countries over many centuries. In his 1976 Richard Dimbleby Lecture Lord Hailsham, the former Lord Chancellor, described the British/English view of state sovereignty as absolute in theory but, until recently, tolerable in practice, and now no longer even tolerable in practice: the British state has become an 'elective dictatorship'. From a Scottish constitutional and theological perspective this English constitutional tradition of state absolutism has always been unacceptable in theory. It is now intolerable in practice. The present unwritten British constitution, founded on the notion of the absolute sovereignty of the British Parliament, offers Scotland no constitutional guarantees over the democratic control of its own affairs, only the frail assurances of political convention and statute laws than can be repealed. Under the existing constitution no Scottish Assembly would be secure from being over-ruled by a British government in Scottish Affairs. The principle of sovereignty in the present constitution cannot conceive of such guarantees for a Scottish Assembly and the present government opposes all moves in that direction. That is the new situation we find ourselves in as a nation within the UK in the late twentieth century. It is that historic problem in its latest manifestation that we must address as a national Church, in the terms of our own theological and constitutional tradition of Reformed thought and practice.

– A Crisis of Principle –

Professor T. F. Torrance has well set out the theological and philosophical nature of the British constitutional crisis in his essay *Juridical Law and Physical Law* (Torrance, 1982). In his foreword to this essay, Lord Mackay of Clashfern, now the Lord Chancellor, stated:

> . . . Professor Torrance identifies two different approaches to the nature of law and sovereignty in Western thought. He argues for the view that all human law-making is dependent on the objective reality of Almighty God for its validity. This divine Justice underpins natural law, in its moral sense, and the fundamental law of written constitutions or a Bill of Rights which in turn provide binding legal norms for the statute laws of parliament and thus limit the state's sovereignty.

A radically different approach can be found in the writings of nineteenth-century English legal theorists like John Austin who argued that all authority within the state is dependent on the will of a sovereign ruler constrained by no equal or superior power. This view of the source of law profoundly influenced the development of the British constitution and its operation in this century. It held that all law is ultimately reduced to statute law passed by a Parliament invested with absolute sovereignty. Analysing the rejection in the British constitutional tradition of the notion of fundamental law and legal norms binding on the state in favour of the prevailing view that law is only the laws which are enacted by a sovereign legislative body, a theory known as 'legal positivism', Professor Torrance concludes:

> Lord Hailsham has reached the conclusion that 'our constitution is wearing out', for its central defects, which consist in the absolute powers we confer on our sovereign body, are gradually coming to outweigh its merits. I am convinced he is right, but I wish to make the further point that a constitution such as ours, with legal positivism built into it, is a scientific as well as a legal anachronism, for it rests upon a theoretical basis which has been tested and found wanting, and from which our science in its astonishingly successful understanding of the rational structure of the universe . . . has had to move far away.
> (pp. 20–1)

Just as the theory that the physical laws of natural science impose only an arbitrary working order on a random universe has been abandoned under the weight of evidence that they are in fact derived from the inherent rational order already existing within the created universe, so the similar notion in theory behind the British constitution, that law is only those laws that a sovereign Parliament may arbitrarily impose on society, must give way to the realisation that Parliamentary legislation can only derive its legitimacy from a more fundamental law constituting and thus limiting the state and its sovereignty. . . . Considered in the light of this analysis of the philosophical roots of the present British constitution, it can be seen that the crisis of the democratic control of Scottish affairs is fundamentally a crisis of principle. Not only is the British constitution proving unable to respond to the political reality of Scottish nationhood. Its theoretical basis is also seriously put into question. Any new constitutional settlement to ensure the democratic control of Scottish affairs through a Scottish Assembly must be built upon philosophical foundations that are more coherent and credible than the notions which underpin the existing British constitution; foundations that are more faithful to the constitutional nature of things in the divine Justice to which under God we are bound.

What is termed the British constitution is in fact the English constitutional tradition in which the doctrine of the 'divine right of kings' to rule without constraining constitutional limits was transferred to the English and then later, after 1707, the British Parliament, and reformulated as the

English constitutional principle of the absolute sovereignty of 'the Crown-in-Parliament'. As Lord President Cooper, perhaps the greatest Scots lawyer this century, stated, 'The principle of the unlimited sovereignty of Parliament is a distinctively English principle which has no counterpart in Scottish Constitutional law' [see MacCormick, 1998]. Despite the contribution made in the seventeenth century to this doctrine of absolute sovereignty by James VI and I, and his son, Charles I, it was never accepted by their fellow countrymen in Scotland; as Samuel Rutherford's great work *Lex Rex* testifies, with its Scriptural case for the limited authority of the king subject to the rule of law and a sovereignty invested by God in the people. In practice, in the twentieth century, this prevailing English principle in the British constitution has meant the growing power of the government in office rather than of Parliament itself.

. . .

The Scottish constitutional tradition, in both its secular and religious streams of thought and practice, has consistently favoured . . . a 'limited' rather than an 'absolutist' notion of sovereignty. Historically, this meant that the ruler was seen as subject to the rule of law and consent of the people. In the original 'Claim of Right' made by the Scottish Parliament in 1689, it stated that King James VII was deposed because he violated 'the fundamental constitution of this Kingdom, and altered it from a legal limited monarchy, to an arbitrary despotic power'. The ruler's sovereignty was seen as relative to the legal limits set on his powers by the nation's fundamental constitution, a bulwark against arbitrary despotic power. In the Scottish constitutional tradition political sovereignty lay ultimately in the people and not the state, both existing under the sovereignty of God. Professor Torrance's call for the re-moulding of our British constitution and political institutions on grounds other than those of the English theory of unlimited parliamentary sovereignty is one that can be traced consistently from the Scottish mediaeval constitutional tradition, through the thinking of the leading Scottish Reformation constitutional theorists and documents, and on into the constitutional writings that arose out of the 1843 Disruption controversy and its final resolution in 1929. For example, at the time of the Scottish Wars of Independence, the Declaration of Arbroath of 1320 asserted that the King of Scots ruled subject to the assent of the community of the realm. This note of limited sovereignty was echoed in the constitutional thought of the great Scottish mediaeval scholar John Mair who wrote that 'the whole people must be above the king'. It can also be heard in Sir David Lindsay's 'Satire of the Three Estates', where the King is rebuked not only by Divine Correction but also by John the Commonweal, a figure representing the people. At the time of the Scottish Reformation and its aftermath, leading reformers further developed the argument for the limited sovereignty of the ruler. John Knox declared the God-given responsibility of the common people for the national reformation of religion in the face of idolatrous secular superiors, in his biblically-charged 'Letter to the Commonality of Scotland'. George Buchanan argued for the Scottish constitutional tradition that kings could be deposed by the sovereign people if they failed to rule according to the law, in his humanist treatise on the principles of Scottish government *Dialogus De Iure Regni Apud Scotos*. Andrew Melville reminded James VI of the divine limits on his kingship when he stated, 'There are two kings and two kingdoms in Scotland. There is Christ Jesus the King and his Kingdom the Kirk, whose subject King James the Sixth is, and of whose kingdom not a king, nor a lord, nor a head, but a member'. The National Covenant of 1638 was a national protest about religious policy which also contained 'a constitutional demand for the rule of law' in Scotland. Mention has already been made of . . . the 1689 Claim of Right's description of Scotland's fundamental constitution as that of a legal limited Monarchy. The second 'Claim of Right' in Scottish history was passed by the General Assembly of the Church of Scotland in 1842, on the eve of the Disruption. The notion that the Church's spiritual life and government stood outside the sovereignty of the British parliament and its legislative powers was the constitutional principle that undergirded its claims for the rights of church and nation in Scotland. Commenting in the decades after the Disruption on its underlying causes, a diverse range of writers such as the philosopher Professor J. F. Ferrier, the churchman Dr James Begg and the advocate Alexander Taylor Innes all recognised its constitutional nature. The alien English constitutional doctrine of the unlimited sovereignty of the British Parliament in matters of church and state was the rock on which Scotland's key national institution, the established Kirk, came to grief.

. . .

By recovering its own historic commitment to the theological and constitutional principle of the limited, relative and differentiated nature of sovereignty within society, and by further arguing that the state's sovereignty must now be relative to and limited by the binding rule of fundamental constitutional law, the Church of Scotland will be open to an ecumenical and international dialogue on the question of the democratic control of national affairs. In the Netherlands, for example, Christians from the Reformed and Roman Catholic traditions have found common ground in their complementary theories that sovereignty should be limited and distributed among several sectors in Dutch national life. The Dutch Reformed tradition developed the principle of 'sphere sovereignty' to establish the autonomy and sovereignty of the various social, economic, and political spheres within society; a principle that also can be discerned in the Kirk's own Constitution with its recognition of the autonomy of the church and the state 'within their respective spheres' (Article VI). The Dutch Roman Catholic tradition embraced the principle of 'subsidiarity' which states that 'affairs that can be managed by lower institutions of the government should not be taken over by higher institutions' (den Hollander, 1979, pp. 167–8). By bringing these two traditions and principles together, their mutually compatible approach to the question of the proper distribution of power and democratic control in a complex, pluralist society is enabling Reformed and Roman Catholic Christians in Europe to co-operate and unite in common Christian concern for national affairs. Similarly, as a European nation, Scotland has been enriched by the shared insights of different Christian traditions in many areas of church and national life. Convergence of thinking on the constitutional question may prove possible as well. . . . Further ecumenical dialogue may establish a common commitment to a Scottish democracy grounded in the principle of limited sovereignty, where state power and democratic control might be distributed among several institutional levels of government, made secure under written constitutional guarantees. Such a principle is compatible both with the Catholic principle of subsidiarity and a modern version of the historic Reformed doctrine of 'interposition'. Derived from Calvin's Biblical expositions, and developed by Knox in his letter to the Scottish Lords, the doctrine of interposition stated that the intermediate levels of authority in society, the lords and 'lesser magistrates' interposed between the people and the ruler, possessed a proper authority to resist unlawful rule by the state. It could be further developed today in a way that parallels the modern recognition of the need in a healthy democracy for 'mediating struc-tures' in government and society between the individual and the state.

Church and Nation: A Catholic View

Tim Duffy

From Stein (1989, pp. 8–10). Duffy was a member of the Roman Catholic Justice and Peace Commission, and represented the Roman Catholic Church in the Constitutional Convention.

. . .

For Scottish Christians who are interested in the destiny of their own country there would seem to be only one question that needs to be asked: Who is my Lord? This is a question of sovereignty and from this question surely all the rest flows. 'No one can be the slave of two masters' puts the choice more sharply (note that it is masters, not politics or religion). It is part of the legacy of western dualism that we talk about 'sacred' and 'secular' as if they had different subjects. The sacred part of us is concerned to save its personal soul by means of religion while the secular part of us engages in accommodation with the world through the muddy compromise of politics. By and large, politicians are too timid to disclaim religious allegiance and [they] attempt to gain religious approval of their policies. If, however, religion presumes to criticise some political act or programme it is accused of improperly mixing religion and politics and decried as a tool of the political opposition. Yet if our faith is to be the expression of what Paul Tillich called our 'ultimate concern', then our religious interaction will inevitably have political consequences. Especially at a time when political ideology aspires to the same status of revealed truth and dogma it is all the more important to debunk the pseudomysticism of the Church being concerned with the purely spiritual. It is no less important to avoid reducing the gospel to this or that political ideology. If our faith involves a call to conversion it cannot happen in solitary splendour. We live socially, through and in history to what is beyond history.

And so while for some people, the problem of religion and politics remains as a dualism, like a circus acrobat astride two horses, it is actually a question of sovereignty, a question of choosing a master.

. . .

It might well be asked what all this has to do with the current debate about Scottish self-determination. I think it is necessary to explain the background to forestall objections of confusing religion and politics. The history and culture of Scotland have been indelibly marked, for good and ill, by the various strands of religion woven into its very fabric. [This] cannot help but remind me of the confessional strand to which I have been consigned by the accident of birth and the recurrent gift of faith. I am in short a Papist! I like the term not least because it is an insult of history and persecution needing to be redeemed. Where confessions describe themselves by the manner of their Church government it is as accurate as Presbyterian, Episcopalian or Congregationalist. Catholic is permissible internally but it is insultingly exclusive (at its unecumenical best it turns up as 'non-catholic'). Roman Catholic always seems to me somehow illogical, a dangerous mixture of religion and politics which Dante called the evil dowry of Constantine. Over several centuries Romanitas regularised the Celtic Church. During the Wars of Independence Scots bishops supported Robert the Bruce despite his excommunication by a papacy resident in Avignon. And from the Reformation legalised persecution was based less on doctrinal than political reliability or orthodoxy, notably demonstrated in the century after the first Claim of Right. For their adherence to a Jacobite cause that did not really merit Scots' loyalty, a form of belief was proscribed by law. And the fear of Rome rule, either directly or through the side door of Ireland, has been the chord harped upon by the no-popery bigot ever since. One of the best ways of exorcising this fear would be to ask Scottish Catholics to define precisely how they are both Scottish and Catholic. There is a body of guidance drawn from the tradition of the Church, especially during the last hundred years, and intensively through the social ferment of the last thirty years, which can be very useful. To deny its usefulness because it is 'popish' would be as foolish as to condemn much modern biblical criticism as 'protestant'. This Catholic Social Teaching is found in papal encyclicals, statements of the Second Vatican Council and statements by bishops at synods and at national conferences. Despite the male, clerical source these materials are increasingly indebted to the advice of specialists in economics, politics and social sciences as well as theology. Increasingly too there is an attempt to understand and to give voice to the victims of injustice.

I have room here only to indicate some of the areas where this social teaching might be properly catholic. . . . Christians have not only the right but the duty to participate in the political life of their country using their talents and abilities. The Church itself, by reason of its role, is not bound to any political system nor identified with any particular political community.

Nevertheless it has the right to speak out when there is flagrant abuse of human rights and when other channels of protest are closed. Political systems must be based on active respect for basic human rights. Those who are in authority must take primary account of the common good, that is all the social conditions which favour the full development of the human personality, since individual human beings are the foundation, the cause and the end of every social institution. This notion of the common good is not to be compromised by ideological, party or partisan interest. The State exists for the benefit of the individual in community, not the other way round. The cultural and ethnic traditions of smaller groups in larger nation states should be respected.

Intervention of government should be at a minimum level necessary for the common good and political power should be exercised at the most appropriate level. This Principle of Subsidiarity is perhaps as near as the papacy gets to 'small is beautiful' and is central to Catholic social teaching on politics. Political power can only be properly exercised where the government has a mandate from the people; indeed the most effective form of government will be that in which authority is accountable to an informed and participatory electorate. Attempts to govern or hold on to power without such a mandate are unjust and frustrating. To these statements one might well add a resolution from the 1989 European Ecumenical Assembly. This Assembly, convened jointly by all the European Churches produced a final document which gained the support of over 95 per cent of those present. One of its sections stated:

> There are in Europe small and also larger national groups whose right to their own culture, religion and political system is not recognised, or only to a very limited degree. We support the efforts of these peoples and national groups towards self-determination and promotion of their own culture and religion.

The problems confronting Scotland then are problems of sovereignty, not simply in a legal sense, but in the basic question 'Who is my Lord?' Our response reveals our vocations as people and as Christians. The answers will not come in the clear-cut terms of party ideology, but rather in the discovered witness of our lives.

Scottish Trades Union Congress Women's Committee

From a submission made by the Committee to the Constitutional Convention's Working Group on Women's Issues, August 1989.

. . .

– The Working Pattern of the Assembly –

The present political system is constructed in such a way as to virtually exclude women from participation. In a society where the main domestic responsibility for child and dependent care lies with women, it is not unsurprising that there are so few women MPs or Local Government elected representatives.

This responsibility, or assumption that the responsibility is a woman's, is unlikely to disappear in the next few years, if even within this century. A Scottish Assembly should, from the outset, therefore, make itself accessible to women. This means that the hours of the Assembly should be suitable to women to allow maximum participation. We do not think, therefore, that the Assembly should meet in constant plenary session, nor in the evenings as is the case of Westminster at the moment. Rather, we believe that the work pattern for elected representatives should be such as to allow them to bridge the diversity of their responsibilities and workload.

We would, therefore, make the following suggestions:

1. that the work of the Assembly's elected representative is a full-time job;
2. that the work of the Assembly should be carried out over a 5 day period, Monday to Friday, during normal working hours, 9–5 pm;
3. that the majority of work of the Assembly should be carried out in Committee stage;
4. that the Committees should, given the perceived need to receive submissions and oral evidence from different organisations and interest groups in Scotland, meet in different geographical locations

(possibly seeking some accommodation within existing Local Government Offices – a Sub-Office of the Assembly perhaps?);

5. that the Committee work should be carried out over 3 days each working week;
6. that elected representatives should work 2 days in Constituencies;
7. that the Assembly should meet once every 4–6 weeks in plenary, at which time Westminster MPs would be able to participate;
8. that through the Assembly administration, there should be regular liaison with Westminster MPs;
9. that the Assembly recesses should coincide with Scottish school holidays.

. . .

– PROVISION OF CHILDCARE ALLOWANCES AND/OR – FACILITIES BY THE ASSEMBLY

. . . [C]hild/dependant care is one of the main domestic responsibilities of women, which affects both their ability to enter or progress in the labour market, as well as to enter or progress within politics. We would, therefore, suggest:

1. that childcare/dependant allowance be available for elected representatives if, without which, they would be unable to participate equally of fully;
2. that crèche facilities and/or childcare/dependants' allowances (whichever is more feasible and practical) should be available to members of the public who select to submit evidence to Committees or attend plenary sessions. For example, anyone with a dependent elderly relative would require to receive an allowance, whereas it may be more practical for a woman with young children to seek crèche facilities. Travelling expenses should also be paid, possibly along the lines operating presently for potential jurors in Scottish courts.

. . .

– Electoral Arrangements/Systems and – their Implications for Women

. . . [M]embership of the Scottish Assembly should represent women and men equally – i.e. 50 per cent of elected representatives should be women and 50 per cent men.

The Westminster model would not, therefore, be appropriate to a Scottish Assembly. We would suggest, rather, that each Constituency should be entitled to return two elected representatives to the Assembly: one woman, one man. Voting could be facilitated by introducing two voting papers – a category for women, who would reflect the different political parties; and a category for men, who again would reflect the different political parties.

If current Parliamentary Constituencies were changed, this principle would still apply, and, indeed, it would work if PR was introduced. If Constituencies were changed to area groups, two categories for voting would still be applicable.

. . .

– Women's Ministry –

We believe that the Assembly should establish a Women's Ministry or Department, the main aims of which would be to:

1. ensure that proposed legislation took account of the views and needs of women in Scotland;
2. ensure that such legislation was implemented;
3. monitor all departments to ensure that each reflected a women's dimension, both in operation and outlook;
4. consult widely and liaise with organisations and groups representing women in Scotland.

– Equal Opportunities Commission –

. . . [C]onsideration might be given to the possible establishment of a Scottish Equal Opportunities Commission, with substantially greater powers and responsibilities than exist at the present time. We would also wish to see a Scottish Women's Commission established, which would work closely with both the Scottish Assembly's Women's Ministry and the Scottish Equal Opportunities Commission.

. . .

– SCOTTISH YOUTH FORUM –

We believe that the Assembly should establish a Forum which can ensure that the views, needs and aspirations of young people in Scotland are fully considered and taken account of in the work of the Assembly. This could assist in making government more accessible, attractive and relevant to the young people of Scotland.

Independence in Europe

Jim Sillars

From a pamphlet of this title published by the Scottish National Party in 1989. Sillars had been elected SNP MP for Glasgow Govan at the by-election in 1988, and was also vice-president of the party. Previously he had been elected as Labour MP for South Ayrshire at a by-election in 1970; at that time, he was opposed to home rule, but in the early 1970s he became an enthusiastic supporter. In 1975, he led a breakaway from the Labour Party (the Scottish Labour Party), and narrowly lost his seat in 1979 (Drucker, 1978). Independence in Europe was the policy of the breakaway party after 1976. He joined the SNP in 1980.

– Introduction –

What is to be Scotland's status within the new Europe? That question now lies at the heart of the Scottish political debate. Without a doubt, the SNP policy of Independence in Europe has set the agenda.

All other political parties are scrambling to find or invent a 'European dimension' to their position on the constitution, in an effort to answer what is the unassailable logic of full member state status. In essence the whole issue boils down to whether Scotland will have a full and equal say in the European policies which will shape our future, or be a province which, at best, will enhance our lobbying ability and, as is likely to be the case, remain as we are, powerless, lacking real influence.

. . .

In the 1970s, the devolution decade, very few people had come to terms with what joining Europe really meant. We still argued with minds moulded by the imperial developments of the 1930–60 period during which England remained at the centre of the complex of nations which evolved from Empire into Commonwealth.

Now, as the European Community starts on a crucial stage of its development, and as other parts of Europe including the Soviet bloc countries begin to fashion new reelations, we have to step out of the old mould. Free ourselves from the constrictive views imposed by the Union set up in 1707 in a different age, and consider and act upon the future, with its new concepts of national relations, much wider and healthier political unions more respectful of small nations, and more relevant forms of government. We cannot allow the past to cling to us while the future beckons.

Turning from the past to the future does of necessity involve looking afresh at old emotional ties. The London establishment did that when deciding it had to find a European role as a substitute for loss of Empire. That meant a significant loosening of the economic and political ties with those who had felt themselves to be, and accepted as, part of the 'British family', the Australians, Canadians and New Zealanders in particular. The London establishment did not hesitate. It turned to Europe, downgraded the Commonwealth, and ever since has dealt with our former kith and kin as friendly but nevertheless foreign powers in the field of trade and finance.

So when that same London establishment and its pro-consuls in Scotland tell us to stick to the old union, reminding us of the years locked in a common embrace with England, and beat the emotional drum of 'Britishness', remember that in addressing their own basic national interests they did not hesitate to put such feelings aside when themselves considering the European option.

– FROM POWERLESS PROVINCE TO A STATE WITH –
POWER AND INFLUENCE

It is essential to compare Scotland's position today, or even in a devolved relationship with the UK, with the position we would have as a full member state of the Community.

Although a distinctive polity, with its own set of economic, social and political values, and priorities, Scotland is today governed by the decisions of another nation, England. In the arena of Europe, Scotland has no means of asserting its national interests, nor of making its own distinctive contribution to the development of Community policy.

Scotland lies on the geographical periphery of the European Community. We are also on its political periphery. We can do nothing about the former in physical terms, but we can and must act to move ourselves from the outer fringe of European politics to the centres of decision making. It is crucial to make such a move because of the creation of the single market in 1992. This is not simply because the internal market is a significant event in itself, which it is, but because it sets in train a process of change in the nature of national sovereignty that cannot be averted or reversed, and which will have a profound effect upon the lives of everyone in the nations of the Community.

There cannot be an internal single market without reference to the role of currencies, monetary policies, fiscal policies, and social policies. These elements of political economy are as crucial to the ultimate working of a genuine internal market as are the elimination of physical and technical obstacles to trade. They will start to loom larger on the political/economic agenda as the current measures inherent in 1992 start to take effect over the next decade, and as the companies and institutions engaged in operating the internal market come to realise that common answers must be found, and pressure is brought to bear on governments to take further steps towards making free trade within the Community a reality.

The crucial factor about 1992 is that it launches an irreversible process of change in the direction of a genuine European economy.

How monetary, fiscal and social policy issues are to be solved is not readily apparent today. The Community is still a diverse grouping of states who, although having surrendered sovereignty in certain areas, retain the bulk of sovereignty in their own hands. Moreover, as well as diversity there is disparity in stages of economic development, and also in political outlook. The 1992 package is relatively easy compared with the next steps that challenge the Community. While in agreeing to the Single European Act the member states have accepted they no longer individually control certain aspects of policy, such as border controls, technical standards and professional standards, they did so knowing that the main instruments of economic power would still lie within their hands individually.

Without a Scottish government in full control of our economy, and having developed its own strategy, it is not possible to say what attitude the Scottish state would strike at the present time; nor is it possible to forecast the exact cast of Scottish attitudes, say, ten years down the line from here. What can be said with certainty is that when the Community comes to address the thorny problems of completing the internal market by further attempts to derogate from member state sovereignty, Scotland will either play a full part in the debate and decision-making as a member state, or we shall be in the familiar position of watching helplessly while others decide what is going to happen to us.

It will matter nothing that Scotland is a small state so long as it is a member state. The moves required in the fields of monetary, direct fiscal and new areas of social policy will require amendments to the basic Treaties. These must be approved unanimously. While the development of the Community must be on the basis of give and take, the future decisions on areas of current residual sovereignty over economic policy will require the most careful examination before any government agrees. If any set of proposals would prove injurious to Scotland's economic future, then our member state government would have the power to block them, and use that power to achieve amendments suitable to our perceived position.

I am not suggesting that we should approach the whole European issue in a negative 'veto-minded' attitude. Despite the impression given by Mrs Thatcher of constantly screeching at and wrestling with our partners, the fact is that the Community works by creating consensus. The Community does not exist to destroy any one of its member states. The national interests of all are taken into account when policies are put forward by the Commission and considered by the Council of Ministers.

. . .

Those outwith the power structure may lobby through setting up information offices, which help delegations make their point to this or that body within the Community. But by definition lobbyists can only cajole and plead, and without sanctions available are kept outside when the doors close and decision-makers decide. When the real players gather round the top table of the Council of Ministers, it is only member states that count. They exercise power.

– [THE ROLE OF REGIONAL POLICY] –

Scotland has been unable to withstand the centralising power of Britain's common market, with the southern centre having stripped away much indigenous control of our economy. Now that we face life in a Community whose greater centralising power will be generated, we must look objectively at our position and seek to produce instruments of policy which create a counter-pull to centralist forces.

It is too pat an answer to say that we must look to regional policy to achieve this. A cool look at British regional policy over many years shows why. While it has helped to mitigate the effects of market forces, British regional policy has not prevented the steady loss of manufacturing or the loss of indigenous control.

Of course, it can be argued that without regional policy the Scottish economy today would be a hollow shell. That is true. But remember that the policy was never meant to be a last ditch safeguard. It was always meant to retain indigenous control and bring in, as additional support, new industries which gave strength to the regional or national economy. 'Regeneration' has always been the key word.

European regional policy need not fall into the same 'last ditch – shore it up' category. But if it is to be more successful, then we have to see why the

British policy, which tried genuinely to re-create industrial and power centres, ended up with Scotland as a branch factory economy with diminished internal control and strength. Perhaps the main weakness of British regional policy has been that it was never formulated in the nation or region which suffered, but in the centre whose growth and increased power created the disparity. The centre, with no first hand experience, was unlikely to produce the solution. Another weakness has lain in the insistence by the centre of uniformity of aid packages whereas each 'regional' area presents different problems requiring varied solutions.

This is not an argument for abandoning the attempt to create regional policies. But it is a call for a more acute examination of the issue, and an acceptance of the fact that power to shape policy is of the utmost importance. It is also a call to acknowledge that a regional policy which is based upon grant-induced development as its main weapon can only be partially successful, and can leave an economy lacking in the quality of investment that guarantees a truly regenerative effect.

. . .

– The Internationalisation of Scotland –

[In assuming Presidency of the Council of Ministers], the Scottish government would not only experience the invigoration of conducting its own business with its partners, but would require to undertake the exacting task of conducting Community business on frequent occasions, including arranging and chairing the summit meetings, which is a Presidency responsibility.

The whole prospect represents a new and different dimension to the administration and diplomatic life of Scotland. It would lift us into a different league, calling for the production and use of skills long buried in our provincial soil. A by-product of such an involvement is of course the experience gained, the foreign contacts made, and the knowledge and identification of Scotland when as President we dealt with the international community on behalf of the European Community.

Of necessity Scotland's people, politicians and media would be compelled to cast our intellectual net much wider than hitherto. The issues that we look at now, as bystanders who know it does not matter what we think, would be central in the sense that we would be required to hold views on them and to cast votes in Europe about them. We would be involved as never before in the big issues, the formulation and testing of big ideas on the future of Europe.

. . .

For Scotland's people and their political class this will be a transformation. In the recent past it has been suspected that some of our more talented politicians have been less than attracted by the thought of being big fish in a small Scottish independent pool. For them the bigger stage of the United Kingdom, as represented by London with its international connections, was much more attractive. But independence in Europe is different, especially when for most the prospect in London is of permanent opposition, winning debates, losing votes, and always denied the chance to bring their talents directly to bear on policy.

Another group to benefit in terms of stimulation to its professional involvement is the Scottish Civil Service. The Scottish Office departments contain people of great talent whose energies and vision are contained within the parochial boundaries set for the Secretary of State by the Prime Minister. They are provincialised, not because they are provincially minded but because that is the only area in which they have a permit to operate.

Serving a member state within the Community, which would call for a metropolitan outlook and a wide range of skills from the technical to the diplomatic, would represent the greatest challenge ever to the Scottish Office departments. These would become departments of state with substantially greater responsibility in Scotland and the Community. New areas of intellectual challenge would emerge in defence and international relations.

. . .

– SOVEREIGN POWER AT HOME –

[T]here is a false notion that Europe now deals with the bulk of policy. Substantial domestic sovereignty remains with member states, and they exercise control over a large range of issues without reference of any kind to the Community. The Community law only applies to those areas marked out by the Treaties. The principal, but not the only, one of these is trade, and thus membership secures the right of access for Scottish goods and services. But all non-Treaty fields of policy are dealt with by members as independent states.

Therefore, having secured itself against separation from its main markets in the Community by member state status, an independent Scotland would have enormous scope at home for pursuing policies based upon our people's own ideas and values.

It is not the European Community that is imposing the poll tax; setting out to destroy the Scottish Development Agency; refusing to upgrade our rail infrastructure; mishandling the oil revenue; driving our young people onto Y[outh] T[raining] schemes of dubious value; failing to produce a training programme to make us fit for the twenty-first century; bankrupting our great universities; attacking the comprehensive basis of our education system; threatening the NHS; cutting family benefit in real terms; failing to address the housing crisis with sufficient resources. All of these, which set out Scotland's case against Thatcherism, are the work of a London government using its domestic sovereign powers.

With Scottish independence in Europe, those domestic sovereign powers are repatriated. They come to vest in a Scottish government, responsible only to the Scottish people, who will surely elect them by proportional representation. None will doubt that a Scottish government using those powers would act very differently from Mrs Thatcher. Thus, not only will Scotland have enhanced political power status within the European Community, we shall have the power to bear directly upon the vexed questions of jobs, housing and poverty which have haunted our society for decades.

. . .

– The David Martin Formula –

David Martin the . . . Labour MEP for Lothians has produced a set of ideas to try and overcome his party's lack of policy for real Scottish representation within the Community. He has argued for a Europe of the regions, and states that while we are waiting for that to happen a Scottish Minister from the [Scottish] Assembly could lead the UK delegation to the Council of Ministers on agriculture, fisheries and oil, and cast the ten UK votes on these policy issues.

A 'Europe of the Regions' is an attractive slogan. It conjures up a Europe which is decentralised yet co-operative, in which there are no states. The problem? It is a nebulous concept. No-one quite knows what it means. No-one, least of all David Martin, can describe it in terms of a practical model. Would a 'Europe of the Regions' be a confederation of the regional/national groupings within the present member states? Would it be a federal structure with a strong central government? When you step outside the confederal or federal structures, no-one has a clue how to get to a 'Europe of the Regions'. Would it require amendments to the Treaties? Would it require the member states to decide unanimously to dissolve themselves and hand power to regions within themselves, or so fundamentally alter the legal bases of the Treaties that they demobilise their own power and influence as states and share it more widely?

There is no chance of that happening in the foreseeable future, particularly as those who have coined the phrase cannot explain it in terms of any substance. As an attitude or expression of the desirable a 'Europe of the Regions' is not to be despised. But without shape or form it cannot be advanced, or even properly examined as to its value. The harsh reality is that it has no place in the present or foreseeable power structures of the Community, from which Scots should not be diverted.

But let us return to his suggestion within the present power structure, of a Scottish Minister for an Assembly leading the UK into the Council of Ministers. It is a proposition bordering on the ludicrous. Can we really be expected to see a Tory cabinet in London handling over its ten votes to a Labourite or Nationalist Assembly Minister? Or even a London Labour cabinet giving the Scots the right to determine how its votes should be cast on oil policy, when such an acceptance would imply Scottish control of oil?

But there is another deep flaw in the Martin formula. He would restrict this Scottish 'leadership' to things he describes as self-evidently Scottish in importance: agriculture, fisheries and oil. But in reality even that small list has to be whittled down. There is no chance of London, Labour or Tory, accepting that the C[ommon] A[gricultural] P[olicy] is a mainly Scottish matter. But leaving that aside, his formula seems to indicate that Scotland has no distinctive position to advance or defend in other vital areas of policy. Finance, Environment, Energy, Steel, Technology, Trade, Transport, Health, Social Policy and Employment! Scotland has distinctive views, reflecting distinctive needs, on these issues which require our distinctive voice and vote. But in the Martin formula the Scots would continue to be represented by a London cabinet answerable not to us, but to a Parliament with a huge English majority.

. . .

– A Word in the Ear of Scottish Business –
and the Trade Union Movement

. . . Scottish independence attained within the Community means no disruption to the trade relations which have been established over many years with both our English and European markets. Scotland will continue as part of the new internal market being created by the 1992 measures. It also means no difference to how we trade with the rest of the world, because our relations there are conducted through the Community. Scottish independence in Europe does mean the end of the political union with England which sees our economic policy dominated by a larger neighbour who frequently has a different set of priorities than those of our smaller nation. The present imposition of punitive interest rates is a case in point.

It does not of course end political and economic co-operation with England, but this will be conducted on a more equal basis within the wider partnership of the Community, rather than by the present lopsided arrangement by which our needs are ignored and our views swamped.

The social union between Scotland and England will be unaffected. That is the easy familiarity with each others' ways, the network of families and friendships, the ease of travel to see each other, the business contacts, and the close working relationship between trade unionists north and south of the border who frequently share a common employer in Britain and, increasingly, with other workers in Europe. Already developing is a new social union with the European Community as a whole.

In terms of economic policy, which is of importance to both trade unionists and business, there are distinct advantages in having an independent government in Europe. We all know that for those engaged in business, particularly the business of exporting, the exchange level of the currency matters. Scotland would be free to do the sensible thing, which is to join the E[uropean] M[onetary] System and thus produce the stability we require at a level of currency valuation suitable to continuity of business and trade effort.

THATCHERISM IN A COLD CLIMATE

David McCrone

From *Radical Scotland* (no. 39, June/July 1989, pp. 8–11). McCrone was a lecturer (now professor) in sociology in Ednburgh University, and convener of the Unit for the Study of Government in Scotland; his ideas are developed further in McCrone (1992).

– WHAT IS 'THATCHERISM'? –

. . .

In the first place, Thatcherism refers to the social movement which mobilised opposition in the late 1970s to Labour rule, a coalition of business groups, traditional bourgeois and disaffected workers. Second, the period from 1979 to the Falklands War (April to June 1982) was one of struggle to consolidate the Thatcher forces inside the Party and the Cabinet. Finally, there is the period of 'consolidated Thatcherism' since 1982, in which a longer term strategy has evolved for restructuring the economy, polity, society and culture of Britain. . . . Ten years on, we can talk of a 'regime' rather than simply a government. Not only has 'Thatcherism' boldly gone where no government has gone before – there are no spheres spared from intervention – but she is credited with recasting the political agenda in such a way that the opposition (both inside and outside the party) finds it impossible to construct a lasting alternative. That this has happened is quite remarkable when one notices that 'Thatcherism' mobilises conflicting strands of thinking. These strands belong to the wider social movement which we can label the New Right.

. . .

The first, and least significant, of these ideological strands has been 'libertarianism', sometimes referred to as 'ethical egoism' or 'rational selfishness'. At the heart of this ideology lay radical notions about being proprietors of ourselves, that no-one – least of all the state – had a right to tell us what to do. 'Doing your own thing' became a political philosophy, and 'market anarchism' an attractive social idea. Certainly, it was vital in the period of the mid-1970s because it seemed to provide an alternative, liberating project to that of an embattled Labour government rapidly running out of steam and ideas.

. . .

In many ways, however, radical economic notions for driving back the state came into conflict with a deeper strand of social or neo-conservative thought. This powerful stream of ideas was quite distinct from 'liberal' thought in most of its forms. Its idea was not to get the state off people's backs, but to reassert the authority of the state. . . . Unlike economic liberals, conservatives were not concerned to produce the minimal state, but to re-establish and extend the power of the state over many aspects of social and political life . . . hence its concern with matters of sex and personal morality, religion, race and family relations. The 'cultural' counter-revolution which has played an important part in Thatcherism derives from conservative, not liberal, thinking.

. . .

The advocacy of the free market was not necessarily at odds with the strong state, because the state was the means whereby the necessary market conditions could be created and protected: the state as the means, the market as the end. More significantly, however, as Thatcherism developed, and particularly after the Falklands War of 1982, it seems that the conservative stream came to prominence.

. . .

A large part of Thatcher's success south of the border derives from the harnessing of these conservative motifs. . . . Its prime success has been in capturing the agenda of British politics, not changing people's hearts and minds. Thatcherism has succeeded in presenting a seemingly coherent game-plan, a vision of the true society, one of small-town, provincial, bourgeois England.

– Is Scotland Different? –

The term which crops up most among those seeking to explain Thatcher's unpopularity in Scotland is 'bewilderment'. Thatcher's upbringing by the Alderman Roberts instilled in her virtues of hard work, self-help and a belief in the immorality of extravagance, virtues which are supposed to have entered the Scottish soul – except in her case they derived from Methodism.

. . .

That Thatcher has a problem in Scotland cannot be denied. . . . Why? There is a substantial body of political science opinion that Scotland simply shares with 'declining' regions like the North of England and Wales a time-lag in industrial prosperity, that Scotland has a surfeit of yesterday's industries, council houses, union members and the like, and that Labour's strength there is ultimately a historic legacy. Scottish Office ministers like to think so too, but it is not a very convincing argument. Certainly, Scotland's share of council housing, manual employment and state 'dependence' are likely to build in for Labour an advantage over the Tories, but these factors do not explain the weakness of the Conservatives in Scotland compared with other 'declining' regions.

The problem with this sort of explanation is that it assumes an automatic transference of social characteristics into political behaviour, a fairly crude 'sociological' explanation which political scientists indulge in from time to time. Nevertheless, it is important to begin our account of Scotland's hostility to Thatcherism with an assessment of material conditions. What is missing from these accounts, though, is any sense of how these character-istics, undoubtedly important, are refracted through the political culture and its associated agenda. And it is the emergence of a distinctive political agenda in Scotland which is the key.

The dominant orthodoxy of the 1950s and 1960s was that politics was about the management of the national economy. The desperate state of Scotland in the post-war years, the collapse of indigenous industry and the need to diversify the economic base brought the state into play as the agent of modernisation quite early on. The embryonic corporate state which Tom Johnston had put together during the war provided the means for state-led economic regeneration, a political goal shared by all political parties, including the Conservatives, to such an extent that it became part of the political 'common sense'. Since the war, the state has played a major part as the corporatist vehicle for modernising Scotland, and collectivism of this sort was approved of by the Right and the Left. The rise of Thatcher and her attack on 'state dependency' came as a rude awakening north of the border. So vital had the role of the state been in economic regeneration that Thatcher's attack on 'state dependency' came to be perceived as an attack on Scotland itself. When the role of the state in the 1950s and 1960s was not a politically contentious issue, then there was little likelihood of one party or the other being perceived as 'anti-Scottish' in ethnic terms. Thatcherism shattered the harmony by politicising all aspects of state activity, and in this respect Scotland had far more to lose than England. And Labour was in a better position to take on the role of protector in this defensive battle, especially through its local government strength.

Of course, in this respect Scotland differed little from the North of England, but was much better equipped in ideological terms to counter the Thatcherite project. Issues of nationality as well as of class were mobilised against this 'alien' attack. And by the late 1970s, the Conservative Party in Scotland was in a remarkably weak state. Thatcherite Toryism fell on stony ground because the historic electoral alliance on which it had depended for more than half a century had collapsed. Right up to the 1950s the Conservative Party in Scotland did much better in electoral terms than its social base allowed. In a country with disproportionately more manual workers and council tenants, the Unionists (as they were) more than held their own. Since the Liberal split over Home Rule for Ireland in 1886, the Unionists (they did not call themselves Conservatives until the 1960s) provided the backbone of right-wing opinion. Its leaders were drawn from the ranks of indigenous capital, mostly in the west of Scotland, reinforced by an officer core of small businessmen and petty capitalists. Its foot soldiers, the Protestant working class, found Unionism with its Protestant patriotism and militarism a congenial political ideology. This coalition between local capital and Scottish workers remained in place until the 1950s when it began to collapse. People like Weir, Lithgow, Beardmore and Fraser are all gone. The Scottish capitalist class went into steep decline, losing out to UK and international competition; and working class politics became secularised, and religious ties were loosened. After the 1950s, Protestants behaved much like the rest of their class – Labour-voting with a wee touch of Nationalism.

Thatcherism in Scotland is unpopular not simply because its political game-plan to roll back the state is inappropriate, but because it no longer has a distinctive social base within which it can 'naturalise', so to speak, its political project.

. . .

In Scotland, the attack on state institutions – the nationalised industries, the education system, local government, the public sector generally – is perceived as an attack on 'Scotland' itself, particularly as this attack is dressed up in the rhetoric of Tory England. It needs, of course, the emotional appeal of (English) nationalism to allow the state to act in this way: state action legitimated in the name of 'the nation'. But Scots have a nation of their own, and Thatcher's vision of recreating bourgeois England is out of kilter not only with Scottish material interests, but with our own sense of identity. Thatcherism is the religion of 'little England'; its 'one nation' is essentially an English concept.

We should not underplay, either, the triumphalist element in this ideology. It comes as a surprise to many English commentators to find how offensive many middle-class Scots find this element of Thatcherism. Her famous 'sermon on the Mound' [1988: see Mitchell, 1990] left many kirk-going Scots shaking their heads at the insouciance of the woman who deigned to lecture them on their moral duties. Her resolute refusal to countenance any form of devolved power to Scotland offends their sense of fairness, particularly in the context of Douglas Home's famous promise that 'a better system of devolution' had to be found to replace Labour's Act of 1978. Hosting a dinner recently to celebrate the tenth anniversary of the referendum seemed to many in Scotland to flaunt what was a dubious 'victory' to say the least. All in all, there seems to be a disregard for Scottish sensibilities in much of Thatcherism which creates a sense of grievance. There is an irony, too, in that in Scotland the Conservative Party pursues the politics of power rather than the politics of support, pushing through contentious legislation without much semblance of moral claim. The irony lies in the fact that the Thatcher tendency rose in the Tory Party on the back of the claim that Edward Heath had failed to build up a politics of support for its policies in the party and the country.

. . .

Finally, the key aspect of the Thatcherite project – to modernise the British economy by privatisation – also drives a wedge into the Disunited Kingdom. Already, many of the state's assets in Scotland have been sold off, and many more proposed. Selling, for example, Govan Shipbuilders to the Norwegian firm Kvaerner severs the remaining responsibilities of the British Exchequer for Scottish yards. Creating private electricity companies once the South of Scotland Electricity Board and the North of Scotland Hydro-Board are sold off helps to sever connections with Whitehall. Imagine a privatised Scotland. What industrial ties would remain with England, apart from the fact that some companies would happen to be English? Until quite recently, we heard a lot from the free-market Right about the economic implications of an 'independent' Scotland. The residue of the Scottish banking system, and especially the issuing of Scottish banknotes, appealed to those who would like to privatise money. Presumably, we hear less of this now because it embarrasses the likes of [Scottish Office Minister] Michael Forsyth who is trying to be Unionist. Once the Scottish economy had been privatised, what would be the political rationale for remaining part of the United Kingdom? It is not difficult to construct a free-market case for Scottish Independence, as well as a socialist one.

. . .

Thatcher has changed politics in a fundamental way. The Conservative Party, undoubtedly the most electorally successful in Western Europe, has taken its chance with a leader and an ideology in stark contrast to its historical antecedents. In Scotland, it is hard to envisage a political message more at odds with what has gone before, and one which runs more directly against the grain of Scottish civil society. Think of it – Mrs Thatcher as the midwife of Scottish Home Rule. Perhaps someone should tell her?

The Implications of a Scottish Parliament for Women's Organisations in Scotland

Alice Brown and Yvonne Strachan

From a report of a discusson held in Edinburgh University on 24 September 1991, chaired by the journalist Ruth Wishart. Brown was a lecturer in politics (now professor) at the university. Strachan was a full-time official in Scotland of the Transport and General Workers' Union, was on the STUC women's committee, and was a member of the Scottish Convention of Women.

. . .

In the event of . . . constitutional reform, the nature of political participation could also change, and it is vital that the views of women in Scotland are represented. There have been debates on how best to improve women's representation as members of a Scottish Parliament and the ways in which the administrtion and conduct of any future legislative body should change to make the participation of women possible. There has been less discussion on how a new Parliament in Scotland could affect women involved in different aspects of Scottish society.

A selection of women representing women's interests in Scotland, including the arts, business, education, church, community groups, employment, health, housing, law, media, pay, rural areas, trade unions and voluntary organisations, was invited to join [a] Roundtable Discussion in order to consider the implications of a Scottish Parliament for women, women's interests and women's organisations in Scotland. It was not possible to make the discussion completely representative and, because of other commitments, not all those invited were able to attend. Nevertheless the Roundtable Discussion provided the first opportunity for women in Scotland to debate the topic openly.

. . .

– Objectives of Roundtable Discussion –

In recognition of the fact that the main focus of attention to date has been on the methods of securing better women's representation as members of a Scottish Parliament within the broader debate on electoral reforms, Alice Brown . . . summarised the objectives of the Roundtable Discussion as follows:

- Broaden the debate to include other women in Scottish society who may not be involved in a political party, but who represent different women's interests in Scotland.
- Allow women a forum in which to consider the new and exciting possibilities which a Scottish Parliament could offer in providing the opportunity to formulate policies and have more direct access to policy-making and implementation, i.e. by being more proactive rather than reactive.
- Increase awareness of the potential possibilities for change for women, so that the statistics on women's under-representation in political and public life and over-representation in low paid work, poor housing and poor health etc can be tackled . . . .
- Stimulate further debate and discussion amongst women, women's groups and women's organisations, in order that strategies for change can be developed.

– Topics Discussed –

. . .

– Problems identified in the present system –

A general lack of confidence and respect for the present political system was expressed. There were feelings that it was inaccessible, unaccountable, unrepresentative, hostile to women and provided few real opportunities for consultation. In particular there were problems for 'non-political' organisations in obtaining access to Parliament and decision-makers and having their views taken seriously. Also, the aggressive, confrontational style in which the two party system is often played out in British politics, the pomp and ceremony surrounding the Westminster Parliament, and the discriminatory attitudes to women and practices of the 'men's club' were all criticised.

The participants identified major problems in enforcing legislation which did exist for improving women's rights and pay and working conditions in a context in which there had been so few changes in fundamental discriminatory attitudes towards women in British society.

It was agreed that the structure, organisation and remoteness of Parliament made real participation unrealistic, but there was a growing demand amongst women in Scottish society to have their views heard and taken seriously.

– Areas of debate –

Various issues were discussed. These included:

- The role of education in changing attitudes, behaviour and expectations.
- Proposals to make the Scottish Parliament truly representative including:
  1. 50:50 proposal for elections.
  2. More open committee structure and the power to committees to initiate legislation.
  3. A new consultation machinery through sampling attitudes of communities, workplaces etc.
  4. Role of ministry for women.
  5. Quotas on appointments to ensure equal numbers of women.
- Strengthening legislation including the introduction of constitutional rights.
- Collection of information, statistics and data on women in Scotland.
- Marketing information on new Parliament – its structures and procedures.
- The approach of women to politics – is it different, less aggressive, more consensual?
- The need to address the contribution made by women in the home and to reflect their views in key policy areas.
- Overcome the marginalisation of women from different ethnic communities.
- Examine alternative routes of representations outwith the party's structure, e.g., lobby. There was also debate about the desirability of a women's party.
- In addition there were proposals for more fundamental changes including changing the present value system, the discriminatory attitudes towards women and the balance of power between men and women in society.

– Proposals for change and future objectives –

It was recognised that moves forward had to be made on many fronts hopefully within a more constructive context which included reforming the electoral system and procedures and structures of Parliament. In general it was agreed that an objective should be for women to gain fair ownership of any future Parliament in order that their confidence in the political system could be restored and that participation is seen to be worthwhile.

Yvonne Strachan summarised the main practical needs identified at the Roundtable Discussion as follows:

- Develop channels for communication of different interests through a lobby, organisation or group.
- Improve consultation and ensure future Parliament works with particular groups and organisations to develop comprehensive and coherent strategy (this has implications for the role of Civil Servants and Politicians).
- Provision of detailed data and statistics on women which could be fed into a ministry for women with obligation on employers and other institutions to collect such information.
- Establish research resource for women and Scottish Parliament.
- Improve political education and training for women, e.g. on how the Parliament works, how people can get access to it and confidence building skills for those wishing to participate.
- Support an open committee structure of Parliament which has power to initiate as well as scrutinise legislation.
- Ensure women are represented in all functions and areas of Parliament, including the Civil Service.
- Review the patronage systems to ensure equal appointment of women in public appointments and bodies.
- Monitor the effectiveness of a Scottish Parliament for women by compiling a National Audit on key statistics.
- Convince people that a Scottish Parliament could be different and increase confidence in the political system.

Yvonne Strachan ended by reminding those attending that the Scottish Constitutional Convention is currently examining the electoral system and procedures for a Scottish Parliament. The topics which had been raised in the Roundtable Discussion were very pertinent to the developments within the Convention in order that the demands on women in Scotland can be fed into the debate.

This is one of the rare occasions in history when there is the opportunity for real change. In this particular instance, unlike the past, there is commitment to provide equality for men and women in a new Scottish Parliament. It is incumbent on us all to seize this unique opportunity so that we do not allow other people, mainly men, to set the agenda for the future.

THE SCOTTISH CONSTITUTIONAL CONVENTION

James G. Kellas

From *Scottish Government Yearbook* (edited by L. Paterson and D. McCrone, 1992, pp. 50–8). Kellas was (and is) professor of politics at Glasgow University, and author of many books and articles on Scottish politics (for example, 1986, 1989).

What is the significance of the Scottish Constitutional Convention? Has it changed Scottish politics in any way, and will it hasten the establishment of a Scottish Parliament?

. . .

A summary of the Convention's Report in terms of academic analysis would place the scheme somewhere between devolution and federalism. The *Claim of Right for Scotland* which prefaces the Report asserts the 'sovereign right of the Scottish people to determine the form of Government best suited to their needs', and asserts 'the right of the Scottish people to secure the implementation of that scheme'. This is federal rather than devolutionary language, because it emphasises the bottom-up (Scottish) aspects of legitimate power, rather than its top-down location (Westminster-based). Consistent with federalism too is the talk of 'entrenchment' of Scottish powers, and the representation of Scotland in international bodies such as the European Community. There are some quite advanced ingredients such as a Charter of Rights 'which would encompass, and improve upon, the European Convention on Human Rights'. This implies that within the United Kingdom civil rights in Scotland might be different from those in England, Wales and Northern Ireland. This might be seen as giving Scotland even more independence than a unit in a federal state.

More reminiscent of devolution, however, is the listing of powers which the Scottish Parliament could exercise ('a defined range of powers and responsibilities') while implicitly leaving Westminster with its old unlimited 'sovereignty' intact. Westminster's primary powers over Scotland are however stated to be confined to 'defence, foreign affairs, central economic and fiscal responsibilities, and social security policy'. While there is a shift in the balance here to Scotland as compared to the Scotland Act 1978, in constitutional terms the status of Scottish Government remains that of devolution from a sovereign Parliament rather than a federal (treaty) arrangement between equal partners, underpinned by a written Constitution of a federal nature. The financial provisions talk of a system of ' "assigned revenues", i.e. revenues assigned to Scotland's Parliament as of right', but that 'right' derives from a British Act of Parliament and a British Government's decision, not from a Constitution. Such rights can in theory be easily revoked by the central Parliament, and the limitations on Scottish tax powers ('there should be some range defined so that the variation in income tax up or down cannot be misunderstood as being by a wide margin') are more restrictive than those normally associated with federalism. All in all then, a hybrid between devolution and federalism, with more practical features of the former than of the latter, but with some federal claims at a theoretical level (e.g. concerning the sovereignty of the Scottish people, and entrenched Scottish powers). However, it must be borne in mind that in academic analysis and real politics federalism and devolution are not always clearly distinguished (for example, Belgium and Spain are not federal countries, but have been partly 'federalised' in the 1980s) (Forsyth, 1989).

What of academic analysis of the Convention? An 'academic' analysis is one which seeks to avoid a partisan or ideological approach, and instead relates the subject to theoretical concepts and uses a comparative and historical method (looking across countries and across historical periods for guidance). But at the end of the day, even academics cannot avoid parading their prejudices, and I declare my sympathy with the primary aim of the Convention, a Scottish Parliament. This does not mean that there is necessarily an 'academic' (scientific) case for such a body, though there might be. Some academics who wrote on the Convention, such as Roger Levy (1990a, b) and James Mitchell (1991, [1996]) were critical or even hostile. I was supportive (Kellas, 1989, 1990), and the well-known political theorist Bernard Crick (1990) was positively ecstatic at the prospect of the Convention provoking fundamental constitutional reforms throughout the United Kingdom.

. . .

– CHANGE AND CONTINUITY IN SCOTTISH POLITICS: –
THE DEVOLUTION RATCHET

While there have been 'Conventions' before in Scottish history (Mitchell discusses those in 1924, 1926, 1927, 1947, 1948, 1949), there has never been a Convention with such a wide membership, and with such an extended series of meetings. Moreover, quite an elaborate organisation was set up, underpinned by the Convention of Scottish Local Authorities, which also provided some of the funding. Thus history does not just 'repeat itself', and a historical framework must take account of change as well as continuity (Levy sees this clearly, though he disapproves of the direction of the change).

Most significant was the presence at the meetings of a large number of MPs, local councillors and delegates of the Churches, STUC, and so forth. From a purely political point of view, the participation or support of leading politicians in the Labour Party and the Liberal Democrats gave added status to the Convention proceedings. It also meant that the main Opposition parties were effectively committed to the Convention's Report, and they promised to legislate on it if returned to power. No previous Convention had this sort of support. It is true that these promises will have to be put to the test. But the ratchet of progress towards devolution has been turned at least one notch by the Convention.

The boycott of the SNP and the Conservative Party clearly dented the devolution consensus, but it is not clear what effect this has had. What these parties feared above all was being committed to policies they did not wish to support by being outvoted on the Convention. This applied also to the Liberal Democrats and Greens, who nevertheless participated. While the final Report confirmed the worst fears of the non-participating parties (and at the end also of the participating Greens), the agreement between Labour and the Democrats was significant in view of the possibility that a future Labour Government might be dependent on Democrat votes in a 'hung Parliament'. So two future possible election results (overall Labour majority, and Labour-Democrat majority) were catered for by the Convention's deliberations. The Leader of the Opposition, Neil Kinnock, declared that a Labour Government would legislate on devolution during its first year of office, and another Labour Shadow Government spokesman Roy Hattersley has backed the Convention scheme. No party leaders had ever before made such a commitment with regard to a Convention scheme. It may be argued that Labour and the Democrats would have introduced devolution anyway without the Convention. But as we shall see, the Convention changed the nature of the devolution proposals, and heightened its priority in the Opposition parties' programmes.

The absence of the SNP and Conservatives probably makes no difference to the strength of the Convention's influence. The SNP has not increased its vote by non-participation, if anything the reverse. It is likely that when the next devolution Bill is introduced, the SNP will split as over the

Scotland Act [1978], but with the same tendency to settle for 'half a loaf rather than no bread'. The Conservatives may also split, for their devolutionists are now re-asserting themselves under John Major's benign regime. In any case, they would be out of power should the legislation be introduced.

– HOW THE CONVENTION CHANGED THE – DEVOLUTION PROPOSALS

Until 1989, when the Convention commenced, devolution proposals were to be found in the programmes of the Labour and Liberal/SDP Alliance parties. There were obvious differences between these programmes, notably in the federalist nature of the Liberal proposals, and in the more devolutionist approach of the Labour Party. By the time the Convention reported at the end of November 1990, the Labour proposals had merged with those of the Liberals. There was even a commitment to change the devolved electoral system in the direction of proportional representation. . . . A new system of 'assigned revenues' was accepted eventually by the Convention (Heald, 1990).

. . .

These proposals show that the Convention has again turned the ratchet of devolution one or two notches higher where it mattered – in the programme of a prospective British government (this is recognised by critics such as Levy and Mitchell, who nevertheless dismiss the Convention's proposals). The reason for this development is entirely due to the Convention process. The Labour Party needed to retain the cooperation of the Democrats if it was to be a Convention rather than the Labour Party Conference under another name. At the same time, the Democrats needed Labour if the Convention was to be a credible exercise in constitution-making. Curiously, the Democrats seem to have taken most of the initiatives and to have prevailed in argument on nearly every occasion. Similar inputs came from the women's movement (representatives in the Labour Party and STUC, and the Scottish Convention of Women) and the Greens. So the tail in effect wagged the dog. Political scientists call this the 'minimum winning coalition', although here it is a moral coalition, since Labour already had a majority in the Convention.

. . .

– The Convention's Proposals: –
Do They Make Political Sense?

The Convention's *Report to the Scottish People* was the result of eighteen months' negotiation between the delegates who comprised the Executive Committee (the plenum merely endorsed without vote). . . . Most constitutions have been designed in this way, the classic case being the American Constitution, cobbled together over four months in the Philadelphia Convention in 1787. It still exists.

. . .

What of *The Claim of Right for Scotland*, with its declaration of the sovereignty of the Scottish people? . . . Political scientists (unlike philosophers) tend to take claims of sovereignty with a pinch of salt, and work out the implications from practice not theory. . . . What it seems to mean is a quasi-federal assertion of 'independence within a sphere' on a coordinate (not subordinate) basis with the British Parliament. Does that make political sense? It probably does, at least as much as the Treaty of Union 1707 (with its two Established Churches, two legal systems etc) and the Government of Ireland Act 1920 and its successors (the despised 'unilateral devolution' rejected by the Conservatives for Scotland, but pressed by them on Northern Ireland). Britain and British politics seem to be capable of almost any twist in territorial constitutional arrangements.

Yet there are many problems of a technical nature still to be addressed. . . . The most tedious of these is the 'West Lothian Question' . . . followed by the existence or not of the Scottish Secretary. . . . More important (but not much more) is the question of the number of Scottish MPs in the House of Commons; quite important is the revenue-raising system for a Scottish Parliament; and crucial may be the nature of the electoral system (without PR, Scotland looks at the moment like a one-party state dominated by the central belt).

. . .

Political scientists (when they are speaking as such and not as partisans) have no clear answers to any of these questions. They tend to let politicians or the people decide for themselves in each country, and then assess 'success' or 'failure' in terms of stability, efficiency, responsiveness, and so on. In other words, all these 'problems' are essentially political rather than 'scientific' questions, matters of preference and will. The analysis of these is not easy, because things keep shifting, and both elite and mass inputs are involved. Reversals of party policies are notorious in devolution, and it might not be too surprising to find the Conservatives espousing federalism or even Scottish independence (there is already some evidence of this, with Conservative Scottish Office Minister Allan Stewart saying that he would give independence his second preference after the status quo (*The Scotsman*, 29 April 1991, p. 3).

. . .

It is possible to attempt political science theory here, using comparisons with other countries facing similar problems, and looking at how in history state structures have changed, especially in Europe. . . . [I]t looks as if devolution is coming to Scotland, and sooner rather than later, if it is accepted that decentralisation of power is a general feature of contemporary politics in Europe.

Where does this leave the Convention's proposals? They are probably more 'advanced' than most devolution systems, for reasons which relate back to the Convention's process of decision-making. The inclusion of the principle of equal representation of men and women can be related to the input of the women's movement, which is particularly strong in the Labour and Democrat parties. Then, the panoply of legalisms regarding 'entrenched powers', a Bill of Rights, and Scottish representation in the European Community seems to have come from the lawyers in the Liberal Democrat delegation. The Churchmen on the Executive . . . topped up the whole thing with morality, sentiment and historic memory. . . . All in all, an impressive array of the 'great and good' within the Liberal-Labour-nationalist establishment, . . . underpinned by the hard and practical men (and some women) of the Labour Party, local authorities (mainly the same people), the STUC and so on.

Part IV: Towards the Parliament, 1992–7

Introduction

The unexpected re-election of the Conservative government in 1992 – and the failure of the opposition parties to reduce Conservative representation from Scotland – inspired the first fresh Conservative thinking on the constitution since the late 1970s. They retained their opposition to any elected assembly, but they were willing to try out various reforms to the ways in which Scottish business was dealt with at Westminster, and to the various committees through which the Scottish Office negotiates with Scottish civil society (ideas which were outlined by the prime minister, John Major, in a speech in Glasgow on 22 February 1992). These reforms were entitled 'taking stock' (and were announced in a white paper in 1993). They are reviewed here by their chief architect, Ian Lang, who was Secretary of State: they are very similar not only to the first of the four options for reform which Pym and Brittan outlined in 1978 (Part II), but also to the proposals which the Labour Party made to Kilbrandon (Part I). The reforms were taken further by Michael Forsyth after he became Secretary of State in 1995, and, unlike Lang, he was prepared to enter into aggressive debate with the supporters of home rule and independence. His speech here was given on the same St Andrew's Day as the Constitutional Convention published its final scheme (which became the Labour government's white paper in July 1997). He coined the term 'tartan tax' to refer to the taxation powers which the Convention proposed for a parliament. The irony – as Donald Dewar pointed out in his 1988 speech in Part III – is that it was precisely the absence of taxation powers which (as we saw in Part II) impelled Alec Douglas Home to advocate a 'No' vote in the 1979 referendum.

Despite the official opposition to a Scottish parliament, some Conservatives continued to support the idea, exemplified here by Christine Richard whose proposal resembles the second model discussed by Pym and Brittan in 1978 and the second model proposed by the Scottish Constitutional

Committee in 1970 (see also Mitchell, 1990). The Convention scheme was refined somewhat – for example, there were more details on the electoral system, and the Liberal Democrat MP Menzies Campbell went so far as to present a Bill at Westminster proposing to set up a parliament (which was inevitably defeated because of the Conservative majority) – but the main development from the home rule groups was a strengthening of the debate about the character of the democracy which a parliament could stimulate. The debate was given rigour by a booklet from Bernard Crick and David Millar, first published in 1991 but revised in 1995; the summary introduction to that second edition is given here. A similar concern with the relationships which the parliament would have with Scottish society was found in the willingness of local government to debate openly the prospect of a parliament and ways of working with it (Alexander, 1997; Fairley, 1997; McFadden, 1996; Midwinter, 1997; Sinclair, 1997). This is exemplified here by the 1996 speeches from Rosemary McKenna and Charles Gray. At the same time, thinkers in London had also noticed what was going on, and that a Labour government would probably treat the setting up of a Scottish parliament very seriously (Marr, 1992; McCormick and Alexander, 1996). A Constitution Unit was set up in University College, London, producing lengthy discussion documents on how to put constitutional change into practice. One of its early publications was a set of detailed prescriptions for a Scotland Bill that would give effect to the proposals of the Convention; these are summarised here by Graham Leicester. And there was a growing interest in how a home rule parliament would relate to the European Union. The Labour MEP David Martin led this debate (as illustrated here by an article written after Labour had won the 1997 general election), but equally significant was the experience of local government in dealing with the EU for grants: see the speech by Charles Gray.

The 1997 general election campaign added little to the debate, and – unlike 1992 – was significant not for the clash of ideas but for its outcome, the defeat of the Conservative government. They lost all their seats in Scotland, and dropped to 17.5 per cent of the vote. The new Secretary of State was Donald Dewar, firmly committed not only to his vision for the Convention as articulated in 1988, but also to his own lifetime support for home rule and to the memory of John Smith's unfinished business. The principles and the summary of the white paper which he produced in July 1997 are given here; it was so closely based on the Convention's 1995 scheme that there is no need to give that separately: as Dewar acknowledged in a speech in July 1997, the formative influences on the paper were the report of the Constitution Unit, the Convention scheme, and the Kilbrandon scheme of legislative devolution (*The Herald*, 12 July 1997, p. 6).

Thus the 1997 scheme went further than the Labour government's proposals of the 1970s (as summed up in *Our Changing Democracy* in Part II). Indeed, in 1970s terms Donald Dewar in 1997 would be a 'maximalist' alongside John P. Mackintosh. It was a sign of how much had changed in the debate that the Labour party could campaign quite enthusiastically for such a white paper only two decades after it had been deeply split over proposals for a weaker assembly.

The debate in the referendum marked a culmination of the whole three decades of discussion. All the strands which were identified in the Introduction were present – good government, nationalism, community, negotiated autonomy. The referendum itself will have entrenched the parliament much more effectively than any legal guarantee of its existence could have achieved, as Peter Jones notes in his essay here (and as he developed in Jones, 1997): for all the controversy that surrounded Labour's proposal in 1996 to hold a referendum, it turned out to be the best way of silencing the Conservatives and of fulfilling the second of the Convention's 'pledges' to obtain the consent of the people (Part III). After all, as we saw, a referendum held for principled reasons (rather than the expediency of the 1970s) was a return to a long tradition of campaigning for a parliament, exemplified here in the article from Paton in 1968, in the Liberal Party's submission to Kilbrandon in 1970, by John Smith in 1981, and in the *Claim of Right*.

The opponents of the parliament in the referendum relied heavily on the arguments of Michael Forsyth, whose castigation of the 'tartan tax' had been one of the reasons why Labour had decided to ask two questions (on the principle of the parliament and on its taxation powers). But the campaigning skills of Forsyth were absent, because, after losing his Stirling seat at the general election, he took almost no further part in the debate. Although Tam Dalyell argued a similar case to the one he had deployed effectively in 1979, the campaign lacked the coherence and cogency of its predecessor. The most (unintentionally) ironic intervention came from Margaret Thatcher herself, whose article published in *The Scotsman* just two days before the vote is given here. It sums up the whole unionist case that had been put by the Conservative party ever since she had changed the line in 1976. Her article stands, then, as both a clear statement of that case and a reminder of why support for home rule had grown. As the *Daily Record* newspaper put it when she visited Glasgow that day, 'if you still need a reason to vote Yes, here's one'. The majority needed little urging: on a turnout of 60 per cent, 74 per cent voted for the principle of a parliament, and 63 per cent for the tax powers.

The future of this debate is, perhaps, indicated by the final set of items here. Europe is bound to be significant, as David Martin argues. The radical politics which drove much of the 1980s campaigning for home rule will not go away, ensuring that the coming of the parliament will mark the beginning of a process as much as a culmination: this is the tenor of the articles by Joyce McMillan and Neal Ascherson. McMillan argues that such a process of re-engaging government with the people is urgently needed right acoss the western democracies. The continuing vitality of Scottish culture will feed this continuing tendency towards radical democratic renewal (as Peter Jones suggests here). The position of the Conservatives was already – in the autumn of 1997 – intriguing. They seem likely to switch track completely, and advocate stronger fiscal responsibility for the new parliament than Labour allows. This is the tenor of Michael Fry's article, was the basis of amendments to the Scotland Bill which the Conservative Party in the Westminster parliament tabled early in 1998, and underlay the tentative move towards federalism of the UK party leader William Hague in February 1998 (*The Herald*, 25 February 1998, p. 6). Some elements of the Scottish party might even come to favour independence, preferable to what they view as the dependency of devolution (a position to which Allan Stewart had come close (*The Scotsman*, 29 April 1991, p. 3)). Moreover, because the parliament will be elected proportionately, Labour will not have this debate all its own way, as Peter Jones argues.

Permeating all these detailed debates will now be fundamental tensions concerning sovereignty and the character of the national community which is about to take democratic control of its own affairs. The issues around sovereignty are summed up by Tom Nairn in his 1997 lecture, and something of the tensions between it and community are discussed by the response to Nairn's arguments from John Lloyd. The *Claim of Right*, assessing the inconclusive 1979 referendum, pointed out that 'no referendum is for ever' (section 4.9): the sovereignty of the people keeps asserting itself against its rulers. The new parliament – and the partially reformed UK which it will usher in – will have to learn that lesson too.

THE SCOTTISH QUESTION

Christine Richard

From *Scottish Affairs* (no. 2, 1993, pp. 121–3). Richard was leader of the Conservative group on Edinburgh District Council.

It is perhaps hard to believe now, but the Conservative Party has not always set its face firmly against Devolution, in the form of a Scottish Assembly. Indeed, in the late 1960s and early 1970s there were two high-powered think tanks working on proposals on behalf of the Party. One was chaired by George Younger and the other by Lord Home (then Sir Alec Douglas Home). The deliberations included proportional representation, were wide ranging, and concluded that there was a real desire among Scottish people to have a greater say in their own affairs. The now famous Declaration of Perth made by Edward Heath at the Party Conference in May 1968 made a clear commitment to bringing this about.

In her turn, Prime Minister Thatcher was just as enthusiastic as Ted Heath had been to advance the cause of Scottish Devolution. Malcolm Rifkind and Ian Lang in the 1970s were equally keen that we should have a directly elected Scottish Assembly.

Scottish Parliamentary representation by Conservatives has not always been at its current low level. Indeed, in 1955, the Conservative Party had not only the majority of seats in Scotland but a majority of votes to go with it.

In many ways I believe the reorganisation of local government in 1974 was the start of the decline in the Conservative Party fortunes in Scotland which has continued since that time. There is, perhaps, a close link which may be established between the decline in electoral support for the Conservative Party and, in turn, the Party's move away from a pro-Devolution to an anti-Devolution stance. This belief would not be popular in the Conservative Party in Scotland and one feels somewhat heretical for suggesting that this should be so. However, I believe it is an issue which must be faced, and there is no doubt in my mind that the connection is well made.

What then happened to cause the complete volte face on the subject during the 1980s and spilling over into the 1990s? The reform of local government produced, with one or two notable exceptions, the rise to real power of the Labour Party in Councils up and down the country. In many cases the actions of local government have a very direct impact on the lives of people, and are seen and felt in a way which actions of Government are not. Local services and the cost of providing them affect everyone on a daily basis, and the increasing power of the Socialists in this field has, I believe, been directly responsible for the centralist approach adopted by successive Conservative Administrations at Westminster.

The present local government reorganisation proposals, based as they are on the concept of the enabling authority, give further evidence of this proposition. Of course, nothing in politics or life – if one can make that distinction – is so simple. I am sure that the Conservative Government of today and its predecessors would deny that there was any connection between the Socialist dominance at local government level and the increasing and frustrating loss of Conservative Party support at both national and local level. There is a school of thought which goes something like this: if the Socialists are taking over local government in its entirety, then a Scottish Assembly would only confuse the two issues. We simply do not know if a directly elected Scottish Assembly would follow the same voting patterns as local government and national government. It is, of course, possible to assume that they would do so. Yet we will not know until we try. There is the spectre held up of increased taxes, frightening away overseas investment and a sort of totalitarian state which harks back to the pre-Cold War days of the Soviet Union. This is, I believe, a very old fashioned view and not borne out by the facts of life in a modern Scottish economy, part of the United Kingdom, which is, in turn, striving to become a leading light in the European Community.

It may be that the first directly elected Scottish Assembly would return a majority of Socialists, and if tax raising powers were available, this could lead to a massive increase in direct, and for that matter, indirect taxation. Such an Administration would not be re-elected in a hurry. Perhaps we should consider an Assembly elected by proportional representation. Local Authorities and MEPs in Northern Ireland are elected by proportional representation.

There are very real fears, not only among Conservatives but among many members of the public and in business, that in these difficult times to take the giant step of setting up a directly elected Scottish Assembly with tax raising powers would be too dangerous a strategy to follow. I think this is a legitimate view and one which is shared by many people.

However, I equally believe it wrong for the Conservative Party to sit back and do nothing. Some Conservatives put forward the view that the whole question is one for the chattering classes and little more than media hype. For many years now, I have not taken this view and I believe that it is not true. There is somewhere buried in all the rhetoric a deeply felt and indeed almost passionate desire for that elusive 'bigger say in our own affairs' which in spite of a Scottish Office, Scottish Established Church, law and education seems to elude Scotland's grasp.

It is my own deeply held view that we are wrong to do nothing and so I have put forward my proposals for a Scottish political forum.

Essentially, what I have suggested is that the Government sets up an official Forum consisting of Members of Parliament and a proportion of Regional and District Councillors (post reorganisation, they would simply represent the single tier authorities). Proportional representation would be considered at least for the Council members. The Forum would be given statutory powers and a block grant. The agreed areas of responsibility for producing legislation would be restricted to domestic issues and probably include at a national level education, infrastructure, social policy and the early stages of all Scottish-specific legislation. It need not have a large bureaucracy as sufficient staff could be seconded both from the Scottish Office and [the] C[onvention] O[f] S[cottish] L[local] A[uthorities] to service the members of the Forum.

I envisage the Forum meeting for perhaps three or four days every month, probably in the old Royal High School building in Edinburgh, which has already been considerably adapted for the purpose. Within its predetermined limits, the Forum would have freedom to propose Parliamentary Bills which would, however, at the end of the day require the Royal Assent through the Westminster Parliament in the same way as Bills generated at Westminster itself.

This would not, of course, answer all the aspirations of the Scottish people, some of whom want independence or nothing. It would, though, give an opportunity for politicians of all political persuasions to work together in a meaningful way for the benefit of Scotland. Instead of being simply 'a talking shop' the ability to initiate legislation and to allocate budgets to meet the expenditure generated by that legislation would give the Forum real political powers and real influence. At a later date it might be appropriate to include the European Members of Parliament, particularly once the Maastricht Agreement is fully ratified.

I am conscious that it will not be difficult to find flaws in this proposition and that it is neither the perfect nor the whole answer. It does represent a genuine attempt at constructive thinking by a Conservative politician who is not afraid to stand out against current thinking in her own Party. The aim of the proposal is to stimulate further debate, and possibly to assist in a small way in bringing about further democracy in Scotland without destroying the balance of the union of the United Kingdom of Great Britain and Northern Ireland.

TAKING STOCK OF TAKING STOCK

Ian Lang

From a speech to the Conservative Party conference in Bournemouth (12 October 1994). Lang was MP for Galloway and Upper Nithsdale and Secretary of State for Scotland.

. . .

[The Union] has led to the growth and expansion of our trade, our industries and our prosperity. In Britain we are part of the sixth largest economy in the world and of the fastest-growing economy in Europe. And the Union has led to Scotland having a front-row seat in the councils of the world – the EU; the G7; the UN – instead of being stuck in the gods. And it has led, not to the submersion of Scotland in its larger neighbour but, on the contrary, to a strengthening of the Scottish identity and the flowering of a distinct Scottish culture.

So, the Union was not up for negotiation when we took stock. And nor was Scotland's status as a full and equal partner in the United Kingdom. But the exercise was of vital importance, nonetheless. For . . . 'taking stock' isn't so much about specific proposals – important though they are – but about . . . a new and ongoing approach to the government of Scotland. And driving forward that new approach to the government of Scotland are three key themes – themes which lie at the heart of 'taking stock' and which are at the heart of the new Conservative approach to the governance of Scotland.

– A NEW ACCOUNTABILITY –

The first of these themes is to make government in Scotland more accountable. Accountability is an essential feature of a democratic society. It has been argued that there is some kind of democratic deficit in Scotland. On the contrary, we are more fully represented than our fellow countries in our United Kingdom Parliament. And we are busily putting in place a robust and more accountable system of local government. The democratic deficit argument we hear in Scotland from time to time is essentially a separatist one, amounting as it does to a rejection of the sovereignty of the United Kingdom Parliament. And many of those who reject the existing parliamentary process do so for reasons not of principle but of expediency.

But although there is no democratic deficit in Scotland there was scope to improve the existing parliamentary arrangements and to enable them to develop organically – and that is what the 'taking stock' proposals were designed to do. Parliament has now approved the various changes to its Standing Orders which we proposed in the White Paper. That means that there will be more parliamentary time available for Scottish business than ever before. More chance to debate Scottish issues and Scottish legislation. More opportunities for Scottish MPs to scrutinise the activities of Scottish Ministers, and ask their questions than ever before. And more opportunities for the Scottish people to see their parliamentarians at work than ever before.

And all of this has been done without in any way reducing the rights of Scottish MPs to participate, as full and equal Members, in the deliberations of the UK Parliament. What 'taking stock' has done is to give the Scottish MPs the best of both worlds: a greater role in the consideration of Scottish business; and as much say as their English, Welsh and Northern Irish colleagues in the affairs of our United Kingdom.

The next session of Parliament, when these new arrangements take effect, will be an innovative and interesting one for all Scottish MPs and a challenging one for Scottish Ministers. We will have to give greater account for our actions than ever before. But I relish the challenge and it will be a real shot in the arm for the way Scottish business is dealt with at Westminster. And it need not be the end of the story. If other ways can be found of extending the role of Scottish MPs at Westminster, without diminishing either their rights or the rights of Welsh, Northern Irish and English MPs as equal United Kingdom Members, then I, for one, shall give them the most positive consideration.

– A Distinctive Policy Agenda –

The second major theme of taking stock is the drive to emphasise the distinctive nature of government policy as it applies in Scotland. There are two aspects to this. The first is that we are deliberately seeking to avoid an ideological approach to the governance of Scotland, in favour of a common sense approach – one that reflects Scottish needs and circumstances. And the second is that we are seeking to pursue specific, home grown policies for Scotland. In that, we have been singularly successful. There is now being pursued by the Government in Scotland a more distinctively Scottish policy agenda than ever before.

The extent to which the Government followed in the 1980s an ideological approach, in Scotland and elsewhere in the United Kingdom, has always been overstated – overstated by those on the right of the political spectrum, as well as by those on the left. Ideology often owes more to hindsight than to foresight. But there is no doubt that the first three Conservative administrations after 1979 were perceived – for good or ill – to have adopted an especially rigorous approach to the business of changing Britain for the better. And there is no doubt, either, that it was an approach with which a number of Scots genuinely felt uncomfortable.

As well as being criticised for adopting too ideological an approach, the Government was accused of compounding the sin by allegedly seeking to anglicise Scotland and her institutions. I found that criticism pretty depressing on two counts. First, because it was manifestly untrue. And, second, because it carried with it the implication that Scotland should have nothing to do with England, English people and English ideas. One of the strengths of the Union is that its partners learn from each other. Scottish patriots have enough confidence in their country to share sovereignty and much else besides with another country. Judged by their anglophobia, Scottish nationalists clearly do not.

But I was anxious for the Government to be seen to adopt a more common-sense approach to the job of governing Scotland, and this we have sought to do. For example, we have responded to criticism of the manner and type of appointments to Health Boards and NHS trusts by appointing a transparently impartial committee to advise on who should be given the job of running these bodies. And there was clearly a need for the Government to emphasise the distinctive policy agenda to be adopted in Scotland. And that is what we have done. In schools, we have brought forward reforms of Scotland's distinctive Highers, built firmly on the traditions of the Scottish education system. In law and order we are bringing forward reforms of the criminal justice system, built firmly on the traditions of the Scottish legal system. In restructuring water and sewerage services, we responded to popular opinion and have built firmly on the tradition of public ownership of these services in Scotland – where they will remain. In economic development, we developed the unique arrangements of Scottish Enterprise and the local enterprise companies. And now we are bringing forward proposals for a new loan scheme for small businesses, built firmly on the traditions of Scottish thrift and enterprise and geared to the needs of small business in Scotland.

. . .

– ALWAYS A NATION –

The third key part of 'taking stock' is the Government's determination to ensure that there is a more wholehearted recognition and understanding of

Scotland's status as a nation. To the vast majority of Scots, who are Unionist, there are few more irksome sights than slogans imploring Scotland to 'rise now and be a nation again'. Scotland was a nation before 1707 and has remained a nation since. And it is part of the Government's purpose to ensure that Scotland's nationhood is properly acknowledged.

This is being done in a number of ways. For example, we are drawing more on Edinburgh's status as a capital city. From the European Council meeting to the State Visit by the King and Queen of Norway, a range of events have taken place designed to underline the Government's – and the international community's – respect for Scotland's status. More of these events will take place in the future.

But the drive to underline Scotland's status as a nation doesn't begin and end with what may appear to be fleeting appearances on the international stage. We are investing in tangible and lasting symbols of Scotland's nationhood. And the progress we are making, for example, in establishing in Scotland new seats of learning and in confirming our country's cultural pre-eminence, amounts to nothing less than a modern Scottish enlightenment.

There are new universities in Glasgow, Edinburgh, Aberdeen, Dundee and Paisley. We now have the highest proportion of graduates per head of population of any country in Europe. A new Museum of Scotland is under construction and a new National Library is almost completed. We have invested heavily in the new Edinburgh Festival Theatre, a showpiece of Scottish architecture and a magnificent showcase for Scottish opera and ballet. And our national galleries and their fine collections continue to fill the headlines.

This modern renaissance and renewal continues with the building of Edinburgh's fine new Conference Centre. In the realm of business, our great financial institutions stand on the threshold of a new prosperity and success, thanks to this Government's drive to knock down barriers to trade and commerce and their ability to grasp with both hands the immense opportunities that are available to them all over Europe. The double benefits of Scotland's skills and environment allied with the UK's sound economic management, low corporate taxation and low inflation are combining to attract inward manufacturing investment as never before. Last month I was in America and [Industry Minister] Allan Stewart was in Japan and it was clear to both of us, not least from the new investment commitments we returned with, that around the world Scotland is firmly on the map and held in a high esteem, unmatched in our history.

. . .

– Taking Stock of the Opposition –

The three themes I have outlined – the new accountability; the distinctive policy agenda; and the emphasis on Scotland's nationhood – are now central to the Conservative approach to the governance of Scotland. They are the impetus behind many specific policies and initiatives. And they are what ensures that 'taking stock' is a vital and organic thing which will continue to have an impact on how Scotland is governed for many years to come.

. . . [W]e must be pro-active in our search for new ways to build on the strengths of the Union and . . . we must seek to make it relevant to a new generation of Scots. The critics are already scoffing as far as the latter goal is concerned. To them, the fact that the most Unionist of parties is presently languishing in the opinion polls would seem to bode ill for the Union as we know it. But before the separatists and the semi-separatists become too gleeful, I should like to utter a word of caution. There is a long way to go before the voters give their verdict on this Government and its policies. The Union has withstood the assaults of its critics in the past, and I have no doubt it will do so in the future.

As far as Labour and the future of Scotland is concerned, time has stood still. The credibility of its scheme for a Scottish Parliament was torn to shreds during the last general election. But, in spite of that, Labour has not only failed to develop its proposals into a less unworkable package, but has openly abandoned any attempt to talk about how their tax-raising Scottish Parliament would work – because they know it wouldn't.

. . .

But Labour cannot ignore forever the loss to Scotland of UK resources, the reduction in the number of Scottish MPs at Westminster, the loss of a Scottish voice in the Cabinet – all of which would be the consequence of their plans for a Scottish Parliament. Nor can they ignore the second-class status that would be the fate of Scotland's remaining UK MPs – upstaged in Edinburgh and down-graded at Westminster. This is all deeply serious, yet it isn't being taken seriously by Labour. It is not even being given a second thought. Given the fatally under-developed and unworkable nature of their scheme for a Scottish Parliament, and given the Parliamentary pitfalls and hurdles that would await a Scottish Parliament Bill, Labour's pledge to legislate to set one up within a year of taking office is not only irresponsible, but undeliverable.

And who would then be circling Labour's constitutional wreckage like vultures, but the SNP? Separation would follow devolution, as night follows day.

– Home Thoughts from Abroad –

But let us just consider one immediate consequence of the constitutional upheaval with which we are threatened: in the field of inward investments. In the last couple of months alone Scotland has secured around £1 billion of new investment securing almost 2,000 jobs. I recently visited Belgium, a country which has played a prominent part in recent European history and which is now home to so many key European institutions. A prosperous country, with so much to offer, Belgium has expended much of its energy in recent years in seeking to resolve differences between Wallonia and Flanders. Far be it from me to tell that country how to order its affairs. But the advocates of constitutional change in this country should be aware of two disquieting things to have emerged from the Belgian experiment with constitutional change.

The first, reported to me by the Federation of Belgian Companies, is a belief among Belgian business people that the instability engendered by the disputes between Wallonia and Flanders has had a negative impact on the amount of United States investment flowing into Belgium. The consequences for the Scottish economy of a fall in US investment in Scotland would be devastating. A key part of our attraction to overseas investors is our stability and our full and equal participation in the United Kingdom. Those who would upset either of those things should be conscious of the price thousands of Scots would pay with their jobs.

There is, now, a new West Lothian question to go with the old one. Would these companies from overseas be investing in West Lothian – or anywhere else in Scotland – against a background of chaotic and schismatic constitutional change? There is an answer to this new West Lothian question. It is no.

. . .

The second point which is becoming apparent as the Belgian constitutional reforms have been implemented is that, far from relieving the tension between the various parts of the country, the creation of a federal system is perceived by a number of Belgians to have institutionalised both that tension and the divisions between Wallonia and Flanders. And that is in a balanced federal system. Can you imagine what would happen if a tax-raising Scottish Parliament were established unilaterally in Edinburgh and Scotland remained, nominally, in the United Kingdom.

Of course, there are occasional tensions between Scotland and England. With two proud countries involved, it would be strange if there were not.

But, as a United Kingdom, we are able to resolve them because we share so much in common. A separate Scottish Parliament of the kind envisaged by Labour would be an engine room for discord and disharmony and would in practice prove to be little more than a staging post on the road to full separation.

– TAKING STOCK FORWARD –

But that is the Doomsday scenario. The paralysis which would afflict government in Scotland if Labour were to win the next election will not happen because I believe that we will win a record fifth term in office. And one of the reasons we will do so is precisely because we and we alone stand four-square behind the Union. The last general election showed that the Union remains for many Scots – and for many people in the other parts of these islands – something to cherish. We have a clear, logical and straightforward view of the Union, augmented by the new approach to the governance of Scotland which taking stock is all about.

The SNP have a policy on Scotland and the Union that is at least clear-cut and consistent, but it is a policy of self-destruction. Labour's is a policy of appeasement and its ill-considered endorsement by this new leader [Tony Blair] says much about his soundbite philosophy.

But this Party and this Government are both consistent and constructive and will stand firm for what we believe in. We are committed to a continuing reappraisal of the way the Union works and of how it can be improved. We'll go on taking stock. But we'll go on backing the Union. And, whatever the ebbs and flows of political fortune, I have no doubt that the Union of 1707 will be around for a long time yet.

TO MAKE THE PARLIAMENT OF SCOTLAND
A MODEL FOR DEMOCRACY

Bernard Crick and David Millar

Extracts from the introduction to the second edition (1995) of a pamphlet of this title published by the John Wheatley Centre (now the Centre for Scottish Public Policy). The first edition appeared in 1991. The pamphlet offered detailed proposals for Standing Orders for the parliament and a framework for a parliamentary and public information service. Crick was (and is) emeritus professor of politics, London University, and an honorary fellow of the department of politics, Edinburgh University. He is close to the Labour Party. Millar had been a clerk of the House of Commons and then director of research at the European Parliament; he was (and is) an honorary fellow of the Europa Institute at Edinburgh University. He had stood as a Scottish Liberal Democrat candidate in the elections for the European Parliament in 1994.

. . .

A new Parliament needs new ideas and adequate resources in three respects:

1. effective procedures relevant to modern Scottish conditions and opinion;
2. an efficient organisation and administration; and
3. a modern information service to serve both members and public.

. . .

Scotland's Parliament will only work as its supporters want it to work, for and with the Scottish people, if from the word go it is bold enough to break from the Westminster mould and to invent and adapt procedures and working practices better suited to and arising from Scotland's more democratic civic traditions. It should draw on experience outwith more than within the United Kingdom. Procedures are not irrelevant to democracy, they are part of its essence. Perhaps they are only means to an end, but the end cannot be reached without the right means. And until now there has been little thought about this.

The tradition-bound procedures of the Westminster Parliament and its excessively confrontational nature are sufficient enough reasons for Scotland's Parliament to make a clean break with Westminster's procedures.

Scotland's Parliament need not suffer from excessive executive control and party domination in what is likely to remain, quite apart from the consequences of a new electoral system, a multi-party system. Too many of the Westminster procedures, formal and informal, seek to perpetuate the English myth of the two-party system, whatever the reality on the ground. The proceedings of the Scottish Constitutional Convention itself have shown that a more consensual approach to decision-making is possible in Scotland, and it has argued that such an approach should and could continue. Party differences will still be strong but procedures should not force party divisions on every issue. Some issues inevitably cut across party lines, and there is no harm in that. Every vote need not be a vote of confidence. Procedures are needed that can work in such a spirit and in such circumstances.

However, not all Westminster procedures need be discarded and doubtless much that is familiar will often be followed or adapted out of habit. We argue for a deliberate and conscious break, otherwise nothing may change; but we know that breaks are never complete in peaceable and constitutional circumstances; so not too much, but not too little either. And we look for rules of procedure to strike a balance between the need to carry on responsible government in a coherent and reasonably consistent way and the rights of the electorate not merely as expressed through their elected MSPs, but by some new devices (new to the United Kingdom at least) to allow the public to express their opinions directly. But such a balance will look very radical to conventional Westminster eyes.

. . .

All of our proposals are consistent with and most follow logically from the Constitutional Convention's main proposals and the supplementary report (*Further Steps Towards a Scheme for Scotland's Parliament*, 1994).

. . .

Parliamentary, not Congressional or Presidential, government is our model. Thus while a case could be made in terms of democratic theory for an American-style separation of powers, with an elected President outside the parliament and the parliament making the major legislative input, we assume, as all parties at the Convention simply took for granted, that the Westminster and Commonwealth Executive-in-Parliament system will continue (much as it did in Ireland, both North and South); but we follow the Convention in trying to show that in such a system the Government need not and should not have such total domination over the legislative process as has evolved at Westminster (as was shown by the late John P. Mackintosh's classic account, 1962, written many years before the Thatcher-Major period). Our proposals are intended to make it possible for much legislation to come from committees, and we envisage the growth of an informal division of responsibilities between Ministers and powerful 'Permanent Committees' of Parliament in agreeing on the need for and preparing legislation or sections of legislation.

We also assume that the proposed, more proportional electoral system, as well as the multi-party nature of Scottish politics, makes it wise to produce rules that would work for a parliament without a continuing majority – quite apart from the hope of the Convention that a Scottish Parliament could operate in a more consensual manner than Westminster, somewhat as the Convention itself operated. The party differences in the Convention were clear but there was a will to reach agreements, to compromise whenever needed, not to push matters to division every time possible. This was easier in the Convention, of course, because of the presence of so many representatives of civic bodies, either non-partisan or whose partisanship was worn lightly and not under discipline. The new Parliament will not be like that. But our proposals for a far greater openness of proceedings than at Westminster to the public at large, and to civic bodies in particular, may help to make the ethos of the new Parliament at least closer to that of the Convention than to the automated dog-fights of Westminster that now plainly amaze, irritate and even disgust the public more than they can possibly (to use some old-fashioned concepts) educate, elevate, inform or inspire.

The structure of government was not commented upon by the Convention. We assume that its silence means a broad consent to have, initially at least, only five departments of state as at present. So the present broad departmental division of functions is likely to continue, at least deep into the first Scottish Parliament, possibly beyond, until Members have experienced actual working relationships between the Parliament and the executive, and both with local government. Then there will be considered grounds for changes. But each department will be headed, of course, by a Minister who is an MSP responsible to the Parliament. We favour few departments in any case for a very important reason. With the related restriction on the number of Ministers that we propose, this would avoid the large payroll vote (about a third of the Government party at Westminster) which gives the Government such excessive power over the House of Commons. The power of back-benchers and committees should be stronger than at Westminster, irrespective of whether elections yield a party majority or not.

. . .

The Convention was also silent on the role and constitutional position of the Secretary of State for Scotland. We assume . . . that the Scottish Parliament will elect its own Prime Minister immediately after electing its President – its Speaker or Presiding Officer. The powers of the Secretary of State for Scotland would then diminish to exercising the reserved powers as they affect Scotland and being the United Kingdom Government's negotiator and adviser on relations with the Scottish Government and Parliament. We . . . [see] the Scottish Secretary's role as vital in the period of transition, but beyond that for one person to hold both functions, even when the one is diminished, would be an almost impossible administrative burden, needing to be constantly in two places at once, but more than that would lead to great political difficulties when governments of different complexion were in power in Westminster and Edinburgh.

The coming of a Scottish Parliament exercising all the powers of the present Secretary of State will inevitably affect the United Kingdom constitution as a whole. The same political considerations and forces that are creating a Scottish Parliament are likely to set afoot other big reforms. Therefore it could well be that a Minister for Constitutional Affairs will emerge in the United Kingdom cabinet, responsible among other things for Whitehall's general relationships with Scotland, Wales and Northern Ireland, replacing in time each of the existing Secretaries of State. The status of the Scottish Prime Minister as the Queen's First Minister in Scotland should be marked by the Secretary of State's official residence in Charlotte Square becoming that of the Prime Minister.

The Scottish Civil Service was not dealt with in the Convention's Report, but we infer from its general principles that the status of the Scottish Civil Service would gradually change. While the Enabling Act would guarantee that conditions of service and pension rights for existing civil servants remained the same as those of the United Kingdom Civil Service, and while they should always remain in law servants of the Crown and not of any Government, yet the Scottish Parliament must exercise no less responsibility for their actions, both in law and practice, than the Parliament at Westminster does at present, if it chooses. There should be a separate Scottish Civil Service and Parliamentary Commission recruiting for the Scottish Civil Service, for officers of the Scottish Parliament, and for senior posts in public bodies designated by Parliament. (Applicants, of course, could apply to either or both civil services and provisions for transfer within the United Kingdom could be simple, as with the Northern Ireland Civil Service.)

A Charter of Rights for Scotland was a strong proposal of the Convention. But a constitutional problem is raised which they noted in passing, but then passed on quickly. That Charter would presumably contain general principles, like the European Convention on Human Rights, that would make not merely the powers of the Scottish executive challengable in the courts, but also those of Parliament.

. . .

Local Government's powers may need protecting even from a Scottish Parliament. The Speaker in the Dáil in 1922 allowed, without giving too much thought to the matter, a question from a Member about the location of a rural phone box. This has been held to mark the diminishment of local government powers in Ireland from what they were even in the days of British rule. The Convention was silent on this problem too, although [we conclude] . . . that, despite a theoretical derogation of the powers of the new Parliament, the Enabling Act should include a commitment to subsidiarity. It should state, as is now common in the EC, that anything specifically not forbidden by a higher level of government can then legally be done. The Enabling Act could thus give local authorities a power of general competence to provide services in their areas. Parliamentary Questions, for instance on particular actions and decisions of local government, would then simply be, on our proposals, as well as legislation, out of order, even though the competence of the Scottish Parliament to debate anything or to hear petitions should be unlimited. Of course it is not easy, political or legally, to define subsidiarity in many actual situations; but were the principle to exist in public law and legislation it would shift the whole focus of political and legal debate. It would change the first assumption: no longer to ask whether a local authority has the legal authority to do this or that, rather to ask if there is any specific law to stop them.

. . .

The main thrust of our proposals is two-fold. First, there should be powerful committees, proportionate to party strength in composition, which can themselves propose legislation as well as consider government legislation, by hearings as well as debate if they choose, and can conduct inquiries into administration or matters of public concern. Second, we propose several new devices for ensuring a general public right of access to proceedings in Parliament, making it more democratic and more informed about and more responsive to public opinion. For instance, Standing Orders could provide that if a specified number of citizens sign up to a

Question or to a Petition, then that Question or Petition would have to be published and answered just as if it came from a Member. And if a still larger number sign a Petition, it would trigger a debate. We assume that committees will regularly want the views of members of the public, representatives of interest groups and civic bodies appearing before them, whether meeting within or without the Parliament House, to be entered into the Record of the Parliament of Scotland.

The Report of the Scottish Constitutional Convention has expressed the general principles admirably and gained massive popular support. Our proposals for Standing Orders cannot, we admit, be read as easily or easily read as a comprehensible and self-contained narrative account of how a genuinely democratic Scottish Parliament would work. But some such entrenched Standing Orders are essential if these good intentions are to be met and if the Parliament is to get down to work without unnecessary delay, is to be made more accessible to women, more consensual, more efficient and less time-wasting, and able to interest and involve the public. Standing Orders should be entrenched (only changeable by a two-thirds majority, we propose) to protect the rights of smaller parties and the public against, it has to be admitted and faced, some of the dangers and abuses of majoritarian democracy, even under some real degree of electoral reform.

THE GOVERNANCE OF SCOTLAND

Michael Forsyth

From the Richard Stewart Memorial Lecture, 1995. This event is held annually to commemorate Richard Stewart, the Labour politician who was the first leader of Stathclyde Region (1975–87), and who died in 1991. Forsyth was Conservative MP for Stirling and Secretary of State for Scotland.

. . .

On this occasion – very appropriately on St Andrew's Night – I want to talk about the governance of Scotland. My central theme is community, by which I mean bringing Government and every tier of decision making closer to our people.

Scotland has long boasted a society that could truly be termed civil. The patriarchal character of our historic monarchy set our kings at the head of a national family. The Three Estates brought the people – at least in some measure – close to the throne. Much of this benevolent constitution may have been more honoured in the breach than in the observance; nevertheless, the aspiration to good governance was there. It is there still. Good government needs at times to be examined, to be overhauled and to be renewed, and now is such a time.

There are moments in the history of every nation when a mood of reappraisal possesses the public mind. Our nation, Scotland, is currently inclined to reappraisal of its constitution and government. I have no illusions about how this mood has largely been induced: the devolution hype has, for six and a half years, been orchestrated through the Constitutional Convention by self-interested politicians for party advantage. Yet sometimes a benefit can indirectly derive from a cynical political exercise; and, provided the people of Scotland have the insight to reject the base currency of the Constitutional Convention, it is good that they should scrutinise the genuine coin of government.

Let me put the record straight on my party's attitude to reform. The caricature image peddled by our opponents is of an English-inclined, intransigent party clinging stubbornly and negatively to the status quo. That is an exercise in black propaganda. We have always been open-minded; we looked at devolution. It was the Conservative and Unionist

Party which first, in 1968, put forward discussion proposals for devolution, including a Scottish assembly. We went down that road and we came back because it led nowhere.

Our opponents have tried to re-write history; but that is a fact. For years – longer even than the Constitutional Convention – the Scottish Conservative Party wrestled with the challenge of devolution. We could find no scheme that would not undermine the Union; or ultimately weaken Scotland's influence; or damage our prosperity. So we desisted from a project that was potentially destructive.

It says a great deal about them that our opponents did not. They picked up our policies; warped them; and tried to sell them to the Scottish people. In 1979, in a referendum, they failed, thanks to the foresight of a Labour MP whose sense of constitutional responsibility impelled him to introduce the 40 per cent rule to prevent the United Kingdom from being hijacked by a minority. Thereafter, devolution was dead. During the 1980s an attempt was made to breathe life into its corpse by leftist politicians hoping to ring-fence Scotland's collectivist and interventionist establishment and protect it from the free-market reforms of the Conservative government. That was the new motive for advocating a Scottish parliament: socialism in one country.

It was on that dismal, reactionary premise – not in any spirit of reform or modernity – that the Scottish Constitutional Convention was founded. For more than six years it struggled unsuccessfully to produce a formula. Academically speaking, I have some sympathy with its travails: Canon Kenyon Wright [convener of the Convention's executive committee], fresh from his defeat as the leading light of CND, and his colleagues, encountered the same insurmountable obstacles that had frustrated us. They found the West Lothian Question and allied problems equally insoluble. Unlike ourselves, however, the Constitutional Convention persisted in a doomed project. They did so, to put it bluntly, because their true objective was not the better governance of Scotland but the gaining of party advantage.

So much for the history. Now consider the events of the past few months. Earlier this year the Constitutional Convention was no closer to a resolution of its problems than it had been at the start of its six-year deliberations. What galvanised it into producing a formula was the recognition that any further delay would destroy its dwindling credibility. And so a deal was struck, in the classic style of backroom politics, to save the blushes of the participating parties.

In truth, they have more to blush about in the grotesque proposals they have produced than if they had come to no determination at all. They are proposing a parliament of 129 members, 73 of whom would be elected in constituencies, while 56 would be nominated by party leaders rather than directly elected. An ill-defined system of gender quotas, to ensure a 50–50 representation of men and women, would further gerrymander the parliament's composition and is both insultingly patronising to women and discriminatory against men. As the Prime Minister observed, during a recent visit to Scotland, these proposals are an alien system of government. What is remotely home-grown or Scottish about them?

All that is bad enough; but the worst flaw in this whole rag-bag is the proposed funding of a Scottish parliament, the Tartan Tax. I did not invent the Tartan Tax: George Robertson [Shadow Secretary of State for Scotland] did. He and his cronies formally and publicly announced a 3p tax-raising power for the Scottish parliament. They have never retracted that proposal; if they did, I would be the first to applaud and rejoice. Jim Wallace [Scottish Liberal Democrat leader] has gone even further. On 8 November he announced that the first 1p of the 3p Tartan Tax would be allocated to further educational spending. Yet George Robertson, his partner in the Constitutional Convention, has taken to denying as 'Tory lies' the existence of a tax which Mr Wallace is already spending.

We all know that the Tartan Tax is a concrete commitment and, increasingly, there is a realisation of the havoc it would wreak. This tax would put an extra £6 a week onto the average income tax bill in Scotland – and only in Scotland. It would not be paid by anybody working in England, Wales or Northern Ireland. It is a proposal to tax people for working in Scotland. It comes from the Labour Party, which gave us the Selective Employment Tax [in the 1960s]. This is the most selective employment tax of all: it victimises Scotland's workforce. It is a tax on Scotland's jobs.

It would fuel wage demands and discourage inward investment. I use no intemperate language; I make no extravagant calculations. Yet that understated phrase 'discourage inward investment' has chilling implications. Since 1981 inward investment into Scotland has amounted to more than £5 billion and has created or secured over 83,000 jobs. The international competition is cut-throat; the effort that is going into this achievement is enormous. We are broadening Scotland's economy, creating a new industrial revolution and going forward confidently into a prosperous new Millennium. To betray this great project would be worse than irresponsible.

Yet the Tartan Tax, for all its malevolent consequences, would only represent a small proportion of the parliament's funding: 97 per cent of it would come in a block grant from the Westminster parliament. That sovereign parliament of the United Kingdom would inevitably have a smaller representation of Scottish MPs once a devolved parliament was established. The Liberal Democrats have already conceded a figure of 54

Scottish MPs instead of 72; if the Stormont precedent were invoked, it could be as few as 40.

The powerful office of Secretary of State for Scotland would be sidelined or abolished, and Scotland's voice at Westminster be hugely diminished. While a Scottish parliament engaged in ever more confrontational relations with Westminster, Scotland would lose much of its real power to influence the block grant.

A further flaw which should be emphasised is the absence of any revising chamber. A vaguely-worded reference in the Convention's document to disputes between the Scottish parliament and Westminster being resolved by an existing body, 'with options including the Appellate Committee of the House of Lords and the Judicial Committee of the Privy Council', provides no reassurance.

Our democracy has been painfully honed over centuries to create a system of checks and balances to protect the freedom of the citizen. If a single-chamber parliament were proposed for Westminster, the people who intend to impose this system upon Scotland would be the first to man the barricades. If it is not good enough for Britain, it is not good enough for Scotland. Here is another affront to democracy in the parliament's composition: it represents single chamber government.

It is a breathtaking affront to Scottish interests to create a constitutional situation which reduces the number of Scottish MPs at Westminster. What kind of MPs would the survivors be? They would have no say in Scottish affairs, since these would be wholly reserved to the Scottish parliament. At their constituency surgeries they could address none of their constituents' everyday concerns and problems. At Westminster, on the other hand, they would vote on all domestic matters relating to England and Wales. The role of this parliamentary rump from north of the border would be nothing more than to provide Labour's United Kingdom majority. In those circumstances, the English backlash would not be long in coming and the outcome would be the destruction of the United Kingdom.

The Convention's scheme is a formula for eventual separatism. Alex Salmond [SNP leader] smiles a lot these days and I can see why. George Robertson and Jim Wallace have become the midwives of Scottish independence. All he has to do is to wait until they deliver his baby. Margaret Ewing [SNP MP] has openly declared that this scheme for a tax raising parliament is the fast track to separatism.

Scottish nationalism is a perfectly legitimate political position, provided it is honestly costed. It cannot be predicated upon Alex Salmond's fantasy calculations on the back of an envelope, which seek to convert a Scottish deficit of more than £8 billion into an imaginary surplus. If independence is the overriding priority, people have every right to vote for it; but they also have the right to be informed in advance about the heavy sacrifices it would entail, rather than being cruelly misled.

Siren voices are luring the Scottish people into support either for direct independence, on the SNP model, or fragmentation of the United Kingdom through an ill-devised tax-raising parliament – sleepwalking into separatism, as the Prime Minister has described it. Before they may be tempted to take an ill-considered and probably irrevocable step, I implore my fellow Scots to think carefully. The benefits of the Union are largely taken for granted; yet they are immense. Government spending per head of population in Scotland is currently running at £4,185 a year, 21 per cent higher than in England. We are not an exploited people.

I make a further appeal to my opponents and to the media: please do not allow truth to become a casualty in a bitter constitutional battle. Our people have a serious decision to make: they have a right to be accurately informed when they do so. Last week the Fraser of Allander survey into Scottish business attitudes to the constitutional question was widely reported as 'confused'. There was nothing confused about it. The plain truth is that 69 per cent of business objected to a tax raising parliament as damaging to its interests.

It is futile for Mr Robertson to pretend – as he now does in his more undisciplined moments – that the parliament's tax-varying powers would be used to cut income tax rather than increase it. In that invincibly hypothetical situation, is it seriously to be imagined that English MPs would continue to vote 21 per cent more expenditure to Scotland than for their own constituents, while simultaneously funding tax cuts north of the border?

And over the whole ramshackle contraption looms the West Lothian Question – the Bermuda Triangle of Scottish devolution. Labour has still not found an answer. George Robertson spent twenty minutes recently on the 'On the Record' television programme, goggling like a rabbit in the headlights at the intractable dilemma of the West Lothian Question. How can Scottish MPs legislate on English matters when English MPs are excluded from Scottish affairs? Therein lies the potential for the break-up of the United Kingdom.

Since Labour cannot answer the West Lothian conundrum they would prefer to silence the questioner. Yet I treat with scepticism reports that the Labour establishment has gagged Tam Dalyell: he is a political opponent whom I have long respected as a strong patriot and fearless defender of the Union. In his book *Devolution: The End of Britain?* he definitively spelled out the case for the Union and the insurmountable objections to a Scottish parliament. I am confident that when Scotland's vital interests are imminently at risk he will again speak out for them as he has so vigorously done in the past.

Like every other Scot, I recognise the emotional appeal of a focus for national self-expression. But our constitutional arrangements and economic prosperity must be guaranteed by more than emotion. The criterion must be: will this improve, or will it damage, the quality of life of the Scottish people? It stands or falls by what it can offer, in the real world, to the people of Scotland. I believe proposals for a Scottish Assembly or Parliament offer nothing but economic ruin, political decline, and the break-up of the UK. Down that road lies disaster.

In anticipation of tonight's lecture some have been indulging in dismissive sloganising: the new proposals are 'only' a beefing-up of the Grand Committee, nothing really effective, and so on. If Labour had been present on Day One of Creation, they would have issued a press release denouncing Our Lord's efforts as 'inadequate', without waiting to see what happened on the other five days.

The Grand Committee is a powerful arm of the Westminster parliament and it can be made more powerful still. The Grand Committee matters and George Robertson knows it. I have proposed more sittings of the Scottish Grand Committee, in Scotland. This is just a beginning. Parliament has been described as the 'cockpit of the nation'. From now on the Grand Committee will carry that intensity of debate into the heart of Scotland.

The principle is that subjects relevant to Scotland will be debated on Scottish soil, with the participation of the Scottish people. There are many towns in all parts of Scotland which could host Grand Committee meetings; local authorities will not be backward in putting in their bids. . . .

Scottish Bills can have their Second and Third Readings in Grand Committee, meeting in Scotland. An all-party committee can take evidence in Scotland. These innovations will be invaluable in arousing Scottish interest and input into legislation and, as a result, we will be able to get more Scottish legislation through the House of Commons . . .

The most significant change is that United Kingdom Ministers will from now on be able to take part in the Grand Committee's debates. The Prime Minister himself will come to Scotland early in 1996 to participate in Grand Committee, as will the Deputy Prime Minister, the Chancellor of the Exchequer and other senior Ministers. The most senior Ministers of the Crown will be accountable to the Scottish people; in Scotland; in a public forum which is also an integral part of the United Kingdom parliament. In this environment, Whitehall must inevitably become more acutely sensitive to Scottish concerns, priorities and needs. In terms of real power, that is a far more potent mechanism than a tax-raising talking shop with no influence at Westminster. Whitehall civil servants will have to burn the midnight oil to prepare their Ministers for Scottish questions they have never had to face before.

Lords Ministers will also make statements and be questioned on them. The Committee can take Statutory Instruments, have Question Times and hold Adjournment Debates. These Grand Committee measures have the dual benefit of bringing government closer to the Scottish people while simultaneously reinforcing Scotland's position in the Union. We can achieve all of this without a Tartan Tax and without the £41.5m [annual] running costs of a Scottish parliament.

In addition, a Special Standing Committee taking evidence in Scotland is an important development in my goal of taking government closer to the people and making it more accountable to them. People in the front line of the war on drugs will be able to have direct input into the new legislation controlling raves. We also hope to establish a new procedure under which a committee of peers can take evidence in Scottish venues for legislation initiated in the Lords. . . .

Consider the significance of these changes. The most powerful members of the Government will come to Scottish towns to account for government policy and be questioned on it. The Chancellor of the Exchequer can explain the excise duty on whisky. The Labour Party has been trying for months to play down the importance of the Grand Committee. The reforms which I have announced could be used by a Labour government with a majority on Grand Committee, to pass legislation and hold the executive to account. There is nothing further which a Scottish parliament could do which could not be done by Grand Committee except raise a Tartan Tax. A Scottish parliament could not hold the Chancellor to account for a Scottish budget determined at Westminster and the Prime Minister would have a place only in the visitors' gallery.

. . .

These innovations are the first outcome of intense consultation. Consultation will continue; it is an essential and permanent feature of good government. One of the people who was most helpful to me during my consultation exercise of the past three months was Campbell Christie, General Secretary of the STUC. Revitalise the Scottish Economic Council, he suggested: strengthen it and use it to enable people to participate in Government policy making. Good idea, Campbell, I said. I asked the members what they thought and they were eager to rise to this challenge.

Together, therefore, we are extending its remit to embrace every issue which affects Scotland's economic performance, including subjects as diverse as Scotland's fishing industry or the economic aspects of health policy . The Council's membership will be broadened to reflect the widest possible range of Scottish opinion: wealth creators, trade unionists, educationalists, local authority leaders and other informed spokesmen. It will meet much more frequently, will hold fuller sessions and will be chaired by the Secretary of State.

The Council's forward agenda will focus on key themes, such as how resources are shared out among different spending programmes; Scotland's place and performance in the global market; Scotland's skills base; and our overall economic performance. We are also establishing committees of the Council and non-members will be invited to contribute, providing a direct line from the people to the Government, so that it becomes truly a Council for Scotland.

Our government must be close to the people of Scotland and responsible to them. We must renew our political culture so that placing a cross on a ballot paper is not the end of the citizen's participation in government, but only the beginning. The electors should instruct the legislators and other government representatives regarding their wishes and needs. This should be done through openness, consultation and participation which will make all government community government.

A Scottish Parliament: Friend or Foe to Local Government?

Rosemary McKenna

Speech to a conference of this title held on 15–16 February 1996 and organised in Crieff by the Scottish Local Government Information Unit. McKenna was president of the Convention of Scottish Local Authorities, and became a Labour MP in 1997.

One of the motivations for a Scottish Parliament – leaving aside the obvious national sentiment in favour of it – is quite simply for better government. That is a need enthusiastically endorsed by much of Scottish local government.

The history of the recent relationship between central and local government has been one of continuous tinkering coupled with the centralisation of power; a relationship exclusively defined by central government on the basis of local government being regarded by the government not as a basic element in the system of government of this country but as little more than a subordinate piece of administrative machinery subject to continuous change and instability.

Our local government colleagues in Europe are astonished when they hear of the level of interference and antagonism from central government, a situation which simply does not exist in any other European country, where local government in its many tiers and manifestations is seen as an integral and important part of the organisation of the country, where there are far more councillors than here and who are held in some regard by their communities.

The present relationship in Britain, and most of all in Scotland, has three major flaws. First there is no agreement between central and local government about the respective boundaries between them. The role of central government is to set the framework and, where appropriate, national standards in which local government operates. But within that framework it is a matter for local authorities to determine choices for service delivery and their own internal management structures. That boundary is simply not accepted by the Secretary of State or the Minister for Local Government as we can see, for example, by their criticisms of the committee and management structures of individual councils, a practice which is not followed by their ministerial colleagues in England.

Secondly, there is no agreement, and thus no stability, about what [are] the functions to be undertaken by local government and [the] timescales that would allow local government to plan effectively.

Last, but perhaps most important of all, we do not have a local government finance system which secures local accountability. Finance is at the root of most of the difficulties that now bedevil the central/local relationship. It is the antithesis of accountability for local government to be accountable for 100 per cent of expenditure when it is only accountable for 15 per cent of its income, an accountability which is skewed by a regressive capping regime.

So I see constitutional change as an exciting opportunity to redefine the role of local government in the governance of the country.

In the scheme adopted by the constitutional convention there are good reasons why the proposals for a Scottish Parliament are to be welcomed – the principle of subsidiarity will be adopted so as to guarantee the important role of local government. That is only logical – if the principle of subsidiarity is to apply from Westminster to the Parliament then it cannot be denied to local government.

Similarly, there is a clear intention to embody the principles contained in the European Charter of Local Self-Government [Bogdanor, 1994], and in particular Article 4 that 'Local Authorities shall, within the limits of the Law, have full discretion to exercise their initiative with regard to any matter which is not excluded from their competence nor assigned to any other authority'.

Adopting the principle of these concepts will fundamentally change the nature of the relationship between local government and Parliament. But we in local government have no wish to enter into sterile debates with the Parliament about what is the correct 'choice' for the division between Parliament and local government as to the responsibility for any particular service. Whilst that might prove attractive to the legal profession, it would be a sterile debate and not conducive to the development of a good working relationship between local government and Parliament. The key issue in my view is to secure agreement on the application of the principle of subsidiarity in the day-to-day dealings between Parliament and local government.

Indeed, how the Parliament operates – its style of doing business – will be as important as what it does. It is vital that the relationships between Parliament and local government are positive, co-operative and stable. Thus the principle of subsidiarity might be best embodied in a protocol between Parliament and local government setting out the respective roles and responsibilities. That will be an early and essential piece of work to be agreed upon between the two bodies.

An important factor in determining the culture of the new Parliament, and in turn its dealing with local government, will be its membership and who is entitled to stand for it. That will ultimately be a matter for political parties to determine but – and here I am expressing a personal view – I hope that there will be a debate about the possibility of individuals being both councillors and parliamentarians. That is not uncommon in Europe and indeed dual membership can strengthen the link between local government and Parliament. Many French Mayors are also Deputies. This should be a serious part of the discussion. I am extremely irritated when I read snide comments from some journalists on this matter. This is not to say that the Parliament is simply another tier of local government, but a Parliament in its own right developing with local government a mutual respect and understanding of their respective roles.

In developing an effective protocol between local government and the new parliament which embodies the principles of subsidiarity and the power of general competence as well as addressing respective roles and responsibilities, we will need to secure agreement about functions and finance.

Scottish Local Government in Europe

Charles Gray

Speech to a conference 'A Scottish parliament: friend or foe to local government?' held on 15–16 February 1996 and organised in Crieff by the Scottish Local Government Information Unit. Gray had been convener of Strathclyde Regional Council and was a member of the Scottish delegation to the European Union Committee of the Regions.

A cynic might suggest that since local government has taken such a battering at the hands of central government in the last decade or so, any directional change would only be an improvement.

. . .

And yet, as the present councils prepare to give way to the new ones . . . I find myself at once pleased and surprised at the healthy resilience and confidence to be found in the new councils and their members. I suppose that part of that feel-good factor might come from the eager prospect of a fresh change of government and the exceptional alliance in the Constitutional Convention which promises major changes in the way Scotland will be managed. Add that to the typical, sometimes dour, determination of locally elected people to get on with their remit as best they can, and you might have a recipe in best practice for local government in Europe as the millennium approaches.

The European Committee of Regions (and Local Authorities, to give it is proper name) is only two years old; was three months late in getting off the ground and within another nine months had to re-organise as members were welcomed from Sweden, Finland and Austria when those nations increased the European Union from twelve to fifteen. The CoR, as it is known in Brussels, meets in plenary four times a year and its twelve commissions (committees) meet almost as often to discuss, and express opinions on, green and white papers whose legislation will have a very real effect on local government which will be expected to enact much of that legislation.

Each commission of the CoR has members from regional and local government from every nation within the EU and each commission has a specific range of subjects in which its members specialise so as to be able to offer expert opinions when asked to do so by the European Commission or

Council of Ministers. Already something like sixty-plus opinions have been given and there is good evidence that some have influenced change in proposed legislation and/or regulations. A unique agreement which CoR has, unlike its sister ECOSOC (Euro Economic and Social Committee), is one with Commission President Santer for a joint follow-up machinery to check up on whether or not opinions expressed have been of good quality, and, if not, how best to improve research and output so as always to get it right. The idea for this agreement came from the five Scottish members of the CoR.

In a sense it is somewhat ironic that the idea for a committee of regions and municipalities came from the European Commission whose members are appointed and not elected, although the notion came from Bruce Millan who had previously formed a small consultative body of about forty representatives of local government from within the then EEC. He convinced his colleagues in the Commission that [the] Maastricht [Treaty] should contain a recommendation to create the CoR and it is interesting to recall that the Council of Ministers were most reluctant to take up the suggestion which, after all, meant the member nations having to recognise – for the very first time – the actual existence of local government!

. . .

Constitutional change here in Scotland by the introduction of our own Parliament will allow the development of Scottish influence in European affairs, but especially with the accent on local and regional policies. The achievements of the Scottish regions, individually . . . will not disappear even if the regions do, and various European institutions will look again to Scots councillors to continue to contribute towards the democratic evolution of the Union as more new member countries are admitted. Indeed, the local government involvement in this is essential if the democratic deficit, which is very real, is to be eliminated.

One advantage which stands out in the aspiration to involve Scottish local government in European matters is the fact that a fair percentage of members of the new parliament are bound to be from local government. Many of them will have had some experience in co-operation with European counterparts. Up until now, perhaps not enough councillors have availed themselves, or their authorities, of communicating with, or membership of, the several European associations, some of which helped persuade Bruce Millan and his colleagues to support the creating of the committee of Regions.

The Assembly of European Regions (AER), the Council of European Regions and Municipalities (CEMR), Regions of Europe of Traditional

Industries (RETI), the Council of Peripheral and Maritime Regions (CPMR) all have had Scottish members and some have played a significant part in whatever progress local government has made in the EU in the last couple of years. Interestingly, it is likely that not a few members of the 'old' councils would have been unaware that, through COSLA, their authorities were full members of CEMR and also by COSLA's membership of the International Union of Local Authorities (IULA) they would have right of access to IULA's researched material. In passing, it is worth noting that in recent years IULA's influence in Central and South America and in the Far East has increased the movement towards local democracy in those regions.

I am convinced that a Scottish parliament with a healthy percentage of ex-local government members will press for individual councils to be active in belonging to COSLA and the appropriate European associations; to make use of modem information communication systems, like Internet, so as to offset any fears of peripherality, which physically, at any rate, can hardly be worse than those ills suffered by local government in recent years. In a sense, looking outward as we must do in order to survive economically, those ills we have suffered from, and still have to endure, are not special to Scotland. Speaking with local government people in and out of Europe, I find that there are very many countries where (dare I say Thatcherite?) fiscal policies have caused difficulties of varying proportions. A small world indeed.

If anyone has doubts about the opportunities to influence European policies through constitutional change here in Scotland, perhaps a look at the diversity of local and regional government in the EU might convince them. The three federal states Germany, Belgium and Austria have quite differing forms of local government.

Belgium has three tiers, i.e.: three regions, nine provinces and about 600 communes. In Germany with its sixteen Länder (states) and various counties, districts and cities one might identify about fifteen or sixteen different systems of local government. Austria has nine Länder and a lower tier where some change is taking place towards direct election of mayors. Greece and Finland have very different single-tier systems while Denmark, Portugal, Ireland, Holland and Sweden have a two-tier system, although the latter is examining the possibility of abolishing counties to make way for regions. Ireland created eight regions in 1994 whose members come from the counties and whose function, one suspects, is to anticipate Ireland losing its Objective I status so that at least part of that country could still have Objective I status. France and Italy have widely differing three-tier systems. Spain might be seen to have three tiers too, but the Spanish constitution permits varying types of autonomy in certain regions, e.g. Catalonia and the Basque region, and the 8,000 municipalities vary in size from Madrid and Barcelona to small mountain villages. Luxembourg has a single tier. The population is about 400,000 and it has an enviable six members on the Committee of Regions. Scotland with population circa five million, has five members.

A deeper examination of the way local government operates in the fifteen member states of the EU might make one wonder how on earth there can be any kind of cooperation, consultation or cohesion – and yet there is, and improvement is taking place by leaps and bounds. This has been happening, not just because of increasing interest by councils in the European associations mentioned earlier, or by the multiplying twinning agreements or protocols involving joint arrangements with educational, commercial and cultural interests, or even the time-honoured Youth Exchange programmes, some of which, like Glasgow's, started in the late 1930s and resumed in the 1950s, but along with all of these, there was, and is, a genuine, noticeable desire on the part of Scottish local government to be European, in the way that can help the electorate most, while reciprocating with their continental partners. Perhaps one dare suggest that the structured gathering of this effort by Scottish councils started off so well at a time when that section of the Scottish Office which dealt with European matters was a 'man and a boy' operation. It probably has a staff of nearer forty now!

The Council of Europe, based in Strasbourg, and not be confused with the Council of the EU because its membership goes beyond the fifteen member nations of the EU, has a local authority and regional section (CLARAE). Although its members include authorities from Poland, parts of Russia, Romania and Norway etc., it is unavoidable that a substantial part of the CLARAE agenda refers to the EU, although, in passing, it has helped tremendously in bringing democratisation of local government to many East European states, and its aid to war-torn Bosnia is immeasurable, but unfortunately unsung. But out of CLARAE some years ago, and echoed by the other European local government associations, and lately by the CoR, came a clear declaration of demand for democratic local self-government. This concept was recognised by the main European Institutions, including the Council of Ministers, but not all of them, including the UK's, have signed up.

If anything else is needed by Scottish local government as a spur to be part of an integrated Europe, it must be a united demand of the British government to sign that Charter. After all, since the UK is without a written constitution, many aspects of its everyday life, including local government, can be abolished at the stroke of a pen. If that sounds far-fetched, remember how quickly Madam Thatcher disposed of the GLC and other Met authorities when they faced up to her, and her actions were never part of her parliamentary manifesto. (Come to think of it, the Scottish similarity must surely be Ian Lang's 'reorganisation' of Scottish local government which we have commenced.)

The Constitutional Convention has put rather well what will be expected of a Scottish parliament, especially in its formative years. So long as its membership comprises a reasonable number of former councillors and, sensibly, women, the writer has no fear of the parliament looking around for mischief for idle hands to perform. Enough of its members, and civil servants, will have sufficient experience, or be hungry to gain experience in Euro-matters, so as to encourage local government to keep doing increasingly that work in the EU at which many have become expert.

Instead of hampering local government activity in Europe, as the present UK government is occasionally wont to do, a Scottish parliament will be able to bring together other institutions in Scotland to work with local government as it shows freshness and innovation in Brussels and Strasbourg which might well be envied.

One of the remarkable things about the Committee of Regions is that the UK delegation of twenty-four, five of them Scots, is reckoned to be the best-served of all the delegations, and this is notwithstanding the positive wealth of, say, the German delegation, which is of equal numbers. The UK group are aided by the amalgam of the five British local authority associations, but the Scots are especially nurtured by COSLA and its man in Brussels, the Scottish MEPs – a very helpful group indeed – and by the Scottish Office and the Scottish Enterprise office in Brussels.

. . .

In anticipation of the Inter-governmental Conference which takes place this year, the CoR was first among the Euro institutions to produce a paper, the Pujol Report (headed by the distinguished president of Catalonia) which sets down certain expectations for local government in Europe. Besides the 'divorce' from the sister committee, ECOSOC, the CoR seeks the absolute endorsement of the charter for local self-government; the re-defining of Subsidiarity and the right to take action in the European Court against any member-nation or Euro-institution seen to fail in the rightful application of Subsidiarity; that the Committee of Regions be recognised as a formal Institution of the EU; that the consultative function of the CoR be strengthened and that it be entitled to consult with the E[uropean] P[arliament], which it cannot officially do at present (a crafty one on the part of the Council!); that the CoR be consulted in the preparing and compiling of European Green and White papers; that in the interest of economic and social cohesion, the Treaty be revised to allow the promotion of cross-border and inter-territorial activities (which the CoR and Euro-local government associations have proved they are good at!); and that the interests of the Citizens become paramount in the promoting of progress in the fields of justice, home affairs and the fundamental rights of Citizens.

Even if the Inter-governmental Conference rejects some, or all, of these demands there is no going back by the member states from the recognition of local government by Maastricht and the voluntary development of the Committee of Regions.

Just as a Scottish parliament dare not be abolished again, one of its underlying strengths will be a strong, vibrant form of local government whose influence, encouraged by the parliament, will be felt and appreciated all over the new Europe to the economic and social advantage of the Scottish people.

FUNDAMENTALS FOR A NEW SCOTLAND ACT

Graham Leicester

From *Scottish Affairs* (no. 16, 1996, pp. 1–6). Leicester was senior research fellow with the Constitution Unit, and later set up the Scottish Council Foundation in Edinburgh.

If there is a change of government at the coming election, it will usher in an administration, either Labour or a coalition of Labour and the Liberal Democrats, committed to legislate for Scottish home rule on the basis of the proposals of the Scottish Constitutional Convention (SCC).

That much is common knowledge. But the bill will need to take its place in a legislative programme which, over the course of a parliament, might include a number of other constitutional measures. All in all there is a heavy legislative agenda, and if Labour honours its pledge, to legislate in the first year of government, Scotland – and Wales – will lead the way. That gives rise to two potential problems:

- the devolution legislation might prove more difficult to enact than expected, might sap the government's energies, and might be fudged and amended to such an extent in order to get it through that it satisfies neither supporters nor opponents. All of these criticisms arguably apply to the devolution legislation for Scotland and Wales passed in the 1970s;
- the legislation could fail to take account of links with other constitutional measures (for example, House of Lords reform, extension of devolution to the English Regions etc.) and effectively close off options which in the long run would make the overall package less satisfactory.

It was with such potential difficulties in mind that the Constitution Unit was established at University College London in April 1995:

- to analyse current proposals for constitutional reform;
- to explore the connections between them;
- and to identify the practical steps involved in putting constitutional reform in place.

The Unit published a detailed report on Scottish devolution at the end of June 1996 [Constitution Unit, 1996]. The report considers how to draft a devolution bill which is sound and workable; what other changes in the UK system of government will be needed to make the devolution settlement work, beyond those included in the legislation; and how Scottish devolution relates to the other proposed changes in the British political system. The focus is less on the internal workings of the settlement in Scotland – how the parliament might operate, what policies it might pursue etc – than on the relationship between a Scottish Parliament and the rest of the UK political system. If the Scottish Parliament is to succeed then it will be necessary, through the devolution legislation and other instruments and agreements associated with it, to carve out a secure constitutional space within the British state in which it can freely operate.

– The Scotland Act 1978 Revisited? –

Naturally the first place to look for guidance is the Scotland Act passed in 1978, which itself drew on some of the lessons of failure from the 1976 Scotland and Wales Bill. There is a good deal of detail in the Act which would need to appear in some form or other in any future devolution Act. But as a model it is deficient in at least two respects – one technical and one political.

The technical flaw is in the way that the 1978 Act assigns legislative competence to the Scottish Assembly. It was put together by trawling through the statute book as it then applied to Scotland and assigning responsibility for each statute either to Edinburgh or Westminster. In many cases even within a single statute some sections were devolved and others not. The result was a list of Edinburgh's legislative competence which ran to twenty-eight pages of the statute book, which made no sense to anybody without cross referencing to other existing statutes, and which in spite of it all still left plenty of scope for argument in any individual case about whether a proposed Act of the Assembly fell within or outwith its authority.

It is very difficult to find any support for following this model again, especially amongst those involved in the interminable discussions of individual statutes which filled over two years of Whitehall committee time between 1974 and 1976. A better model exists in the Government of Ireland Act 1920, which specifies only the powers retained at Westminster rather than those devolved to the Stormont Parliament. A devolution Act on that model would still be a complex piece of legislation. But it would be clearer; it would be more firmly based on a principled division of powers; it would be more workable in practice (not least for the courts to interpret); and it would probably be easier and quicker to draft.

The second point is a political one. The 1978 Act contained a significant role for the Secretary of State for Scotland as the guardian of the devolution settlement. He was to act as the channel of communication between the two political systems, the interpreter of the devolution legislation to colleagues, the initiator and defender of policy in Scotland where it remained the responsibility of Westminster, and most importantly the person responsible for policing the Scottish Assembly's use of its powers.

It is this last role in particular which is troublesome today. The late John P. Mackintosh described the role as a 'one-man House-of-Lords' [Mackintosh, 1976]. The Secretary of State had the right to recommend that Parliament strike down a proposed Scottish Act if he considered that it might affect a matter reserved to Westminster and that its enactment would not be 'in the public interest'. In effect, the 1978 provisions thus allowed a political decision about the extent of the Assembly's powers to trump any judicial interpretation of what the devolution legislation actually said. That arrangement, under which a Westminster representative enjoying perhaps little support in Scotland has a qualified veto over decisions of the Scottish Parliament, is surely politically unacceptable today.

The key to coping with such potential conflicts between the two Parliaments will be the provision of institutional machinery to allow an agreed political outcome to be reached if possible, and tight and efficient judicial procedures to resolve any disputes that remain. The Constitution Unit recommend a fast-track procedure for judicial challenge in advance of entry into force of an Act of the Scottish Parliament, and a reference procedure, by analogy with determining questions of European Community law, where devolution points arise in the course of other matters. The choice of the final court of appeal is a finely balanced one, but less important than framing the legislation in a clear and helpful fashion and devising straightforward procedures for the adjudication of disputes. The Unit favour the House of Lords over the Judicial Committee of the Privy Council.

– SCOTLAND'S RELATIONS WITH CENTRAL GOVERNMENT –

This article referred earlier to carving out a constitutional space within the United Kingdom in which a Scottish Parliament and government will have room to operate. The framing of the legislation is crucial, but so too are several other factors which will have a strong impact on Scotland's policy autonomy in practice. England will always be the dominant partner within the Union: the devolution legislation needs to recognise this and entrench institutional and procedural safeguards which prevent as far as possible any abuse of that position in practice.

The first possible area for dispute is finance. Changes in the Scottish Office budget each year are currently derived by increasing Scottish programmes by a fraction of the planned increase in equivalent English and Welsh programmes. The fraction is based on Scotland's population share, and is embodied in the 'Barnett formula'. The Unit suggest that in the future an independent Commission should be established, comprising representatives appointed by both governments: to audit the Treasury's application of the formula; to highlight any difficulties in applying it (for example if there is no 'English equivalent' spending on which to base Scottish increases); and to conduct a needs assessment exercise across the UK to determine whether the present distribution of public spending between the regions and nations accurately reflects the differences in need that they clearly exhibit.

The second important area is European policy. Some overlap of legislative competence between the Scottish Parliament and the European Community will be unavoidable given the extent of the latter. Thus under EU rules it will formally fall to the United Kingdom to agree EC law even where domestic legislation in the same area would be the responsibility of the Scottish Parliament. Cooperation in this area is therefore essential – to make sure that the UK's position accurately represents the Scottish interest, and to allow the Scottish Parliament to implement European directives for itself to reflect local concerns. The Unit propose a formal agreement between the UK and Scottish governments covering consultation over new legislative proposals, levels of representation in the Community institutions, and attendance at all relevant Council and working group meetings and at inter-governmental conferences to review the treaties. Special provisions in the devolution Act should also make clear where responsibility for failure to apply EC law lies.

European policy is a special case of a general need for the Westminster and Edinburgh political and bureaucratic systems to liaise with each other closely. That liaison will need to happen at all levels: officials, parliaments, governments. The Unit suggest a number of features which might help to make sure that the relationship functions smoothly. One is that the civil service should remain a unified UK-wide organisation, although with an enhanced degree of autonomy in Scotland. Another is the establishment of a Joint Council of the two governments, at least for the early years. Scottish – and other – MPs at Westminster might also join a Scottish Affairs Select Committee to monitor the devolution settlement. In time its terms of reference would probably expand to cover other devolved nations and regions: in other words, 'Devolution Affairs'.

The Secretary of State for Scotland will also have a key role to play in establishing this machinery in the early period, and in interpreting the devolution settlement to his or her colleagues. But the role may diminish, and – although it will still be open to the Prime Minister to fill it – will be difficult to justify once the Parliament becomes established.

Finally, the question of Scotland's level of representation in the Westminster Parliament will again be raised in the context of devolution, as it was in the 1970s when it became known as the 'West Lothian question'. The fact is that the question will still be asked so long as one Scottish MP remains at Westminster, and the only two genuine answers – no representation at all, and 'in and out' (Scottish MPs taking no part in Commons business dealing only with the rest of the UK) – are unjust or unworkable.

A political response might lie in reducing Scotland's representation at Westminster. But there are practical difficulties involved in implementing any change with so many other relevant factors to consider. They include, potentially, Welsh and Northern Irish representation, conflicting Boundary Commission rules in the different parts of the UK, the speed of development of English regional government, and the need to put a ceiling on the overall size of a constantly expanding House of Commons. It is not in any government's gift simply to change the level of representation unilaterally: any revision would have to emerge from a trusted process. That might be a Speaker's Conference, or perhaps a review by a new UK Electoral Commission. Both would need clear cross-party political guidance about the objectives of the review before commencing. That might prove difficult to obtain, especially with a referendum on change in the Westminster electoral system itself also in prospect (as proposed by the Labour Party).

– CONCLUSION –

This article has touched on a number of the fundamentals for success in legislation for devolution in the 1990s: the form of the legislation and the nature of the administrative infrastructure which will have to be provided to make it work. The Unit's report covers a good many other areas in significantly more detail. Even so, it does not claim to be comprehensive: there are still questions to answer, details to be sketched in, political judgements to be made.

It will have succeeded in its purpose, however, if it moves the debate in Scotland on from the point represented by the 1995 St Andrew's Day report of the Constitutional Convention, and if in addition it succeeds in stimulating a wider debate south of the border. It suggests a number of areas where public and private discussion might usefully now focus: on what needs to be retained at Westminster rather than what can be devolved to Scotland; on the means of securing stability in the financial settlement rather than the mechanism for varying it potentially at the margins (tax-raising powers); on the implications for central government on which the Convention remains silent, and in particular the practical implications of the overlap in Brussels and Edinburgh competences; and on the wider implications of a rolling programme of devolution for the way in which the Scotland/UK political relationship is to be managed.

In all of these areas the report has suggested possible solutions and responses, a range of possible options. It is not intended to be in any way prescriptive, or exclusive of other ideas. It is offered not as a blueprint, but as a contribution to the debate. Above all, it recognises that devolution – if it occurs – should not be considered as a gift graciously offered by the centre, but as a response to a demand from part or parts of the state which has to be met.

Scotland's Next Step

Peter Jones

From the magazine *Prospect* (April 1997, pp. 48–51). Jones was (and is) Scotland and North of England correspondent of the *Economist*.

. . .

[The] underground layers [of Scottish society] are much more fissured than is suggested by the rolling surface undulations of a country seemingly united by a desire for a political means of self-expression. Assuming the desire is satisfied after the election the fissures will soon become more visible.

– Scotland: Less United Than It Seems –

The Highlander and the Lowlander, while they might agree that they are both Scottish, would find it more difficult to agree on what bonds them in their Scottishness than the Cornishman and the Cockney would concur on the essence of their shared Englishness.

Yet it seems clear that the Scots are moving towards self-government. Opinion polls, although an uncertain barometer of mood, nevertheless indicate a steady wish for some form of home rule. For a decade, the mercury has shown a constant 25–30 per cent of voters favouring independence, 45–50 per cent wanting self-government within the UK, and only 15–20 per cent supporting the constitutional status quo.

This points to one crucial difference between politics north and south of the border. South of it, sovereignty is something under threat. North of the border, sovereignty is a prize yet to be gained. But, should this sovereignty be attained through the election of a Labour government which then sets up its long promised Scottish parliament, this will not be an end to the matter. It will merely be another twist in a long road which curls around the debris of previous 'solutions' to the Scottish problem.

The problem began in 1707 with the Act of Union which ended the independence of the Scottish parliament and integrated Scotland politically with England. By the early nineteenth century, attempts to expunge the notion of Scotland from popular consciousness and replace it with the idea of North Britain were in full swing. But by the late nineteenth century the pendulum was swinging the other way. Scotland gained its own department of government, the Scottish Office, and its own government ministers, whose power has grown steadily during the twentieth century.

The limits to this solution – the administrative devolution of education, health, local government, the still distinctive legal system, industrial development, the arts, aid to farmers, police and prisons, which occupies 12,000 civil servants spending £14.3 billion a year – have now been reached. The devolution of political power over this administrative empire is the next, logical step. It is only a step, not an end. The interesting question at this stage in the process is not the West Lothian one, but the dynamics of political and cultural change that will occur within Scotland after devolution and the opening up of public debate.

Seen from a British perspective, Scottish politics are as democratic as anywhere else. Viewed from within Scotland, however, they are profoundly undemocratic. The Scottish Office machinery of government has been controlled for the past fifteen years by a party for which only a quarter of Scots have voted and whose ideology is comprehensively rejected. This has warped public debate in Scotland. Political issues such as privatisation, the constraints on local government and education reform are analysed not so much according to their merits, but according to their relationship to Scottish values, whether they are an external imposition or a response to a demand within Scotland. The Scottish Tories, because they have been perceived to be essentially an English party, have suffered accordingly.

Scottish culture, on the other hand, seems to have flourished vigorously. This seems to owe something to the indecisive vote (one third said 'yes', one third 'no', and one third stayed at home) in the 1979 referendum. Devolution is, after all, an obsession of the chattering classes, and writers and artists are innate chatterers. The paintings of Ken Currie writhe with the muscular power of shipwrights and boilermakers, a power that is useless against the relentless tides of market forces. The books of James Kelman boil with the same frustration. Works such as these speak with an inchoate nationalism, expressed more clearly still by pop groups which proliferated in the 1980s, such as Hue and Cry, The Proclaimers and Deacon Blue. The titles of their albums were clear political slogans: *Remote, When the World Knows Your Name* and so on.

This subliminal nationalism also pervades Scottish political debate far beyond the press releases of the SNP. For example, the Scottish media's coverage of last year's decision by the Labour party leadership that there should be a referendum on devolution before the legislation is introduced into Westminster was not conducted in terms of whether this was a good idea which would assist the process of devolution. Instead the media speculated endlessly on just how much this was a diktat by Tony Blair, and how offensive it was to Scottish opinion. The real explanation for the referendum idea – that it was devised in a shadow cabinet subcommittee composed mostly of Scots who thought it was the best way to ensure that the legislation was passed and would endure [see Jones, 1997] – was not sought out.

This is alibi politics. If the Scots do not like something, then the English make a convenient scapegoat. Scottish hands remain clean. It will not do after devolution.

– SCOTLAND'S PARLIAMENT: NO MORE ALIBIS –

Responsibility for all the work done by the Scottish Office will pass from five government ministers (and two law officers) appointed by the prime minister to an elected 129–seat Scottish parliament. The buck – for closed hospital wards, dilapidated schools, or cuts in council cash – will stop with them.

True, while the parliament can decide how to spend taxpayer's money, it will have to rely on Westminster to keep sending a cheque to Edinburgh. If it is not able to reopen hospital wards, mend the schools and restore money to councils, it may choose to blame the meanies in London.

But this would be an unwise tactic for Labour and Liberal Democrat members of the Scottish parliament. They would be taunted from both sides. The nationalists would say that here was proof that they had been right all along; that this much vaunted parliament was no more than the powerless talking shop they had always said it would be. The Tories would also claim to be vindicated – that the parliament was indeed the cancer that they had predicted would destroy the Union. And should the parliament be granted the power to raise taxes, the politics of complaint would have even less meaning. This power, to levy up to 3p on the basic rate of income tax, may raise at most £450m, a mere 3 per cent of the budget which would be granted by Westminster, but it would be enough for Scottish voters to see the lie in any claim that Scotland's problems cannot be cured except through greater generosity by English taxpayers.

A new Scottish politics will emerge after the election. Some of its new fault lines can already be detected within the Scottish Labour Party. Labour in Scotland is not the left-wing leviathan sometimes portrayed. It has produced Gordon Brown and Donald Dewar, men as essential to new Labour modernisation as Peter Mandelson. It voted as overwhelmingly for Tony Blair to be leader as the rest of the Labour party. Even in its Red Clydeside heartlands, in the very tenements which nurtured the radicalism of Keir Hardie and James Maxton, it voted to abandon Clause Four.

But it is still different. It has factions. The trade unions, mainly because the Scottish Trades Union Congress (STUC) has been politically cleverer than the TUC, are a stronger force and still believe in the virtues of tax-and-spend. Last year, the STUC produced a document showing how many jobs could be created in construction and related industries if the Scottish parliament decided to raise its own revenue and spend it on housing projects. The other side of the equation – how many jobs might be lost through a levy on income tax applicable only to Scottish residents – was not calculated.

Because more of them have been in Labour hands for longer than in England, the local authorities have a big say in the party. And councillors, frustrated by years of having their powers and finance curtailed by the Tories, are desperate to get some back. At meetings of Labour-controlled councils the air is thick with half-veiled attacks on Gordon Brown for pledging to maintain the Tories' straitjacket on council finances and public sector workers' pay for another two years.

And Scottish Labour has a nationalist wing, which thinks that the parliament will have to accumulate more power than Blair will permit; and that the Labour party in Scotland will have to become more autonomous and separate from Labour south of the border. Dennis Canavan, MP for Falkirk West, is not alone in thinking that the 3p income tax supplement is a puny power, and that the Scottish parliament would be better to gather all taxes levied in Scotland and pay a portion to Westminster to cover the cost of shared services such as defence.

Against all these tendencies are ranged Blair's supporters. They see devolution not so much as the restoration of the pre-1707 landscape, but as a modern exercise in the decentralisation of British politics, bringing those parts of the political system which are Scottish closer to those it is supposed to serve, while maintaining the integrity of those aspects which are and need to remain British. Such politics, to adopt European jargon, is all about subsidiarity.

This suggests that Scottish Labour, post-devolution, could be an unruly mob. Indeed the elections to the party's Scottish power base, the Scottish executive committee, at the recent party conference in Inverness would have been a bloody affair but for the impending general election.

Although these divisions will become more obvious after the election, there are also constraints which will prevent Scottish Labour from exploding in fissiparous disarray. The Scottish parliament is to be elected by proportional representation: seventy-three of the seats will be elected by first-past-the-post within the existing Westminster constituencies (Orkney and Shetland is to be divided), and fifty-six seats will be filled by members from party lists according to the party's share of the popular vote.

Under this additional-member system, Labour is most unlikely to win an outright majority. In the past two decades, it has never had more than 42 per cent of the vote. According to John Curtice, of Strathclyde University, the voting pattern at the 1992 general election would have given Labour 54 seats, the Tories 30, the SNP 28 and the Liberal Democrats 17. If Scottish Labour spends its time between the general election and the first Scottish parliamentary elections fighting itself, then even 54 seats, 11 short of an overall majority, would be impossible to achieve.

– NEW COALITIONS –

Once inside the Scottish parliament, the politics of alliance and coalition rather than acrimony and confrontation are more likely to predominate. There are two reasons for this. First, the parliament will operate on fixed four-year terms, [and] so forcing an election to unblock a political logjam will not be an option. Second, Labour and the Liberal Democrats have agreed that their seats should be filled by equal numbers of men and women. The effects that this will have are uncertain, but it seems likely to make macho posturing less fashionable.

The likeliest coalition is easier to predict. While there is a left-right spectrum in Scottish politics, the nationalist-unionist continuum is a more powerful determinant of alliances. This places the SNP at one end, the Tories at the other, with Labour and the Liberal Democrats in the middle. Since both the latter parties have been, through their joint work in the Scottish Constitutional Convention, the architects of the present home rule plan, they have an interest in making it work.

Labour's nationalist wing may therefore be under some pressure to join the SNP. The SNP, however, will have its own factionalism to contend with. Quite a few SNP members see their role as a pressure group aiming to ensure that Labour delivers a Scottish parliament. These people will want to make a success of the parliament. But others will argue that it needs to fail, because only out of the ruins of failure will come the determination to push for full independence.

The Tories will have problems, too. Throughout the years of strident Unionism, the small band of pro-devolution Tories have kept quiet. But once the parliament is seen to be on its way, they will come out of hibernation to argue that the Tories' best course is to accept that it has lost the war on this issue. Their main difficulty will be not so much Scottish Tories wanting to carry on a resistance battle, but the party in England which will want to address the West Lothian question and perhaps cut the number of Scottish MPs at Westminster.

These problems are unlikely to cause a sudden dash for independence. If Labour's devolution scheme does run into trouble, it seems unlikely that the electorate, having been persuaded to take one problematic step towards autonomy, will think that the best cure is to take another more dangerous step.

– OPENING UP THE SCOTTISH ESTABLISHMENT –

In any event, the new politicians will also have to contend with another part of Scotland's hidden sub-strata that devolution will expose to daylight. This is the Scottish establishment elite which has quietly got on with running the country while the politicians have ranted and raved.

Sometimes too much is made of the distinctiveness of the Scottish education system, but the policies which guide its development have not, in the main, been devised by politicians, but by a largely unknown elite – the administrators of the Scottish Office education department, Her Majesty's Inspectorate, the certification and curriculum authorities, the General Teaching Council and the local authority directors of education – who make up a formidable array of bureaucrats.

From these people has come a seamless robe of policy changes which can be traced back to the 1960s and which has flowed on unperturbed by changes in government and politicians. Only one politician, Michael Forsyth, has been able to introduce changes which the bureaucracy did not approve of. Yet even he, perhaps the most determined politician the Scottish Office has seen in two decades, found it a difficult task. Despite all inducements, only two of Scotland 3,700 local authority schools have opted out for [self-governing] status.

And yet there is much need for reform. Scottish education rests too much on the laurels of being superior to English education. In terms of exam results, it is not as good as a Northern Irish education; and measured by other forms of achievement, it does not match up to France or Germany.

Much the same goes for the Scottish legal system, which quietly prospers away from the spotlight which shines on its English counterpart. Why are there so few women judges? What is being done to speed up court procedures? What can be done to lift the pressure on the public prosecution service? Is sentencing policy right? None of these questions receive any serious political or public debate.

The people inside the education and the legal system are inherently hostile to any idea or innovation which comes from south of the border. Devolution should cure that. If the new Scottish politicians rise to the challenge, they can abandon the ramparts of defensiveness in favour of serious examination of the internal workings of Scottish society. In time, self-confidence can replace self-doubt. True, there is much to be doubtful of in Scotland. The myth that Scottish society is not racist needs to be destroyed. The cancer of religious sectarianism which afflicts many communities in the west of Scotland needs to be rooted out. Parochialism and parish rivalries are rife. Enterprise is still a vaguely unsavoury word, profit still close to being a swear word.

The one area which does not need a boost to its self-confidence is the arts. They could hardly be healthier. But the thesis that English oppression is responsible for producing the cultural exuberance of recent years hardly stands up to examination. There has been no oppression of language or identity as there was in Catalonia or the Basque country in the days of Franco's dictatorship. James Kelman and Irvine Welsh have been able to pioneer the vernacular novel of the urban underclasses uncensored, and have been lauded for it. Pop is so over-loaded with Scottish bands that the music critics moan about their proliferation. Scottish films, such as *Shallow Grave* and *Small Faces*, are critical successes. Gaelic culture has turned from being a dying minority interest in the Highlands and Islands to being a renowned treasure, from the susurrating poetry of Sorley MacLean and Norman MacCaig to the insistent beat of Runrig and Capercaillie.

A good deal of this work has been motivated by the search for a national identity. That will go on, just as French, German or American writers gnaw at the bone of their national identity and dissect the complexities of their societies. If you can detect in contemporary art the portents of the future, as you could hear the breaking of chains in the theatres of pre-1990 Prague, then the state of Scottish art bodes well. Where Scottish art has travelled in the last twenty years, Scottish politics and Scottish society can, with luck, follow in the next twenty.

Sovereignty after the Election

Tom Nairn

From a lecture given to a Charter 88 meeting in London, June 1997, and reprinted in *New Left Review* (no. 224, July/August 1997, pp. 3–18). This lecture both reiterates some of the main themes that Nairn was already dealing with in his 1970 essay in Part I, and also marks significant changes in his view towards endorsing Scottish independence. (See also Nairn, 1977; and Nairn, 1997.)

– Sovereigntyscapes –

The week before the 1 May General Election, Robert Harris wrote in his *Sunday Times* column [27 April 1997, p. 5.4] that the interminable electoral campaign had probably been a waste of time for the outgoing government. It had made no difference to voting intentions because 'the tectonic plates had shifted' already to determine the outcome. I think this was more than just a striking phrase. Deeper pressures had indeed asserted themselves, and are continuing to do so. The fault-lines are still widening, and we are still trying to work out just what they are.

Theorists of nationality-politics have invented the term 'ethnoscape' to describe certain aspects of traditional national identity. By analogy what we are dealing with here might be called the 'sovereigntyscape' of the United Kingdom – the deeper configuration of central authority inherited and taken for granted, and in practice grafted on to most ideas (including popular ideas) of the nation, of 'what it means' to be British or English. I think it is in this zone that the tectonic shifts are occurring. The two outstanding manifestations so far have been the precipitous decline of the Monarchy since around 1990, and 1997's electoral earthquake – 'the Labour landslide' as most comment called it (appropriately enough in the context of Harris's metaphor). But there is another old-fashioned metaphor which might be applied too. It could equally be said that 'a crisis of the State' is going on. Marxists used to be fond of this idea, which implied that social forces (notably economic ones) were outpacing and undermining the existing power structures, and hence bringing about an inevitable 'collapse' (with any luck, a 'revolution') from which Progress would emerge victorious, guided by Marxists. A crisis of the State is by definition a crisis of Sovereignty.

Sovereignty is the ultimate or last-resort power over a given population and territory. . . . Everyone knows that in Great Britain a peculiar mysticism attaches to the notion, reflecting the metempsychosis of the late-feudal Crown into a representative Parliament, after the Revolutions between 1640 and 1688. Given the aristocratic or patrician nature of the resultant English representation, an extraordinarily centralised and elitist apparatus of power and administration was created. . . . At the moment of birth of the British Union, . . . the Crown-in-Parliament became the sovereignty-mode of what Liah Greenfeld (1992) has called 'God's first-born' – the early-modern or primitive template of the nation-state. This lasted three centuries, plenty of time to acquire delusions of immemoriality. Round about its 300th birthday in 1988, however, in the thirty-fifth year of the reign of Elizabeth the IInd and Ist (and the ninth of Counter-Sovereign Margaret), it began to exhibit serious symptoms. As if stricken by a premonitory curse, the Crown abruptly de-metempsychosed into a tacky Heritage side-show, leaving Parliament as sole manager of the national team-identity. Westminster was poorly equipped for the role: hauteur, immemoriality and Empire had long ago immured it into a traditionalism immune from 'that sort of thing'. So the deposition of Margaret in 1990 consigned Britain to a sort of Hades, John Major's grey nether Kingdom of dinge, sleaze, rigor-mortis constitutionalism, tread-water triumphalism and anti-European xenophobia.

. . .

The locus of debate has at last shifted decisively from the economy to the state. It always used to be said by conscious and unconscious apologists of Old Corruption that the people 'had no interest in constitutional questions'. Well, they seem to be acquiring one fast. That was in any case always a piece of Westminster dullardry. Ah for the days of such pseudo-shrewd-ness and unflinching self-admiration! Naturally there was little popular concern with reforming a Constitution which everyone had been taught to revere alongside the State Opening and Vera Lynn. But all this meant is that people used to behave themselves. In the 1980s they stopped behaving themselves too. And finally Britain's last hope of rectitude, the Labour Party, embarked upon a noisy and compromising (though possibly brief) affaire with democracy. About the same time as the National Lottery, identity-Angst crept at last into the British soul and led it to query 'the way we're governed' – which means sovereignty.

. . .

– IRREFORMABLE UNITARISM? –

The underlying demography and economics of the archipelago – with England representing more than three-quarters of the whole – meant that [the post-1707 British] state could . . . behave pretty well 'as if' it were a unitary polity. Approaching the year 2000 we still inhabit 'as if' land. Although [they were] the most significant of the national minorities, the Scots were (and maybe still are) too few, far off, ill-organised and (in European terms) 'unconnected' to interfere with such a de facto interpretation of Britishness. In practice the English Parliament simply turned into the United Kingdom Parliament and got its own way with a name-change. Later such unitarism was buttressed by a nineteenth-century reconstruction of the Monarchy. Transformed into a popular ideology-code, this worked as a state-ordained nationalism substitute until the collapse of the 1990s (Nairn, 1988).

The old interpretation still prevails, of course. But it is ceasing to do so, because of the new crisis of sovereignty created by a combination of British decline, the European Union, and the advance of non-elite (or anti-elite) democracy. As a result, the crisis of dis-formation of Crown-in-Parliament absolutism is now seriously upon us. 1997's electoral lurch was another symptom of this (whether or not it indicates any deeper will to escape). And one of its victims now seems certain to be the style of multinational sovereignty.

Occluded multinationalism depended completely upon the absence of political voice in its 'satellites'. That was the single most important meaning of 'incorporation'. More exactly, it was that meaning from the majority or main-body standpoint. But the point has never been taken in the same way by the satellites themselves. As Harris pointed out in the article quoted before, not much was said of any importance during the longest election campaign in history. Among the important statements, however, were some made at its outset by Conrad Russell on the constitution (1997). Re-reading the Treaty of Union, he underlined how it was in fact 'an international treaty between two equal sovereign states . . . (which) may be thought by some to be capable of re-negotiation', and also recognised 'a residual Scottish sovereignty'. This may be a museum-piece in England, but lives on in the satellite:

> What the Scots have wanted ever since 1603 is recognition as equal partners in a union with England. This the English, because of their unitary theory of sovereignty, have consistently denied them.

In other words, when Scots have talked about 'being British', staying in the Union (etc.) most of them have never meant what the English – and especially English political leaders – thought they meant by these apparently harmless phrases. Such misunderstandings are vital to an unwritten constitution. Though less blatantly obvious than in the case of Northern Ireland, Scottish and Welsh mésententes are just as profound, and just as reflective of the present crisis. Hence (Russell goes on),

> For Scots the point of devolution is to destroy this unconscious English supremacism. . . . Something like two thirds of Scots want to preserve the Union with England, but they do not want, and have never wanted, to preserve it on exclusively English terms.

Some other conclusions seem to me to follow from his acute observations. 'Devolution' is for London precisely that: 'power retained', or a way of preserving the old terms, while affecting the more democratic or liberal approach made obligatory by the post-1989 climate. Lady Thatcher's version lay in pretending to devolve power to 'the individual' (entrepreneurs, families, etc). Blair, on the other hand, in the phrase which the election campaign made sadly famous (though naturally more in Scotland than in England), would rather give nothing away to a northerly 'parish council' [Butler and Kavanagh, 1997, p. 110]. Since his Scottish Party is fixated on this aim, he has no option. But like nearly everyone in England he interprets the Scots assembly as simply a more democratic form of administration, a benign modernisation-move in no way affecting the existing structure of sovereignty. The Scots by contrast (including many in the Labour Party, and many conservatives) will welcome the reconstituted parliament as a reappearance (albeit one-legged) of sovereignty among them – something more like equality, 'their due' in the sense of what the Treaty should have meant, and so on. Could misunderstanding be deeper, or more total?

. . .

– West-Lothianitis –

. . .

In general terms, there is likely to be less ground for the negotiation of novelty into the system than appears at first sight – particularly in a period of euphoric expectation. A state in steepening long-term decline will tend to consolidate or fall back upon its essence, even while it searches (avidly, as at present) for new survival-formulae. Everybody knows that the Labour government inherits easily the most dense, refractory and metropole-centred power-system in Europe. That historical unitarism was borne to a new level altogether by the reforming passion of Baroness Thatcher, who in some respects remains Blair's heroine and model. He wants to move in a different direction, but 'as she did' in the sense of rapidly, popularly and decisively (even ruthlessly). Furthermore, he has something she didn't: a new party. The new Premier's authority enjoys the crucial vehicle of a 'modernised' party where greater individual democracy has been counter-balanced by intensified central domination. To regain office, in other words, Kinnock, Smith and he were forced to transform Labourism along parameters which were (immediately) those of 'Thatcherism' but (more profoundly) could not help also being those of an ultra-centralist polity near the end of its tether. They made Labour a party of power rather than protest; but 'power' is not an abstraction. A party reconfigured in these circumstances unwittingly became the prime bearer of actual 'sovereignty'. For all Britannic subjects power has the defined form of Crown-in-Parliament, the airless courtroom-Chamber by the Thames, the wondrously flexible Constitution (and so on – all the rest of it). Also, we know how New Labour has attained its object: through the kind of absurd tip-over inherent in the ancient electoral system – too great a victory, in other words, and one owed to the mechanism of elite representation rather than democracy. It would seem to follow that the 'Presidentialism' so many commentators have depicted is not a passing or merely personal phenomenon. It is most probably . . . a farther phase in the crisis of the state: from Monarch-substitute to pretend-President.

. . .

There is no way in which some sense of sovereignty regained can be prevented from informing a new Scottish parliament. And hence, no way in which a counter-sense can be prevented from arising in the old British-English parliament. No way (consequently) of avoiding some kind of struggle over where the last word lies – on what, eventually, might be any number of subjects.

For [Tam] Dalyell and his numerous class (the artificers and loyal servitors of Union) such a struggle must be prevented at all costs. The only sure way of doing so is by abortion. Unfortunately, this particular abortion lobby has got used to phrasing its message in the deliberately quaint litany imposed by its author: legislating on sewage, road-signs, toilet-paper, class-sizes and e-coli outbreaks 'in West Bromwich but not in West Lothian', or an English resentment of over-many Scots at Westminster. . . . Such matters have of course been straightforwardly resolved by other regional or subordinate-national constitutions round the world, and there would be nothing to prevent that here – if we had a new, general, written constitutional settlement to replace 1688 sovereignty. A redrafted, democratic Union could then build in some new quasi-federative, confederal or other partnership scheme for the ethnies. But this is Tam's real point, one to which he has never wanted to draw overmuch attention. Heavy concentration on hypnotically engulfing detail dispels the uneasy radicalism attaching to such notions. The truth is not only that we do not have such a settlement. In itself that might just be a remediable accident. The more effective truth (best not dwelt on for the sake of democratic sanity) is that in this Kingdom – which 'one' (Dalyell, the Queen, Tony Blair, etc.) wishes to keep united to the world's end – we never will.

– MAKE UP OR BREAK UP –

. . .

There is actually only one solution to West-Lothianitis and the quandaries of devolution: recognition of the sovereign character of the new (or more precisely, the restored) Scottish parliament. If that is not given it will end by imposing itself. The 'New Britain' everyone has heard so much about for the last six months requires a new Treaty of Union. This has to be re-negotiated: in 1998–9, it can no longer be imposed. But re-negotiation needs at least two parties, in order to guarantee consent, whole-hearted democratic agreement (and all the other watchwords). If a substitute for equal partnership is imposed by one side alone – as appears likely – it can only end up as provisional, incessantly contested, and probably bad-tempered.

If there is anything in the longer-term perspective I have argued for here, then 'Devolution' will be like the application of a Band-Aid to a broken leg. Thus far it remains founded (like Labour's previous 1978 [Act]) upon solemn listings of discrete 'powers'. These may be either given to the new assembly, or (in the formula reputedly more favoured by Blair) 'withheld' from it as the imperial responsibilities of Westminster. That may make a difference to legislative progress through the House of Commons but in no way affects the principle. In the light of sovereignty, both formulae are absurd. They disregard and offend the 'residual

Scottish sovereignty' which Russell has rightly diagnosed in the post-1707 legacy. The only way this can be avoided is by treating the resurrected assembly as a constituent or 'convention parliament', one of whose tasks – probably the most important – will be to strike a new deal with Westminster and replace the old Treaty, on behalf of the Scottish nation.

If people feel uneasy with the abstraction of the nation, let me remind them of something more concrete, and recent. The Scottish Constitutional Convention was a broadly-based body which included the Labour Party, the trade unions, the churches, and representative of the most important institutions. Not without reason was it parodied as a constellation of the Scottish great-and-good, convened in definitely Godly style by a cleric of the Episcopalian Church, Kenyon Wright. The Convention met patiently for years in the 1980s and produced the over-modest Home-rule scheme on which any new legislation will largely be founded. But in 1988 – the 300th anniversary of William's accession – it also published a Scottish *Claim of Right* signed by most Labour and Liberal Democrat MPs, which attributed all sovereign rights in Scotland to the Scottish people, rather than to the Crown in Westminster. Did they mean it? Well, presumably the signatories did mean it, at least while their pens were scratching the Declaration paper. Some of them may now be telling themselves it is irrelevant, or has been superseded by the newly Glorious & Bloodless Accession of 1997. If so, they are mistaken.

. . .

It may not be so easy to distinguish death-throes from the stirrings of the new. Any suggestion of this kind – that nation states are the likely inheritors of the British Union – is bound to encounter the accusation of archaism. All think-tanks seem to have it in for nationalism and nation-states: out-moded, narrow, obstructive, reactionary, inward-looking and immune to alternative intellectual medicine. As a modernising addict I sympathise with much of this. None the less, if the question of sovereignty is taken seriously, then the emphasis has to be put the other way. A degree of anachronism remains inseparable from solutions to that question in the United Kingdom, because the context itself remains so deeply anachronistic. There can be no magic leap out of it. Democracy won a remarkable victory on 1 May, but so (unavoidably) did archaism. We don't know yet which aspect will be the more important, but of course the argument advanced here implies the second. Power may or may not corrupt 'absolutely'; it will as sure as Hell tend in that direction. In such an old-fashioned framework, old-fashioned solutions remain not only inevitable but at least provisionally desirable. If the President continues to successfully appropriate the former charisma of Royalty, and the framework gets even more old-fashioned beneath the New trappings, then they will become that much more desirable. This is why the Convention and its *Claim* remain justified – and much more justified in principle than in the over-praised detail of the self-rule schemes which it and other bodies have so laboriously considered.

– Trapped in the Interim –

The present British Sovereignty-system arose in the interim era between Absolutism and (with 1776 and 1789) the advent of democracy. Its terminal crisis is occurring in another interim: that between the national identity states of 1789–1989 and the formation of a European polity. Historical and developmental location explains most of what matters about nationalism. The point can be put more crassly too: things happen when they have to, usually at the 'wrong time'. There is a deeply (and in its own way essentially) accidental side to progress, which has consistently mocked blueprint-makers from the Enlightenment onwards. This has nothing to do with irrationalism or 'human nature' in the fatidic sense, though it helps to explain the formation of mythologies of that kind. The wrong time we happen to be in is the one between the endlessly-analysed 'decline of the nation-state' and a European successor in which ethno-linguistic and political differentiation can assume renewed and stable forms (Milward, 1992; Gowan and Anderson, 1997).

It would of course be awfully convenient if Scotland, Wales and Ulster could fast-forward into that regional/national condition of the future. There is no lack of voices urging them to do so, and thus avoid the perils of nation-statehood and atavism as well as the delusions of sovereignty in a globalized world. These same admonitory voices have discovered how the abandonment of old-style sovereignty can be awfully good for you – how societies may actually gain in effective authority (as well as in economic terms) through a pooling or merging of statehood, and this without sacrificing 'identity' in the psychic or communitarian sense. Well, that may be so, and be absolutely splendid, for those with the stuff to give away. For those without it, who possess nothing resembling sovereign power to 'pool', 'merge' or gallantly sacrifice, the prospect is necessarily a bit different. Sovereignty-rich metropolitans may enjoy such snakes-and-ladders; sovereignty-deprived satellites wouldn't mind just getting into the game. For the latter the UK and French Leviathans appear quite differently: not only did they appropriate smaller-nation sovereignty, they think they can give it away on our behalf as well.

Scotland has plenty of its own fast-forwarders, some of them in the Scottish National Party (which has been brandishing 'Independence in Europe' for many years). As usual I suspect they actually mean something different by it, not necessarily appreciated from a distance. As a formulaic long-term solution the thought may appeal of being an autonomous Region, or Region-Nation, inside European Union (whatever 'independence' turns out to mean there). In the shorter term, however, as a way of avoiding trouble, strife and secession, there is always another implication present, but possibly less evident in the London/Home County conurbation. It is that England (or maybe even regions of England) must move at the same time towards some similar or equivalent status. Indeed – since that happens to be where Sovereignty is unjustly concentrated – it would plainly be easiest for the metropolis to at least temporarily lead the way in such sacrifice.

So on with the pooling and merging, Britons. Until merger is achieved and 'Sovereignty' decently buried, however – i.e., until the interim becomes a bit less interim, just to be going on with – could the peripherals please have some ordinary, boring, narrow, dangerous, egotistical, potentially atavistic (etc.) sovereignty? In an epoch of the provisional, the sole solution remains the actually attainable one: that which looks back as well as forward – sovereign statehood, also known as independence, and prescribed by the general rules still prevalent in Europe and the United Nations world. Though some of its members-to-be may not yet grasp the implication, the new Scottish parliament does have a sovereignty-ambit defined for it in advance by the history I have tried to over-view here: from the 1689 Claim of Right down to the new 1988 one squeezed out by the pressures of Thatcherism. That is where it will really start from. In the new parliament there may also be plenty of 'good boys' (including I hope 50 per cent of women) who wish above all to conduct themselves with devolved propriety inside the pseudo-immemorial rules of Ukanian hegemony, antique and New. This is already known as 'making the parliament work'. I suspect they will be wasting their time. Seen in the sovereignty terms we have been looking at – the rise and fall of Britishism – ordinary nation-statehood and responsibility (also known as freedom) may turn out to be a lot less trouble.

. . .

This can be put in another way, by asking what the Scottish electorate now votes for. In one sense, of course, it votes via the Westminster table d'hôte menu of different parties inherited from the long epoch of political incorporation. However it can also be seen as voting in a fairly unanimous (70–80 per cent) manner for a decided if ill-defined direction of affairs, described in innumerable surveys and polls as 'more say in our own affairs', 'home rule', and so on. With a degree of relief, some commentators regularly point out that only one part of this registers on the Thames-side Richter scale as overt 'separatism' – the 20–25 per cent supporting the SNP. This is true, but the relief is misplaced. The point can be put more Irishly: in Scotland, Home Rule is too serious a matter to be distracted by Independence.

What most voters may really be supporting is (so to speak) the Sovereignty Party, a movement now addressing itself to the people in many different party and non-party guises (and with increasingly open support from within the ranks of Scottish Conservatism). It could also be called the right-to-decide party. The most important thing for a recalled parliament to decide (I need hardly point out) is not raising or lowering income tax by a few per cent. It will be whether to try and alter the conditions of UK affiliation. Like many (possibly most) adherents of 'right-to-decide' I think that once it comes into existence only a Scottish parliament will have the right to decide such questions. Of course this body might meet only once and decided to follow 1707 precedent, by requesting re-incorporation at Westminster with a few modernising touches. I would be disappointed by the verdict but would certainly accept it on democratic grounds; just as I assume opponents would accept any eventual verdict on dis-incorporation or seeking 'independence in Europe'.

The right-to-decide party is about democracy, not ethno-cultural nationalism. At the same time, it recognises that democracy retains a predominantly national configuration capable of transformation but not (or not yet) of supersession or transcendence. British Unionism was a short-lived pseudo-transcendence whose day is over. The 1997 election result opens the door to (at least) begin an escape from it. I hope we can get some way through that door before it closes again.

THREE-LEVEL PATH TO FLOURISH IN EUROPE

David Martin

From *The Herald* (24 July 1997, p. 16). Martin was (and is) Labour Member of the European Parliament for the Lothians, and a vice-president of the parliament.

The White Paper on Scottish devolution could herald a major boost to Scottish involvement in mainstream European progressive politics: the dynamic development of a Europe of the Regions balancing and complementing the movement towards European Union (EU). Scotland's unique position and history could mean it joining one of the leading groups in EU development.

The two historic European 'nation regions' which Scotland most resembles are The Free State of Bavaria, and Catalonia. These are prosperous states where the citizens have no problems in dealing with triple identity. Their people are proud to be Bavarian, German and European: Catalonian, Spanish and European. Similarly, the White Paper could offer Scots the best of all worlds, the flexibility of a Scottish Parliament; the strength of the UK's ten votes in the Council of Ministers; and the benefits of being part of the largest trading bloc in the world – the European Single Market.

With the imminent arrival of the European single currency the importance of the concept of a Europe of the Regions cannot be overestimated. Catalonian president, Jordi Pujol, put it well: 'the regions must look to develop co-operation with other regional authorities since political and economic union will inevitably lead to the reshaping of the European space along the lines of coherent and competitive macro-regions'. Catalonia is a historic nation with its own culture, and an existence which goes back a thousand years. Like Scotland, both historically and in terms of its economy, Catalonia has always had strong ties with the rest of Europe. It took on autonomous status within the Spanish state in 1979. Since its entry into the European Community in 1986 its gross domestic product has risen more than the average for the countries of the Community partly as a result of forming collaboration and co-operation agreements with economically buoyant regions like Baden-Württemberg, Lombardy and the Rhône-Alpes.

A progressive White Paper and a successful referendum campaign could see Scotland enter the European game at a crucial stage. What

Scotland needs to become a major player in the current European developments is:

- A Scottish European Office in Brussels, staffed by civil servants and accountable to the Scottish parliament, as the official voice of Scotland in Europe;
- Similar observer status to the German Länder (states) – Catalonia negotiated a similar figure known as the regional *aggregate* – with automatic representation on the appropriate UK delegation to the Council of Ministers;
- Co-operation between the Scottish and European Parliaments to scrutinise new European laws which relate to areas covered by a Scottish parliament;
- The appointment of a Scottish Minister of European Affairs.

The last measure, which might have to be left to the Scottish parliament itself, would signal to the various European institutions and our partners the high priority we attach to our relations with the European Union.

The Free State of Bavaria, with its centuries of political and cultural unity, is regarded as the main champion of what is known in Europe as 'three-level development': the region, the member state, and the European Union. Just how effective the Bavarians have been in putting across their case at the European level was brought home to me recently when I contacted the Bavarian Office in Brussels ('the white and blue Embassy') to ask their opinion on the establishment of a Scottish parliament, and the effectiveness of regional representation. Dr Hubertus Dessloch, director of the Bavarian Representation in Brussels, stressed the need to be involved at the European level because 'EU institutions are generating the content of national law up to 60 per cent on average. We must be able to influence this.' On economic development Dr Dessloch was equally as forthright: 'The German Länder take care of themselves. That is why we have a sound economic structure in Germany.' But the head of the Bavarian Office had no fear that an autonomous parliament would lead to calls for independence: 'The German Länder are loyal partners within the structure and are not inclined to separatist tendencies at all.'

A Scottish parliament within the United Kingdom could be equally effective. It would give the Scottish people the best possible representation in Europe. It would put us in the mainstream of European Union developments as part of a major global player while at the same time maintaining our unique identity, history, and increasing autonomy. Devolution will enable us to be Scottish, British and European, and play a major role in the Union's further development.

Scotland's Parliament

General philosophy and summary contained in the government's white paper of this name in July 1997 which was endorsed in the referendum of 11 September 1997.

– Introduction and Background –

The Government are determined that the people of Scotland should have a greater say over their own affairs. With their agreement we will change the way Scotland is governed by legislating to create a Scottish Parliament with devolved powers within the United Kingdom. This Chapter sets out the historical background and developments since the 1970s.

Following the Union of Crowns of Scotland and England in 1603, the Union of the Scottish and English Parliaments in 1707 created a Parliament of Great Britain meeting in London. A Secretary of State for Scotland was appointed in the first post-union Government. After 1745 however no such appointment was made; and while responsibility for Scotland during the majority of the ensuing period lay with the Home Secretary, most of the effective political power was exercised by the Lord Advocate. This system lasted until 1885 when the office of Secretary for Scotland was created. The status of the office of Secretary for Scotland was enhanced in 1926 to that of Secretary of State. As the Secretary of State's responsibilities gradually increased, St Andrew's House in Edinburgh became the headquarters of The Scottish Office in 1939 and the functions of The Scottish Office in London were transferred to Edinburgh. In recent years, further administrative devolution to The Scottish Office has taken place, resulting in the addition of major functions such as industrial support, training, higher education and the arts.

During the 1970s, in the light of the deliberations of the Royal Commission on the Constitution (the Kilbrandon Commission), the then Labour Government brought forward proposals to establish a Scottish Assembly. In November 1977 a Scotland Bill providing for the establishment of a Scottish Assembly was introduced; it received its Royal Assent on 31 July 1978. The Act required that a referendum be held; and an amendment carried during its Parliamentary passage required that, if less than 40 per cent of the electorate voted in favour of its provisions, an Order repealing the Act should be laid. The referendum was held on 1 March 1979. 1,230,937 voted in favour of an Assembly – a majority in excess of 77,000 – but this represented only 32.9 per cent of the electorate; the Act was repealed by Order on 26 July 1979.

Since 1988, the cross-party campaign for change has been led by the Scottish Constitutional Convention, comprising Members of Parliament of the Labour and Liberal Democrat parties, Labour members of the European Parliament, local authorities, the STUC, business, church and civic groups and other political parties. The Convention's final report *Scotland's Parliament. Scotland's Right*, which was published on St Andrew's Day 1995, set out their proposals for a Scottish Parliament.

The Government have a manifesto commitment to a comprehensive programme of constitutional reform. In its scope, scale and significance this programme will bring about the most ambitious and far-reaching changes in the British constitution undertaken by any Government this century. The aim is to make government more accessible, open and accountable. It includes devolution to Scotland and Wales; greater regional government for England and a strategic authority and elected mayor for London (subject to referendums); reforms to both Houses of Parliament; the incorporation of the European Convention of Human Rights into UK law; and a Freedom of Information Act. This comprehensive programme will give the United Kingdom a modern constitution fit for the twenty-first century. The manifesto promised legislation to allow the people of Scotland and Wales to vote in referendums to be held by the autumn of 1997 on proposals to be set out in White Papers. That legislation will shortly complete its passage through Parliament and this document is the White Paper on the basis of which the people of Scotland will be invited to make their historic choice.

– A Summary of the Proposals –

The Scottish Parliament will have law-making powers over a wide range of matters which affect Scotland. There will be a Scottish Executive headed by a First Minister which will operate in a way similar to the UK Government and will be held to account by the Scottish Parliament. The Scottish Parliament and Executive will be responsible for:

- Health including the National Health Service in Scotland and public and mental health;
- Education and training including pre-5, primary, secondary, further and higher education; and training policy and programmes;
- Local government, social work and housing including local government

structure and finance; social work; the voluntary sector; housing policy; area regeneration; building control; and the statutory planning framework;

- Economic development and transport including responsibility for the economic development of Scotland; financial and other assistance and support for Scottish business and industry; promotion of trade and exports; inward investment; tourism; functions in relation to the energy sector; the administration of the European Structural Funds; and a range of road, rail, air, sea transport and inland waterways matters;
- The law and home affairs including most civil and criminal law and the criminal justice and prosecution system including police and prisons; fire services; legal aid; parole, the release of life-sentence prisoners and alleged miscarriages of justice; certain Crown, church, ceremonial and local government electoral matters; and civil defence and emergency planning;
- The environment including environmental protection policy and matters relating to air, land and water pollution; the natural and built heritage; and water supplies, sewerage, flood prevention and coastal protection;
- Agriculture, fisheries and forestry including The Scottish Office's existing responsibilities for promoting agriculture and fisheries in Scotland and those of the Forestry Commission in Scotland;
- Sport and the arts including the Scottish Sports Council, the Scottish Arts Council and the national institutions;
- Research and statistics in relation to devolved matters.

The legislation setting up the Scottish Parliament will specify those powers which are reserved to the UK Parliament. These matters include the constitution of the United Kingdom; UK foreign policy including relations with Europe; UK defence and national security; the stability of the UK's fiscal, economic and monetary system; common markets for UK goods and services; employment legislation; social security; and most aspects of transport safety and regulation. Scotland will remain an integral part of the United Kingdom, and The Queen will continue to be Head of State of the United Kingdom. The UK Parliament is and will remain sovereign. Scotland's MPs will continue to play a full and constructive part at Westminster. The number of Scottish seats will be reviewed. The Secretary of State for Scotland will work with the new Scottish Parliament and represent Scottish interests within the UK Government.

The Scottish Executive and the UK Government will work closely together at both Ministerial and official level. There will be arrangements for resolving disagreements about whether legislation is within the powers of the Scottish Parliament.

Relations with the EU will remain the responsibility of the UK Government, but the Scottish Executive will be involved as closely as possible in UK decision-making on Europe. Ministers of the Scottish Executive will participate in relevant meetings of the Council of Ministers and in appropriate cases could speak for the United Kingdom. The Scottish Parliament will be able to scrutinise EU legislative proposals. There will be a Scottish representative office in Brussels to further Scotland's interests and complement the role of UKREP. The Scottish Executive will have an obligation to implement EU legislation on devolved matters. The UK Parliament will continue to have the ability to legislate to give effect to EU obligations in Scotland.

The Scottish Parliament will set the framework within which other Scottish public bodies – local government, non-departmental public bodies and health bodies – operate. The detailed arrangements will be for the Scottish Parliament and Scottish Executive to develop.

The financial framework for the Scottish Parliament will be closely based on existing arrangements for financing The Scottish Office, and will allow the Scottish Parliament to approve spending decisions in accordance with Scottish needs and priorities. The control of local authority expenditure, non-domestic rates and other local taxation will be devolved to the Scottish Parliament. Subject to the outcome of the referendum, the Scottish Parliament will be given power to increase or decrease the basic rate of income tax set by the UK Parliament by up to 3p. Liability will be determined by residence in Scotland. Income from savings and dividends will not be affected. The Inland Revenue will administer any tax variation, with the Scottish Parliament meeting the administrative costs.

The Scottish Parliament will consist of 129 members, 73 directly elected on a constituency basis, plus 56 additional members (seven from each of the eight current European Parliament constituencies) allocated to ensure the overall result more directly reflects the share of votes cast for each party. Eligibility to vote will be based on residency. Each Scottish Parliament will have a four-year fixed term. The Scottish Parliament is expected to adopt modern methods of working; and to be accessible and responsive to the needs of the public. Detailed arrangements will be left to the Scottish Parliament itself.

The Government are looking at options available in Edinburgh for the Scottish Parliament building. The staff of the Scottish Executive will continue to be part of a unified Home Civil Service. The annual running costs are estimated to be between £20 and £30 million a year, i.e. about £5 per year per head of Scottish population.

Scotland will be asked to vote on 11 September in a referendum on the proposals set out in this White Paper. Following a positive referendum result, legislation to establish a Scottish Parliament will be brought forward as soon as possible. Once the legislation has been enacted, elections to the Scottish Parliament will be held in the first half of 1999, and the Parliament will become fully operational in the year 2000.

WHAT'S THE STORY?

John Lloyd

From the New Statesman (8 August 1997, pp. 37–8). Lloyd was (and is) associate editor of the New Statesman.

The Scots are great ones for presenting the English with stories. They now give their neighbours two narratives about themselves: a diminution, perhaps a relief. There had been three.

Lost is the unitary, British one. It is futile to lament it, though it had (in my view) evolved into the best system available and will privately be much missed: especially by the Scots diaspora in England, whose interests were best served by having a cultural homeland and living in a unitary state; by the very many who live in Scotland, one or neither of whose parents were Scots; and by the uncountable numbers who prefer party politics to be far from them, as long as civic freedoms are thought to be secure. Constitutional conservatism used to be possible within the left; the last two decades have driven it out of the left, and confined it to Conservatism.

At the same time Conservatism itself has shrunk in Scotland to 20 per cent of the electorate, and its representation in parliament to zero. William Hague, the new Tory leader, has set the seal on the loss by committing his party to retain the Scottish Parliament if it is successfully established. He had little choice: inevitabilities, no matter how drear, have to be recognised in politics.

The official narrative now, long growing in the womb of the old, is that of Donald Dewar, Secretary of State for Scotland, a man whose determination to have a devolved parliament created in Scotland has borne fruit while he is still in his political prime. His white paper on the devolved parliament is a detailed document which gives the Scottish Parliament authority over most of what is currently handled by Dewar's office – that is, everything except foreign and defence policy, macroeconomic strategy, social security and pensions.

In an interview last week, however, he was concerned to stress that the 'genuine feeling for change' would be contained and channelled by the proposed parliament, and that the 'slippery slope' towards separation, though still existent, was now 'significantly flatter'.

I reject the argument that this is a diminution of sovereignty. There is a diminution of workload on [the Westminster] parliament. It clearly changes the day-to-day distribution of power. But no-one denies that sovereignty remains at Westminster. We rely on Westminster for our authority. We are inviting people to endorse reform within the UK.

If I control a given situation and decide to pass my authority to someone else while retaining my right to that authority, I am not diminishing it. I accept the logic of the phrase that power devolved is power retained.

But parliament now is trusting Scotland to run many of its own affairs. The difference between now and 1978–9 [when the last Labour government attempted to devolve power to Scotland] is that there were substantial override powers retained for the Scottish Secretary. We don't have these now – it is a genuine devolutionary settlement. But of course Westminster can still dispose, which is why Hague's statement is so important.

I believe this will strengthen the Union. But I don't argue it in those terms. I argue it in terms of greater democracy, of enriching Scotland's place in the Union. I don't see it as dishing the Nationalists: I argue it in terms of a democratic imperative. Yet if people in the future vote clearly for independence, I would be the last to deny it to them.

Inevitably, Dewar's proposition is seen as a halfway house, splitting the difference between the unitary model (the phrase inadequately describes the complex arrangements between Westminster and Scotland over the past two and a half centuries) and full-blown independence. It can be seen as an agenda unfulfilled, a final settlement halted, even stillborn

This helps to drive the separatist version: Alex Salmond, the Scottish National Party leader, managed to persuade his party to support Dewar on the basis that this would be seen as a stepping stone towards independence rather than, as some nationalists continue to see it, as a diversion from it that will deflate nationalist pressure. In an essay in the current *New Left Review*, Tom Nairn continues, as he has for two decades, to provide the intellectual grist for the nationalist mill. More fastidious than he has sometimes been, he separates himself from the SNP and from nationalism, holding the latter was never really the issue in recapturing sovereignty for Scotland but that regaining 'a voice' is.

Nairn sees the Dewar proposal as 'absurd'. The only way in which the popular desire for a Scots sovereignty is to be served, he argues, 'is by treating the resurrected assembly as a constituent or "convention" parliament, one of whose tasks – probably the most important – will be to strike a new deal with Westminster and replace the old Treaty, on behalf of the Scottish nation . . . Further conventions are needed to establish democracy'.

In Nairn's version, there are a number of crucial statements or assumptions; that 'Britishness' (and perhaps Britain itself) is in terminal decline; that the incorporation of Scotland's into the English parliament was 'a devious form of strangulation'; that the new Labour Party is simply a modernised form of English imperialism; that there is a 'Sovereignty Party' in Scotland that expresses the views of the vast mass of the electorate, reaching into the Tory Party, which wants and should have the right to decide on the future of Scotland; and that that decision, if freely taken, will result in sovereignty being demanded back by a Scottish Parliament (which may decide to stay in a federation, or confederation, called the United Kingdom).

Nairn's argument is an essentialist one. It depends on the view that within Scotland there is a democratic polity, waiting for its expression, which will be much more democratic than that available under the 'pseudo-transcendence' that was British unionism. The right to decide, for him, is about democracy, not 'ethno-cultural nationalism' – though how the two are to be separated in practice, when the latter observably gives the former its vital energy, in Scotland as everywhere else, he does not say.

He has cruder supporters. Ian Bell, *The Scotsman* columnist, provides a sour, cynical commentary on any efforts to stop short of the nationalism he invokes yet never manages to describe. His latest piece, this Monday [4 August 1997, p. 15], took off into a never-never land in which the literary invocations of Scotland, especially those of Irvine Welsh, the author of *Trainspotting*, are counterposed against the white paper, to the latter's disadvantage.

> They [the Westminster politicians it seems; the 'they' is not precise] have mistaken Scotland because they did not know it in the first place. They have overlooked the people . . . The parliament, should we manage it, will succeed only when it begins to give a voice to the culture within which it is planted. If it only echoes the insensate mediocrity of Westminster it will fail.

'They' have overlooked the people, mired in their 'insensate mediocrity'. What this means is that there is an essential people from whose culture can be constructed a political system that transcends mediocrity. Behind this (genuinely absurd) belief is a thickening hinterland of appeals to Scots democracy, wisdom and courage through the centuries: a tradition betrayed, now clamouring for expression, flowers of Scotland long crushed, now slowly uncurling in a little sun.

For all Nairn's devotion to democracy, he will not save Scotland from the horrors of ethno-cultural nationalism that his road opens up. It found something of a solvent in the now discarded unionism. From now on, the best that can be hoped for is that Donald Dewar does know his own country, and that he is right about it.

Losing Sight of Tinkerbell

Joyce McMillan

From *The Herald* (16 August 1997, p. 32). McMillan was (and is) a freelance journalist, broadcaster and theatre critic.

. . .

[A] civil society, like the one in which we still live, is like Tinkerbell [in J. M. Barrie's *Peter Pan*]; if we stop believing in it, it begins to fade away. And if I read the cultural signs right, what seems to be happening, beneath the surface of things, is that the shared belief in the positive role of government in improving the lives of its citizens, which enabled us to shape the decent outlines of post-war British society, is now dwindling to vanishing-point . . .

And it seems to me that the despair of a generation that no longer believes in society's power to improve itself is something that Scottish voters should consider long and hard, as they approach the referendum on Scottish home rule; if only because so many of the arguments being deployed against a Scottish Parliament seem to belong to this same culture of intense negativity about the power of peaceful democratic politics to change lives. Of course, there are a few arguments against home rule which address themselves straightforwardly to the specific situation of Scotland now, without seeking to smear the whole idea of democracy. There are questions about whether Scotland is really the right size and kind of unit for effective devolved government; there is the anxiety that the UK, alone among large west European states, may find itself unable to take the strain of accommodating a devolved historic nation within its borders.

But by and large – and rather oddly – these are not the arguments against change which appear most often in the current debate, particularly in the letters pages of Scottish newspapers. On the contrary, most of those opposing the Government's proposals seem to take the view that an elected parliament for Scotland is a bad idea because – well, because it is an elected parliament. It will cost money, they say, paying all those MSPs; although in fact it seems we could run the whole show from now until 2020 for less than the cost of the Millennium Dome at Greenwich. It will be full of party politicians, they say, and the last thing we need is more of them; although in fact the number of elected politicians in Scotland was so drastically reduced by the last Government that they are now outnumbered four-to-one by members of unelected quangos. And the people may vote for a government that will do silly things, they say, since half of them are not even income-tax payers; as if Scottish voters were so uniquely dim and feckless as to require a return to a system of property-based voting rights that was abolished for Westminster more than a century ago.

Now it may well be that most of those who deploy these arguments do not really intend to imply that all democratic government is a waste of time and money. Most of them never seem to think, for instance, of applying the same criteria – cost, politicians, danger of silliness – to the UK parliament at Westminster, and advocating the abolition of that; and it strikes me that their real aim, in conjuring up the image of a Scottish Parliament as a ghastly and pointless body, is not so much to rubbish democracy in general, as to appeal indirectly to that underlying Scottish lack of confidence about our own classiness and competence as a nation which so easily degenerates, at moments of decision, into a kind of self-hating conviction that we'd better keep hold of the Westminster nurse, for fear that a Scottish Government might actually be worse.

And naturally, the current grandstand view of the corrupt and disgraceful faces of old Labour politics in the west of Scotland only strengthens this half-spoken implication that any parliament elected by the Scots would inevitably be a chamber of low-life Old Labour horrors. Rationally speaking, there is not the smallest chance of a Scottish Parliament elected by proportional representation bearing any resemblance to local councils whose defining characteristic has been the colossal dominance of a single party over a period of almost a century. But we are not talking here about rational argument. We are talking about the fomenting of ancient fears and inferiority complexes; we are talking about making the Scottish people feel in their hearts that they alone among the nations of Europe are too ignorant to be able to run their own affairs, or to sort out their own corruption scandals.

'You can't seriously have democracy in a country where people think it's OK to shop at Blanks', I once heard a Scottish business leader argue in private; and he named a cut-price High Street store that is a god-send to countless thousands of hard-up Scottish mums. But that language of contempt for the intelligence and opinions of the Scottish people, ugly though it is, is not language that many people dare use in public. And so in public these opponents of home rule tend to do what is finally worse. They simply reach for that dark rhetoric of anti-politics that now exercises such a grip on the Tory party at Westminster; a rhetoric that imputes the worst possible motives to everyone involved in political life and public service, that comes close to trashing the whole concept of political authority legitimised by the consent of the people and that colludes in the idea that there is no realistic alternative to a brutal economic free-for-all, in which political authorities intervene at their peril.

And then, having operated that kind of scorched-earth policy on the very possibility of political idealism and hope, they wonder irritably why young people nowadays seem so nihilistic and self-destructive; why they smoke and drink and get involved with drugs, why so many seem to lack motivation and hope for the future.

So what I would say to those opponents of home rule is that they themselves should perhaps 'think twice' about the profoundly negative implications of some of the arguments they are using; that they should avoid, in particular, forming a devil's alliance with that kind of destructive cynicism about human motives and possibilities which, if we do not resist it, gradually destroys the fabric of trust that sustains civil peace, real freedom, and the kind of sage public space in which children and young people can thrive. If the voters of Scotland say 'no' to home rule, on 11 September, because they have suddenly become convinced of the positive qualities of our present system of government, then that is fair enough. But if they vote 'no', or stay away from the polls, in a spirit of apathy and despair about the very possibility of changing their lives for the better through democratic politics, then we will have turned a very dangerous corner. For we will have moved into a world where one of the most basic yearnings of the human heart – to feel part of a good society – is increasingly dismissed as a naive pipe-dream and where young people who want to live in a world driven by something other than brutality and greed increasingly get the message, unspoken but unmistakable, that if they need that kind of relief from harsh realities, they will have to follow in the footsteps of despairing Scots down the ages and search for it in the bottom of a bottle, or at the heart of a little white pill.

Don't Wreck the Heritage we all Share

Margaret Thatcher

From *The Scotsman* (9 September 1997, p. 17). Thatcher was by now a
Baroness, and hence a member of the House of Lords.

If a professional politician says that something is more important than party
politics it is generally time to take a large pinch from the salt cellar. But
perhaps former prime ministers can get away with making this point, as I do
in the case of the proposals for Scottish devolution on which the Scottish
people will shortly vote. What is at stake – in the case of both the
propositions on the ballot paper – is nothing short of the Union of the
United Kingdom itself. And the constitution of our country is a matter of
the gravest moment for all of us, north and south of the Border, although
you would never think it from the shallow and cynical manner in which the
Government is proceeding.

The argument for a devolved Scottish assembly, with or without tax-
raising powers, is, of course, not new. In fact, it belongs by right to the 1960s
and 1970s when too many people thought that more government was the
answer to our national problems. Creating a new set of politicians, with new
powers and spending more money is essentially what all the airy talk about
devolution is about.

The true way to give the Scots more control over their future is, by
contrast, to cut back what government spends and controls, leaving more
freedom of choice for the people. That, though, is the last thing which so
many still socialist-minded Scottish politicians want.

Indeed, it is hard to imagine how Scotland could conceivably benefit
from what is proposed. Will there be more firms and jobs in Scotland after
devolution than before it? Hardly. It is the excellent education, entrepre-
neurial flair and hard work of the Scots – along with low inflation and
competitive tax rates – which have brought business success and more
employment in recent years. But the prospect of more political interference,
regulation and taxation – particularly at a time when global not local
competition is what increasingly counts – can only deter foreign investors
and drive talent south of the Border or beyond our shores.

The adverse consequences of the 'tartan tax', which a Scottish parliament
would have the power to impose, have already been criticised by businessmen, and the Scottish people would do well to listen. Nor should they be

beguiled by the Labour Party's undertaking that it will not, in fact, raise tax. Let's remember some home truths. Powers are given in order to be used; politicians love to spend and, in the end, they have to tax; all that ever deters them is the unpopularity of taxation. But, in this case, with the vast majority of the budget still coming from general Exchequer taxation, Scottish politicians will be able to shift the blame to Westminster for all that goes wrong.

So much for the gloomy jobs prospect under devolution. But would the Scots at least have a better deal on public spending? Almost certainly not. Public expenditure per head in Scotland is already substantially higher than in England, and this arrangement has continued unchallenged for many years. It is, though, doubtful whether it would last if the whole financial relationship were subject to fundamental re-examination on the basis of proven need. Certainly, the majority of English MPs would have little sympathy for the predicament of a Scotland that had its own assembly and its own tax-raising powers when it came to the distribution of public money. And within the Cabinet, the ability of the Secretary of State for Scotland to argue persuasively for Scottish interest would be radically diminished, since he would have no responsibility for most Scottish services, and, for that matter, no obvious function at all.

But the longer term consequences, both for Scotland and for the rest of the UK, go far beyond economics. As the present Prime Minister tactlessly but accurately blurted out in the course of the general election campaign, sovereignty will continue to rest with him in the Westminster Parliament. The outcry in Scotland which greeted this remark demonstrated, however, that the enthusiasts for a Scottish parliament do not accept that. The support of the SNP for what is proposed also shows that while the Government pretends that devolution will help keep the UK together, those who have set the agenda for change (and who intend to keep on setting it) are hell-bent on separation and will not be appeased.

As the case of the Quebec parliament in Canada confirms – and as the assertiveness of the European Parliament reminds us nearer home – directly elected assemblies which claim to represent the interest of peoples are naturally driven to assert ever wider claims. And, of course, the opportunities for conflict between Westminster and the Scottish parliament are legion. I have already mentioned some of the predictable and potentially destabilising clashes over spending and taxation. But what if, say, the Scottish parliament, which would have control over training, runs up against Westminster, which has control over social security benefits? How can these two aspects of labour market policy be disengaged? Or again, what if the Scots who would have control over industry policy, wanted to bail out a firm against the general policy guidelines, which would still be set by Westminster? Whose judgement would prevail? Still more seriously, what if the Scottish parliament refused to have nuclear weapons in Scotland, while the Westminster government was determined to keep our nuclear capability there? The agitators would have a field day.

Already, the constitutional absurdities of what is proposed are clear. The so-called West Lothian question has not been answered – this is, of course, the monstrosity whereby Scottish Westminster MPs would be able to vote on English domestic affairs but not on Scottish domestic affairs. It is but the thinnest edge of the wedge, which will – along with the proposed transformation of the House of Lords into a glorified quango, the sapping away of authority to Brussels and this Government's arrogant disregard for the rights of the House of Commons – ultimately undermine the respect due to our laws.

Over the centuries in the UK, we have created something of which we should be proud, a history to which the Scots have made a special contribution and from which they – like the English – have received enormous benefits. Scottish engineers, scientists, doctors, economists, philosophers, businessmen, soldiers, explorers and statesmen have helped make Britain what it is. And the spread of British civilisation, by trade, by conquest, by settlement, by education and by example has provided Scots with opportunities that would otherwise have been unthinkable. The UK is that rare thing – a multi-national state. We can, accordingly, be passionately proud to be Scotsmen, Englishmen, Welshmen and Ulstermen, without any diminution in our pride in being British.

But such ties of unity are inevitably fragile, because they are ultimately emotional; they can, like those of any relationship, unravel; and they may do so with unforeseen consequences. Scottish politicians do Scots no service if they lead them to believe they can always pick and choose the terms under which they wish to remain in the UK. They should not be surprised if the result of doing so is to awaken a resentful English nationalism, which questions other aspects of present arrangements that the Scots themselves take for granted.

I do not believe that most Scots want to end the Union. But separation is the destination towards which the present devolution proposals lead. They represent a negation of our shared history and an abdication of our joint future. Scottish voters can do no greater service to their country than to reject them.

Free, on our Own Terms

Michael Fry

From *The Herald* (19 November 1997, p. 19). Fry was (and is) a historian and a regular columnist on the paper, and had been among the small group of Conservatives who had retained a public commitment to a Scottish parliament throughout the 1980s and 1990s.

It comes as no surprise that Scotland has a structural deficit in her public finances. The astounding thing would be if there were no such deficit after half-a-century in which Scots have bent every effort to building one up.

From Walter Elliot and Tom Johnston onwards, the policy pursued by each administration at St Andrew's House has been to dun the English for money. An entire Scottish industry, employing thousands in public authorities and agencies, with hangers-on in media and academe, has emerged in consequence.

By its own lights, by patronage and subsidy, this industry has achieved a lot. It has given us a string of other industries as wasteful in itself, symbolised by the names Ravenscraig, Linwood, Bathgate, Corpach. It has endowed us with sectarian leisure centres and drug-running security companies. It has created urban paradises such as Ferguslie Park and Craigmillar. It has showered freebies and gongs on its votaries. All this on the argument that the Scottish economy is doomed by the market, and that only expenditure by the state can ever save it.

The argument is wrong but it has had the inevitable result that the state spends more than it raises in Scotland. If things are otherwise, then we must count the careers of every Secretary of State from Willie Ross to Michael Forsyth to have been complete failures, and judge that the expertise of the thousands of officials and pundits working with or for them went for nothing.

They all, on this view, achieved the precise opposite of what they intended, not more but less money than Scotland should have got. Such an interpretation flies in the face of reason and common sense. I just do not believe it. But in another sense I do not think it matters a whit.

Quite apart from ham-handed interventions by the British state, there would anyway have been a flow of funds from England, or more precisely the South-East of England, to Scotland. Such flows, from relatively rich to relatively poor countries, have been observed since the eighteenth century, in a natural operation of the market which makes investors seek out cheap factors of production. Germans and Japanese arrive for the same reason, without inducements from their governments. In the process, some countries become creditors and others debtors, but these things even themselves out over time. It does not matter.

In fact the whole of this line of argument is irrelevant to the questions it is supposed to illuminate, how and to what extent the imminent system of devolution should finance itself or depend on hand-outs from London. The issue of national income or expenditure is and in principle must be different from the issue of public expenditure. Similarly, the issue of devolved expenditure is and in principle must be different again.

Why? Because we are dealing not with the whole field of public expenditure but only with certain devolved services, the existing functions of the Scottish Office. I do not myself see why those services have to be financed out of the Treasury (for the sake of the argument I shall treat the Scottish parliament's power to vary income tax by 3 per cent as too paltry to bother about).

On the Government's own figures, the expenditure of the Scottish Office in the last fiscal year was £14.6bn. The amount of taxation raised in Scotland was £25.5bn. It is as plain as a pikestaff that the entire expenditure of the Scottish Office, and so of the devolved parliament, could be met out of Scottish resources if that was what we decided to do.

The devil, of course, lies in the residue, the £10.9bn which, hypothetically, Scotland would have left over from the taxes she raised after satisfying her own needs. Is this a fair contribution towards the public expenditure of the entire United Kingdom, considering that the budget of St Andrew's House covers only about half of all money spent by the state in Scotland?

We must again examine the figures. The amount in 1996–7 for all programmes which cannot be territorially allocated (such as defence and foreign affairs) or which are common to the United Kingdom (such as social security or trade and industry) was £126.7bn. Of this, £10.9bn represents 8.6 per cent.

Would that be a fair contribution to those programmes, when our share of gross domestic product is 8.8 per cent and our share of population not very different? I think myself it would be perhaps not exactly fair, but pretty much so. And I would be happy to hand over that amount to the Treasury to spend on our behalf, especially as we are likely to get more out of a programme such as social security than we put in, on sound grounds of equity rather than silly grounds of subsidy.

I must add that my account of public expenditure still has to be completed, because I have so far left out the Government's purely financial transactions arising mainly from the national debt, as opposed to its current balance-sheet of revenue and expenditure. The residue of Scottish taxation would not stretch to covering Scotland's proportion of them, even if I added to the residue, as I would like to do, a bit of the oil revenues. But this problem is not so great that it could not with goodwill, over a transitional period, be solved.

The general picture I wish to present is this: we could if we wanted stand the Government's scheme of devolution on its head, do without the block grant and have a sort of reverse block grant. Then we in Scotland would raise all our own taxes, control all our own spending, and still contribute a fair share to the common expenditures of the United Kingdom. The advantage of doing things that way is that we would have a responsible system of government, with no time for patronage and subsidy, not an irresponsible one such as Labour proposes.

Some Poetry, Pipers and Politics for the People

Neal Ascherson

From *The Independent on Sunday* (14 September 1997, p. 17). Ascherson – one of the UK media's most eloquent foreign correspondents and political commentators – had been involved in the debates throughout the 1970s (when he was on the staff of *The Scotsman*), and intermittently also after his return to London following the 1979 referendum.

It was midnight, at the top of Drumochter Pass. We stopped the minibus and climbed out into the darkness, scented with invisible heather and bog myrtle, to look up at the sky. It was uncannily clear, the Milky Way lying like a silver fleece across the north-west. As we stared, a brilliant meteor flashed out of the constellations and slid towards the Pole.

We sensed a good omen. As the bus set off again, its occupants began to recite and sing. One repeated Alexander Montgomerie's old poem 'The royal palace of the highest Heaven/The stately furnace of the starry round . . .'. Deep in the small hours, I half-woke to hear William McIlvanney softly rendering Sinatra ballads. Chancellor Seafield signed away the Scottish parliament in 1707 with the famous words 'Here's ane end to ane auld sang'. But old songs never end.

The 'Bus Party' was making an overnight run from Inverness to our next date at Biggar in the early morning. Then it would be Lesmahagow, Peebles, Galashiels. We were campaigning through the last 100 hours before the Referendum, trying to use every moment left to meet people. But this was no conventional 'yes-yes' effort, nothing to do with political parties. We were a travelling conversation and ceilidh, haring round the land to listen and learn as well as to speak and entertain.

The idea came from Germany. Back in the 1960s, at a time of suffocating conformity in West German politics, the novelist Günter Grass decided to stir up trouble. The opposition Social Democrats had the right ideas, he felt – reconciliation with eastern Europe, a bolder public life – but were too timid to voice them. So he hired a bus, stuffed his friends into it and set out round the small towns and villages. There he would throw parties, make heretical speeches and encourage local people to open up their private hopes and fears. But his 'Bus Party' was not just a new, ribald style of politicking. It was a two-way process. The band of big-city intellectuals on board were also discovering their own country, a Germany they only knew about from reading novels. They listened to the fantasies and nightmares of people with little education – people they would normally have avoided with a snigger. They argued with local politicians, and with one another. They preached but also they learned.

Could something like this be done in Scotland? Some of us thought it could and should. The chance to revive a Scottish parliament after three centuries was – or ought to be – a choice calling for the most profound reflections on responsibility and liberty, history and the future. But as early as last year, the menace of dire, routine Scottish campaigning began to emerge. The same old faces were preparing to squabble about the same old petty conundrums; the people would watch with gloomy scepticism as the politicians rattled on about the tartan tax, the West Lothian Question, local government sleaze and the business rate. Passion would be monopolised by the inanities of the Braveheart tendency. There was a danger that the Scots would be so alienated by this debate that they would not bother to vote, or return such a lukewarm, indecisive verdict that – as in 1979 – devolution would be stillborn.

So the Bus Party was dreamed up. The journey of Günter Grass had not swung an election; neither would we. But by word of mouth, and the media, the rumour of a different way of doing politics – maverick, enjoyable, coaxing people to speak their hearts rather than obey slogans – had filtered into German awareness. Perhaps we could achieve something like that.

We soon found our Grass. William McIlvanney is the best-known novelist in Scotland; every small-town bookshop stocks a row of his works. His tall, spare figure, the lean face with the Clark Gable moustache, is recognised everywhere. Better yet, he has orator's magic: that West-of-Scotland eloquence that thaws a wary audience into laughter then seizes their hearts as the wit turn serious. With him came the critic Joyce McMillan, the teacher Margaret Macintosh, the young piper Fin Moore, the minister Willie Storrar, who organised the whole journey, the radical lawyer Alan Miller. Billy Kay, promoter of popular song and oral history, was there and the historian Isobel Lindsay. Poets – Douglas Dunn, Robert Crawford, Matthew Fitt – came and went: we were joined by folk singers such as Sheena Wellington, Rod Paterson and Mairi Campbell, whose baby daughter slept on our laps as the bus toiled across the Border hills.

We seemed always to be crossing rivers: Forth and Tay, Don and Dee, Deveron and Spey, Ythan and Ugie, Gala Water and Tweed. Amateurs at campaigning, stress and lack of sleep pitched us into peaks and troughs of feeling. But emotion was close to the surface in the audiences too. An old man in the town house at Inverness said, 'Never again will this chance come. Your fathers and grandfathers look down at you', and I heard a hiss of indrawn breath all around me. 'Let politics look after itself – this is a moral and a spiritual decision', and the sober citizenry broke into applause. At Galashiels, the night before the poll, Mairi Campbell sang 'Auld Lang Syne' to the touching melody which was Burns' first choice for it. It was a reminder that old times were enduring and a new time opening, and – I swear it – I saw tears on solid, red-cheeked Borders faces.

But there was fun too. There was the Arbroath schoolboy who said 'I want the parliament to help wee-bitty Third World companies to compete wi' multinationals. And mair flags!' There was a couple from the Home Counties visiting Forres: 'Good luck to you. But mind you don't get a rotten government like we've had in England for the last twenty years!'. There was the chippie in Stonehaven which pressed on us the local delicacy of fried Mars bar in batter (a killer but tasty). There was the man in St Machar's cathedral at Aberdeen who shouted: 'Comparing Scots to sheep is an insult to sheep. Sheep don't have the vote, and if they did they wouldn't vote for mutton pie!'

And there were topics which never came up. Where were the scab-picking orgies, so dear to intellectuals about Scottish identity? The pupils at Mintlaw Academy knew just who they were, and only wanted their 'Doric' speech – now taught in the school – to be better respected. 'Why should some shopkeeper force me to use a language that's no mine?' a boy asked me. Willie McIlvanney commented 'Scottishness is like an old insurance policy you can't lay your hand on when you need it'. But people we met on this journey knew exactly where to find it. It follows that the other thing we didn't encounter was anglophobia. A girl from Biggar High School told me: 'I don't feel put down because I am Scottish. The English and the Scots put each other down in a perfectly normal way.' At Forres we met English families from the RAF base at Kinloss who were happily preparing to vote 'yes'.

But there are places a parliament cannot reach. We went to the desolate housing scheme at Middlefield in Aberdeen. 'Powerlessness to the people' said a social worker. 'I see families come here and disintegrate month by month.' Local authorities foster this dependency culture by refusing to trust self-help community groups with money. It was a microcosm of the worst aspect of Scotland – an archipelago of undemoc-racies run by power cliques who want as few people as possible to participate in running their own lives.

At midnight on Wednesday we returned to our starting place: the Calton Hill in Edinburgh, where the empty parliament building waits. The vigil veterans, who had squatted at the gate for just 1,979 days to demand a Scottish parliament, greeted us with whisky. Speeches, embraces, a last tune from Fin Moore's pipes as passing cars hooted greetings. We agreed that we had learned much and shared much. Then William McIlvanney recited the ancient lament for King Alexander III, one of this small country's many lost leaders: 'Succour Scotland and remede/That stayed is in perplexitie'. And quietly, without trumpets, Referendum Day began.

References

Aitken, K. (1997), *The Bairns O Adam: the Story of the STUC*, Edinburgh: Polygon.

Alexander, A. (1997), 'Scotland's parliament and Scottish local government: conditions for a stable relationship', *Scottish Affairs*, no. 19, spring, pp. 22–8.

Ascherson, N. (1997), 'Some poetry, pipers and politics for the people', *The Independent on Sunday*, 14 September, p. 17.

Beat, L., W. Walker and B. Jones (1991), *Real Devolution: an Equal Union of Regions and Nations*, Edinburgh: privately published.

Bennie, L., J. Brand and J. Mitchell (1997), *How Scotland Votes*, Manchester: Manchester University Press.

Bochel, J., D. Denver and A. Macartney (1981), *The Referendum Experience*, Aberdeen: Aberdeen University Press.

Bogdanor, V. (1979), 'The defeat of devolution', *Spectator*, 10 March, pp. 13–14.

Bogdanor, V. (1979), *Devolution*, Oxford: Oxford University Press.

Bogdanor, V. (1994), *Local Government and the Constitution*, Isle of Wight: Society of Local Authority Chief Executives.

Breitenbach, E. (1989), 'The impact of Thatcherism on women in Scotland', in A. Brown and D. McCrone (eds), *Scottish Government Yearbook*, Edinburgh: The Unit for the Study of Government in Scotland, pp. 174–206.

Breitenbach, E. (1990), ' "Sisters are doing it for themselves": the women's movement in Scotland', in A. Brown and R. Parry (eds), *Scottish Government Yearbook*, Edinburgh: The Unit for the Study of Government in Scotland, pp. 209–26.

Brown, A., D. McCrone and L. Paterson (1998), *Politics and Society in Scotland*, London: Macmillan, second edition.

Brown, A., D. McCrone, L. Paterson and P. Surridge (1998), *The Scottish Electorate*, London: Macmillan.

Brown, A. and Y. Strachan (1991), *The Implications of a Scottish Parliament for Women's Organisations in Scotland*, report of conference at Edinburgh University.

Brown, G. (ed.) (1975), *The Red Paper on Scotland*, Edinburgh: Edinburgh University Student Publications Board.

Buchan, N. (1975), 'Scottish devolution: why democracy demands a referendum', *The Times*, 4 November, p. 12.

Buchanan-Smith, A. (1976), Speech to parliament, *Hansard*, fifth series, vol. 922, columns 1290–5, 14 December.

Butler, D. and D. Kavanagh (1997), *The British General Election of 1997*, London: Macmillan.

Campaign for a Scottish Assembly (1988), *A Claim of Right for Scotland*, Edinburgh: Campaign for a Scottish Assembly.

Carty, T. and A. McCall-Smith (1978), *Power and Manoeuvrability*, Edinburgh: Mainstream.

Church of Scotland (1989), 'The government of Scotland', in J. Stein (ed.), *Scottish Self-Government: Some Christian Viewpoints*, Edinburgh: Handsel Press, pp. 14–23.

Clarke, M. G. (1976), 'The assembly and local govermment', *New Edinburgh Review*, no. 31, pp. 37–42.

Cole, G. D. H. (1950), 'Democracy face to face with hugeness', in *Essays in Social History*, London: Macmillan, pp. 90–6.

Conservative and Unionist Party (1970), *Scotland's Government*, Edinburgh: Conservative and Unionist Party.

Constitution Unit (1996), *Scotland's Parliament: Fundamentals for a New Scotland Act*, London: Constitution Unit, University College.

Cook, R. (1983), 'Interview: devolution', *Radical Scotland*, no. 4, August/September, pp. 9–11.

Crick, B. (1990), 'The growing threat from Scotland', *Observer*, 4 March, p. 20.

Crick, B. and D. Millar, (1995), *To Make the Parliament of Scotland a Model for Democracy*, Edinburgh: John Wheatley Centre.

Dahrendorf, R. (1959), *Classes and Class Conflict in Industrial Society*, London: Routledge and Kegan Paul.

Dalyell, T. (1977), *Devolution: the End of Britain?*, London: Jonathan Cape.

Dewar, D. (1988), Williamson Lecture, Stirling University, 21 October.

Douglas Home, A. (1979), Speech at Edinburgh University, BBC Scotland, 13 February.

Douglas Home, A. (1980), Interview, 'Current account', BBC Scotland, 12 February.

Drucker, H. M. (1978), *Breakaway: the Scottish Labour Party*, Edinburgh: Edinburgh University Student Publications Board.

Drucker, H. M. (ed.) (1982), *John P. Mackintosh on Scotland*, London: Longman.

Duffy, T. (1989), 'Church and nation: a Catholic view', in J. Stein (ed.), *Scottish Self-Government: Some Christian Viewpoints*, Edinburgh: Handsel Press, pp. 8–10.

Edwards, O. D. (ed.) (1989), *A Claim of Right for Scotland*, Edinburgh: Polygon.

Elcock, H. and M. Keating (1998), *Devolution in the UK*, London: Frank Cass.

Fairley, J. (1997), 'The democratic reform of Scotland?', *Scottish Affairs*, no. 18, winter, pp. 18–23.

Finlay, R. J. (1997), *A Partnership for Good? Scottish Politics and the Union Since 1880*, Edinburgh: John Donald.

Forrester, D. (1993), 'The Church of Scotland and public policy', *Scottish Affairs*, no. 4, pp. 67–82.

Forsyth, M. (ed.) (1989), *Federalism and Nationalism*, Leicester: Leicester University Press.

Forsyth, M. (1995), Richard Stewart Memorial Lecture, Strathclyde University, 30 November.

Fry, M. (1987), *Patronage and Principle: a Political History of Modern Scotland*, Aberdeen: Aberdeen University Press.

Fry, M. (1997), 'Free, on our own terms', *The Herald*, 19 November, p. 19.

Fry, M. and J. Cooney (1979), *Scotland in the New Europe*, Dublin: Dublin University Press.

Gowan, P. and P. Anderson (1997), *The Question of Europe*, London: Verso.

Gray, C. (1996), 'Scottish local government in Europe', speech to a conference *A Scottish Parliament: Friend or Foe to Local Government?*, 15–16 February, Crieff.

Greenfeld, L. (1992), *Nationalism: Five Roads to Modernity*, Cambridge, Mass.: Harvard University Press.

Grimond, J. (1979), 'The Scottish assembly: why it will not work', *Spectator*, 10 February, pp. 14–5.

Hanham, H. J. (1969), *Scottish Nationalism*, London: Faber.

Harvie, C. (1976), 'The devolution of the intellectuals', *New Statesman*, 28 November, pp. 665–6.

Harvie, C. (1981), *No Gods and Precious Few Heroes*, 1st edn, Edinburgh: Edinburgh University Press.

Heald, D. (1990), 'Financing an assembly', in D. McCrone (ed.), *Financing Home Rule*, Edinburgh: Unit for the Study of Government in Scotland, pp. 16–38.

Hearn, J. S. (1998), ' The social contract: re-framing Scottish nationalism', *Scottish Affairs*, no. 23, spring, pp. 14–26.

Heath, E. (1968), Speech at annual conference of Scottish Conservative and Unonist Party, 18 May.

HM Government (1975), *Our Changing Democracy*, London: HMSO, Cmnd 6348.

HM Government (1997), *Scotland's Parliament*, Edinburgh: HMSO.

Hodge, P. S. (ed.) (1994), *Scotland and the Union*, Edinburgh: Edinburgh University Press.

Hogg, Q. (1947), *The Case for Conservatism*, West Drayton: Penguin.

Hogg, Q. (1967), 'Regionalism – all for one and one for all?', *Scotland*, vol. 11, no. 11, pp. 20–4.

Hogg, Q. (1969), *New Charter: Some Proposals for Constitutional Reform*, London: Conservative Political Centre.

Hollander, C. den (1979), *Christian Political Options*, The Hague: AR-Partij-stichting.

Jones, P. (1997), 'Scotland's next step', *Prospect*, April, pp. 48–51.

Jones, P. (1997), 'Labour's referendum plan: sell-out or act of faith?', *Scottish Affairs*, no. 18, pp. 1–17.

Keating, M. (1996), *Nations Against the State*, London: Macmillan.

Kellas, J. (1986), *The Scottish Political System*, Cambridge: Cambridge University Press.

Kellas, J. (1989), 'Prospects for a new Scottish political system', *Parliamentary Affairs*, 42, pp. 519–32.

Kellas, J. (1990), 'Constitutional options for Scotland', *Parliamentary Affairs*, 43, pp. 426–34.

Kellas, J. (1992), 'The Scottish Constitutional Convention', in L. Paterson and D. McCrone (eds), *Scottish Government Yearbook*, Edinburgh: Unit for the Study of Government in Scotland, pp. 50–8.

Labour Party (1970), *The Government of Scotland*, Glasgow: Labour Party.

Labour Party (1981), *Interim Policy Statement on Devolution*, Glasgow: Labour Party.

Lang, I. (1994), 'Taking Stock of Taking Stock', speech to Conservative Party conference, Bournemouth, 12 October.

Lawson, A. (1985), 'Towards a Constitutional Convention', *Radical Scotland*, no. 17, October/November, p. 6.

Leicester, G. (1996), 'Fundamentals for a new Scotland Act', *Scottish Affairs*, no. 16, pp. 1–6.

Levitt, I. (1996), 'The origins of the Scottish Development Department, 1943–62', *Scottish Affairs*, no. 14, pp. 42–63.

Levy, R. (1990a), 'Eleventh-hour questions as Convention prepares to deliver its findings', *Glasgow Herald*, 30 November, p. 17.

Levy, R. (1990b), *Scottish Nationalism at the Crossroads*, Edinburgh: Scottish Academic Press.

Liberal Party (1970), *Forms and Consequences of Federalism*, Edinburgh: Liberal Party.

Lindsay, I. (1976), 'Nationalism, community and democracy', in G. Kennedy (ed.), *The Radical Approach*, Edinburgh: Palingenesis Press, pp. 21–6.

Linklater, M. and R. Denniston (1992), *Anatomy of Scotland*, Edinburgh: Chambers.

Lloyd, J. (1997), 'What's the story?', *New Statesman*, 8 August, pp. 37–8.

MacCormick, D. N. (ed.) (1970), *The Scottish Debate*, Edinburgh: Edinburgh University Press.

MacCormick, D. N. (1989), 'Unrepentant gradualism', in O. D. Edwards (ed.), *Claim of Right*, pp. 99–109.

MacCormick, D. N. (1998), 'The English constitution, the British state and the Scottish anomaly', in L. Paterson (ed.), *Understanding Constitutional Change*, special issue of *Scottish Affairs*, pp. 129–45.

MacKay, D. I. (ed.) (1979), *Scotland: the Framework for Change*, Edinburgh: Paul Harris.

Mackintosh, J. P. (1962), *The British Cabinet*, London: Stevens.

Mackintosh, J. P. (1967), 'A bed of thistles', *Socialist Commentary*, December, pp. 11–12.

Mackintosh, J. P. (1968), *The Devolution of Power*, Harmondsworth: Penguin.

Mackintosh, J. P. (1974), 'The new appeal of nationalism', *New Statesman*, 27 September, pp. 408–12.

Mackintosh, J. P. (1974), *The Government and Politics of Britain*, London: Hutchinson.

Mackintosh, J. P. (1975), *A Parliament for Scotland*, Tranent: Berwickshire and East Lothian Labour Party.

Mackintosh, J. P. (1976), 'The role of the Secretary of State', *New Edinburgh Review*, no. 31, pp. 9–16.

Marr, A. (1992), *The Battle for Scotland*, Harmondsworth: Penguin.

Marshall. G. (1992), *Presbyteries and Profits*, Edinburgh: Edinburgh University Press.

Martin, D. (1997), 'Three-level path to flourish in Europe', *The Herald*, 24 July, p. 16.

Massie, A. (1978), 'Scotland and Europe: two responses to the decline of the nation state', *Nevis Quarterly*, no. 1, pp. 37–48.

Massie, A. (1984), 'Scotland – omega one', *Spectator*, 14 January, pp. 9–10.

Massie, A. (1991), 'Can Scotland be cured of socialism?', in *Scotland and Free Enterprise*, London: Aims of Industry.

Maxwell, S. (1973), 'Scotland: Europe's hard case', *Scottish International*, January, pp. 12–4.

Maxwell, S. (1977a), 'The trouble with John P. Mackintosh', *Q*, no. 24, 18 March, p. 5.

Maxwell, S. (1977b), 'Women in Scotland', *Q*, no. 29, 27 May, pp. 4–5.

McCormick, J. and W. Alexander (1996), 'Firm foundations: securing the Scottish parliament', in S. Tindale (ed.), *The State and the Nations*, London: Institute of Public Policy Research, pp. 99–166.

McCrone, D. (1989), 'Thatcherism in a cold climate', *Radical Scotland*, no. 39, June/July, pp. 8–11.

McCrone, D. (1992), *Understanding Scotland: the Sociology of a Stateless Nation*, London: Routledge.

McFadden, J. (1996), 'The structure and function of local government under a Scottish parliament', *Scottish Affairs*, no. 17, autumn, pp. 32–41.

McKenna, R. (1996), 'A Scottish parliament: friend or foe to local government?', speech to a conference *A Scottish Parliament: Friend or Foe to Local Government?*, 15–16 February, Crieff.

McMillan, J. (1997), 'Losing sight of Tinkerbell', *The Herald*, 16 August, p. 32.

Midwinter, A. (1997), 'Local government in a devolved Scotland', *Scottish Affairs*, no.18, winter, pp. 24–35.

Midwinter, A., M. Keating and J. Mitchell (1991), *Politics and Public Policy in Scotland*, Edinburgh: Mainstream.

Milward, A. (1992), *The European Rescue of the Nation State*, London: Routledge.

Mitchell, J. (1990), *Conservatives and the Union*, Edinburgh: Edinburgh University Press.

Mitchell, J. (1991), *Constitutional Conventions and the Scottish National Movement*, Strathclyde Papers on Government and Politics, no. 78, University of Strathclyde Department of Government.

Mitchell, J. (1992), 'Shibboleths and slogans: sovereignty, subsidiarity and the constitutional debate', in L. Paterson and D. McCrone (eds), *Scottish Government Yearbook*, Edinburgh: Unit for the Study of Government in Scotland, pp. 98–113.

Mitchell, J. (1996), *Strategies for Self-Government*, Edinburgh: Polygon.

Morton, G. (1994), *Unionist Nationalism: The Historical Construction of Scottish National Identity, Edinburgh, 1830–1860*. Ph.D. thesis, Edinburgh University.

Nairn, T. (1970), 'The three dreams of Scottish nationalism', in K. Miller (ed.), *Memoirs of a Modern Scotland*, London: Faber, pp. 34–54.

Nairn, T. (1977), *The Break-up of Britain*, London: Verso [2nd edn 1981].

Nairn, T. (1988), *The Enchanted Glass*, London: Radius.

Nairn, T. (1997a), 'Sovereignty after the election', *New Left Review*, no. 224, July/August, pp. 3–18.

Nairn, T. (1997b), *Faces of Nationalism*, London: Verso.

Parliamentary Debates (1966), *House of Commons Official Report*, fifth series, vol. 737, 30 November, cols 456–9.

Parliamentary Debates (1977), *House of Commons Official Report*, fifth series, vol. 939, 14 November, col. 87.

Paterson, L. (1994), *The Autonomy of Modern Scotland*, Edinburgh: Edinburgh University Press.

Paton, H. J. (1968), *The Claim of Scotland*, London: Allen and Unwin.

Paton, H. J. (1968), 'A parliament to run Scotland', *Glasgow Herald*, 26 February, p. 8.

Paton, H. J. (1968), 'The economic argument for home rule', *Glasgow Herald*, 27 February, p. 10.

Paton, H. J. (1968), 'An appeal to right and reason', *Glasgow Herald*, 28 February p. 10.

Payton, P. (1993), *Cornwall Since the War*, Redruth: Institute of Cornish Studies.

Pym, F. and L. Brittan (1978), *The Conservative Party and Devolution*, Edinburgh: Conservative and Unionist Party.

Richard, C. (1993), 'The Scottish question', *Scottish Affairs*, no. 2, pp. 121–3.

Royal Commission on Scottish Affairs (1954), *Report*, London: HMSO, Cmd 9212.

Royal Commission on the Constitution (1972), *Written Evidence 5: Scotland*, London: HMSO.

Royal Commission on the Constitution (1973), *Report*, London: HMSO, Cmnd 5460.

Russell, C. (1997), 'In search of the constitution', *Times Literary Supplement*, no. 4901, 7 March, p. 15.

Scott, P. H. (1997), *Scotland: an Unwon Cause*, Edinburgh: Canongate.

Scottish Trades Union Congress (1974), 'Scottish government', *Annual Report*, Glasgow: STUC, pp. 157–61.

Scottish Trades Union Congress Women's Committee (1989), *Women's Issues and the Scottish Assembly*, submission to the Constitutional Convention's Working Group on Women's Issues, Glasgow: STUC.

Shanks, N. (1996), 'Constitutions, conventions and values: the Scottish churches and the constitutional debate', *Scottish Affairs*, no. 16, pp. 18–35.

Sillars, J. (1989), *Independence in Europe*, Edinburgh: Scottish National Party.

Sinclair, D. (1997), 'Local government and a Scottish parliament', *Scottish Affairs*, no. 19, spring, pp. 14–21.

Smith, J. (1973), 'A matter of debate', *The Scotsman*, 7 November, p. 12.

Smith, J. (1980), 'Interview: portrait of a devolutionist', *Bulletin of Scottish Politics*, no. 2, spring, pp. 44–54.

Steel, D. (1968), *Out of Control*, Edinburgh: Scottish Liberal Party.

Steel, D. (1976), 'Getting devolution right', *New Society*, 23/30 December, pp. 608–9.

Stein, J. (1989), *Scottish Self-Government: Some Christian Viewpoints*, Edinburgh: Handsel Press.

Stewart, A. (1987), 'The devolution maze', in *Apostles not Apologists*, Eastwood: Eastwood Conservative and Unionist Association.

Storrar, W. (1990), *Scottish Identity: a Christian Vision*, Edinburgh: Handsel Press.

Surridge, P., L. Paterson, A. Brown and D. McCrone (1998), 'The Scottish electorate and the Scottish parliament', in L. Paterson (ed.), *Understanding Constitutional Change*, special issue of *Scottish Affairs*, pp. 38–60.

Taylor, T. (1978), 'Why it must be "No" when assembly is put to the vote', *Glasgow Herald*, 19 May, p. 6.

Thatcher, M. (1997), 'Don't wreck the heritage we all share', *The Scotsman*, 9 September, p. 17.

Tindale, S. (1996), 'Devolution on demand: options for the English regions and London', in S. Tindale (ed.), *The State and the Nations*, London: Institute of Public Policy Research, pp. 47–71.

Torrance, T. F. (1982), *Juridical Law and Physical Law*, Edinburgh: Scottish Academic Press.

Wright, E. (1968a), 'Why enmity and conflict?', *Glasgow Herald*, 29 February, p. 10.

Wright, E. (1968b), 'The biggest truth omitted', *Glasgow Herald*, 1 March, p. 10.

Wright, E. (1970), 'In defence of the UK', in D. N. MacCormick (ed.), *The Scottish Debate*, Oxford: Oxford University Press, pp. 103–20.

Index